Never Will I Leave Thee, Never Will I Forsake Thee

Heather Wilber

Edie,
In God we Believe!
God Bliss,
Heather
Wilber
♡

Deutronomy 31:6

Never Will I Leave Thee, Never Will I Forsake Thee

Trilogy Christian Publishers A Wholly Owned Subsidary of Trinity Broadcasting Network

2442 Michelle Drive Tustin, CA 92780

Rights Department, 2442 Michelle Drive, Tustin, CA 92780.

Trilogy Christian Publishing/TBN and colophon are trademarks of Trinity Broadcasting Network.

For information about special discounts for bulk purchases, please contact Trilogy Christian Publishing.

Manufactured in the United States of America

10 9 8 7 6 5 4 3 2 1

Library of Congress Cataloging-in-Publication Data is available.

ISBN: 979-8-89041-105-1

E-ISBN: 979-8-89041-106-8

DISCLAIMER

In the following text, the names of certain individuals have been altered in an effort to protect and uphold their privacy and confidentiality.

I dedicate this book to my Lord and Savior, Jesus Christ. This is His book of miracles. I am the vessel He used to carry out His divine plan to give hurting mothers hope in Him alone. I am honored with this special opportunity to write *Never Will I Leave Thee, Never Will I Forsake Thee* to glorify God's never-failing love for all who seek Him.

TABLE OF CONTENTS

Chapter 1: "You Are My King"—Newsboys 15

Chapter 2: "Word of God Speak"—MercyMe 21

Chapter 3: "Above All"—Michael W. Smith 29

Chapter 4: "God, You Are So Good"—Passion............................ 41

Chapter 5: "Always"—Chris Tomlin.. 57

Chapter 6: "Here in the Presence"—Elevation Worship 65

Chapter 7: "Who Am I"—Casting Crowns 75

Chapter 8: "How Great Is Our God"—Chris Tomlin..................... 85

Chapter 9: "I Can Only Imagine"—MercyMe 99

Chapter 10: "Here with Me"—MercyMe 107

Chapter 11: "The Blessing"—Kari Jobe 115

Chapter 12: "Same God"—Elevation Worship.............................. 123

Chapter 13: "There's Nothing That Our God Can't Do"—Passion ...129

Chapter 14: "Battle Belongs"—Phil Wickham 141

Chapter 15: "Graves into Gardens"—Elevation Worship............... 151

Chapter 16: "Surrounded"—Michael W. Smith 161

Chapter 17: "God Who Listens"—Chris Tomlin.......................... 169

Chapter 18: "Yesterday, Today and Forever"—Passion 179

Chapter 19: "Million Little Miracles"—Elevation Worship 189

Chapter 20: "Even If"—MercyMe 201

Chapter 21: "Gratitude"—Brandon Lake 217

Chapter 22: "Then Christ Came"—MercyMe 227

Chapter 23: "I Speak Jesus"—Charity Gayle 235

Chapter 24: "My Testimony"—Elevation Worship........................ 245

Chapter 25: "Oceans (Where Feet May Fail)"—Hillsong UNITED... 257

Chapter 26: "Imago Dei"—Sean Feucht.. 269

Chapter 27: "Run to the Father"—Cody Carnes 275

Chapter 28: "Raise a Hallelujah"—Bethel Music.......................... 287

Chapter 29: "God Really Loves Us"—Crowder 293

Chapter 30: "Too Good Not to Believe"—Brandon Lake.............. 303

Chapter 31: Testimonies.. 313

About the Author 321

PREFACE

I sit here writing God's story and realize He made me for a time such as this. God helped me resist Satan's schemes of destruction for my children. I was blessed with visions and guidance through Christ for His book. I didn't think I could write a book, but God showed me the path to write this book on "God's victories."

He blessed me with a loving family and friends to help me through the hard times. My mom was my number one prayer warrior and spiritual advisor. I thank Him that He blessed me with her spiritual foundation. She showed me that I can conquer anything through Christ.

I tried different avenues of writing this book, but when I realized the path He set for me, everything fell into place. Sometimes we try different routes in life, but God has already laid the perfect path for us.

The writing was very emotional. I had ups and downs. God inspired me to write this book to help other mothers who have children with critical health conditions to "never" give up! Mothers who need hope and encouragement that there is someone out there who cares for them and is the ultimate healer. That is Jesus Christ!

God hears our prayers and our cries. Life is so precious, and sometimes it is for a short time. Sometimes things are not fair. Life is full of trials and tribulations. But God did say He would never leave us nor forsake us. I stand on that promise! When friends and material things come and go, God never leaves!

This scripture is the foundation scripture and the reason for my title. God gave this to me in a time of desperation. To this day, when I am desperate or feel Satan attacking my family, I fall back on this scripture. This scripture is a promise from God and comforts me. I pray it comforts you too.

"The Lord himself goes before you and will be with you; He will never leave you nor forsake you. Do not be afraid; do not be discouraged" (Deuteronomy 31:8).

God is just that good! He is there when we cry. He is there when we are joyful. God is everywhere. All we have to do is give our whole hearts to Him and believe that He is Jesus Christ, our Lord, and He will listen to our prayers. I stand on that faith!

As God guided me through every word, chapter, scripture, and song, He was healing me. There was trauma from near-death experiences with Katelyn that I had shoved back to forget. I didn't want to remember or relive some of them. But God showed me those experiences were an important part of my life. A valley that I went through to see God's healing on the other side. We have to go through valleys to strengthen our faith in God. I am honored to say I am one of God's loyal followers.

I pray our family's legacy gives you hope and trust in our Lord Jesus Christ. When God gives you trials, give Him your whole heart. God will bring you through. I am living proof!

Acknowledgements

First and foremost, I would like to thank Jesus Christ, my Lord and Savior, for choosing me to glorify Him through my book.

I want to thank my husband, Shane, for withstanding the trials with me. Through Christ, we have endured more obstacles in twenty-six years than most married couples do their whole life. When I was overwhelmed writing this book, Shane was there to reassure me. His famous reminder to me was, "God will provide! You can't out-give God! This book is going to touch many lives, and you are doing exactly what God has led you to do!" I thank God He put Shane by my side to help me weather these storms.

We are blessed with our three beautiful kids and their support. Shaelyn, Katelyn, and Chance were some of my biggest encouragers. Shaelyn and Katelyn's little notes of how proud they were of me gave me confidence. There were days I did not feel worthy. Chance knew the importance of the book and was always willing to help in any way.

My mother's prayers and love got me through some of the hardest situations with Katelyn.

She taught me the importance of prayer and faith in Jesus Christ.

Her prayers and spiritual guidance have made me into the woman I am today.

Rebecca Nidey was my main editor. I am pleased to call her my new friend. Her talent in editing was a blessing. Thank you, Becky, for your hard work and determination.

Kendra Jones has always given me moral support. We have been best friends since Katelyn was two years old. I knew Kendra was always praying for my family. We are great travel buddies for beach therapy! I thank God for Kendra's friendship.

I would also like to thank these wonderful clients whom I consider friends. Anita Bush and Susan Lockart for helping edit and read my manuscript. They didn't have to accept the responsibility, but they knew how important it was to get Katelyn's story into publication.

Laura Ayres—the Lord sent her into my beauty shop to give me the final confirmation to start my book. If it wasn't for her encouragement and word from God, I would still be questioning writing it. Thank you, Laura June.

Multiple other clients helped give me advice and confidence when they unknowingly contributed to my book. They are dear friends and will be blessed.

I thank God for everyone who was mentioned and those not mentioned who encouraged me in the spirit and prayer. Everyone who contributed and sewed a seed into this miraculous book will be greatly rewarded. May the Lord our God bless everyone who supported and helped unselfishly along the way.

Introduction

Katelyn's quote: "God gives His hardest battles to His strongest warriors. I am proud to say I am one of God's strongest warriors!"

Katelyn Wilber is a twenty-year-old young lady from Flat Rock, Illinois. She was born with a heart disease called complete heart block. This congenital disease is where the electrical system at the bottom of the heart does not receive the signals from the top of the heart to inform it to beat. Statistics show that one in 500,000 babies diagnosed with this condition lives. If they do survive, life expectancy is eighteen years old. Katelyn has had a pacemaker that she is solely dependent upon because of this heart condition since she was six hours old. She has had nine complete pacemaker systems and a total of ten big surgeries. Katelyn has beat the medical data and is now living to tell her story.

The Lord has performed at least thirteen miracles in her young life. Two of which were before birth.

In 2017, the Lord impressed on me to write a book on all the miracles He performed in Katelyn's life. This book is to help other mothers who have children with life-threatening illnesses to never give up and rely solely on our Lord and Savior, Jesus Christ. Without Him, Katelyn would not be with us today. Her story is a sign and wonders from God.

The title comes from a near-death experience with Katelyn. I broke down and asked God what He wanted me to do. I was tired and weak. As I cried out to Him, I vividly heard Him say,

"Never will I leave thee, and never will I forsake thee." I have held onto that promise. He has never left us or forsaken us.

The book was also derived from our family's experiences and how we all adapted and lived with a chronically ill family member. Katelyn's siblings share their testimonies of how she impacted their lives. God worked in miraculous ways but not without trials and tribulations. Her younger brother, Chance, was diagnosed with trisomy 18 and had a miracle as well. Abortion was suggested and urged by our medical professionals for Katelyn and Chance. Satan seemed to always be in a tug-of-war with God over our family. He knew the plans the Lord had for us, and he tried everything in his power to destroy our unity. We stood on our faith in Jesus Christ, and I am proud to say we are here today glorifying Him. Katelyn was the inspiration for the book, but God was the center of our family's legacy.

Katelyn battled back multiple times after surgeries to play the sport she loves, softball, and to continue onto the collegiate level. She was urged by her doctors not to continue playing, but with her faith and determination, she made her dreams come true! Satan continued to attack her at college, and she learned to overcome his schemes. When you are loyal to God, he opens doors that nobody realizes could be opened. Sometimes the doors are not what we anticipated, but they are His divine plans.

When the Lord gave me the ending to my book, I thought to myself, *This is not the ending I prayed for.* Then the Lord said, "This is the book's ending, but not an ending to the big things I have in store for Katelyn. I want *all* of her!" I believe this book will have a sequel. The way the Lord left it, this season is over, but He has big plans for the next season of her life.

Katelyn has beat the odds with the statistics the doctor provided. She now boldly gives her testimony at churches, church camps, sports clubs, sports teams, Softball World Series, and Softball Nationals. She has touched thousands with her story. I believe it is now time to tell the whole story through a book guided by God.

Thank you for reading, and I pray this book touches your life. God bless!

Chapter 1: "You Are My King"—Newsboys

I received a phone call from a dear friend that her nephew, twelve years of age, had tried to commit suicide. She asked me to please pray as they were transferring him to a hospital in St. Louis, Missouri. I knew I was supposed to go physically and pray with my friend and her young nephew. I did not know this young boy but wondered what could be so bad in his life to want to end it at twelve years old. *Where are the parents? Do they have hope in God?* All I knew was I needed to be by my friend's side for spiritual support. My drive to St. Louis was consumed with prayer for guidance to do His will through me. As I walked into the hotel to meet my friend, I could feel nothing but the presence of God. As we sat talking, we began to pray, and the Holy Spirit overcame her and me. I heard the Lord say, "This baby will be okay."

On the way to the hospital, my friend informed me of the struggles in the family. Her sister was addicted to drugs, and her nephew was tossed around from home to home. They were not church attendees, and she was not sure of her sister's or nephew's salvation. This information made the suicide attempt clearer to me.

As I entered the hospital room, the little boy was so peaceful and beautiful. I stood by his bedside and was taken by the amity I felt in the room. I knew that either here on earth or in heaven God had this young boy in his arms. I looked at the sadness and hopelessness in the mother's eyes, and it broke my heart. I asked for permission to pray with her and her son, and she welcomed my offer. After prayer, I felt such peace and reassurance that God was in control.

Later that week, I received a phone call from my dear friend. Her sister decided to take him off his life-saving devices. Within a few days, he went to be with our Lord and Savior.

After I heard this child had passed, I cried and mourned like he was my own. I wondered what I could have done differently. The comfort I had was knowing that the child was in God's presence now and he was no longer in pain or struggling on this earth anymore. The Lord confirmed this to me in my spirit with these precious words, "This baby will be okay."

It was a confirmation that I was to write a book about my life on the miracles and struggles of a mother with a child facing death or congenital illness. If I could help one mother to have hope and faith to believe in the power of prayer, I would be fulfilling God's promises.

One year before this incident, I believed in my spirit that I was to write a book on my journey with my daughter Katelyn, who was born with complete heart block, a congenital heart disease. I thought, *How in the world can I write a book? I don't even read books! I'm just a hairdresser from Flat Rock, Illinois. I don't have any connections, and we can't afford to pay someone to publish.* I had excuse after excuse. I told God, "If You want me to write this book, You have to guide me and open doors." I had no clue how to even begin! What it boiled down to was I didn't have faith and believe in God to guide me through this journey. One day during my devotion time, the Lord said, "Fear not." I knew exactly what God was advising me. Since I was a young child, my father always told me I could be and do anything I put my mind to. I have lived by that my whole life. I know now that was Dad's way of saying, "Fear not." Wow! That was a huge revelation! God has perfect timing.

After that revelation, God kept sending confirmation through people and random situations. Here are a few instances. As I said above, I am a hairdresser. I had a lady whom I'd never met or done her hair before. I knew she was a wonderful godly woman. I do live in a small town, and as a hairdresser, I hear a lot. After I finished cutting her hair, she left the beauty shop. I heard the door open again, and there she was with her Spirit-filled smile. She looked at me, radiating with the Lord's Spirit, and said, "Write that book." You can only imagine my expression and response. I'm pretty sure my jaw hit the floor! Yes, after she left, I thanked God and cried like a baby.

Another instance that I'm reminded of was when I took Katelyn to a new specialist in Chicago. It was by the grace of God we found this wonderful doctor. After our initial visit, he just sat there for two hours talking to us and going over Katelyn's history. He said in thirty-five years of being a heart surgeon he had never met anyone like Katelyn. Let me tell you, any specialist who will sit for two hours just conversing is a blessing. As we got up to leave, he looked at me and said, "Have you ever thought about writing a book?" I just smiled and said, "Yes, I have." God works in mysterious ways. We just have to be willing to listen to Him when He is working.

Before I get too far into our miraculous journey with Katelyn, I feel I should give a little of my background. It will come in later in our journey. I was raised as a "PK," which stands for a preacher's kid. Was I perfect? Not! Was I loved? Absolutely! I was always called the "black sheep" of the family. My sisters all had blonde hair and green eyes. I had dark brown hair and dark brown eyes. Not only was I physically different, but I believe I was more headstrong and determined. Like I said earlier, my father always expressed to me that I could do and be anything I put my mind to. As I look back, that is exactly what I did and still do. That was a proclamation of my life from God. I had no idea that my father was speaking life into me.

"The tongue has the power of life and death, and those who love it will eat its fruit" (Proverbs 18:21).

My father taught me at an early age that there was a heaven and a hell. He impressed me with the power of prayer and that only God can save us from destruction. He showed me how to defeat demons and proclaim Jesus over my life. My mother worked very hard, sometimes holding down three jobs to help provide. She was a wonderful woman of God as well. My mother had a special connection to me, and later she told me it was because of the difficulties I had with health issues as an infant. She and I spent a lot of time together in hospitals and at doctor's appointments. I almost died as an infant because of an allergic reaction to a family member smoking around me. She said after prayer and faith, the Lord brought me through and defeated death. She knew God had something special in store for me and my life. After my father passed away on January 21, 1993, my mother and I became very close. You could say she was my best friend. My mother prayed for me to return to the church. I strayed after my father's passing. My mother never gave up on me, and because of her prayers and determination, I am the strong woman of Jesus Christ that I am today.

Now, as I continue into our miraculous journey of twenty years with Katelyn, you will hear Katelyn's testimonies of how she saw her illness through her eyes and mine as well. I believe both testimonies are important to proclaim God's greatness as we walk together. The Lord has guided me through each step of this book. In my quiet time, God gave me the title of my book. You will see later how special the title is. He directed me to use praise and worship songs for the chapter titles because they were my comfort to help me get through all the trials and tribulations. The one song I remember that I used to play over and over again to worship God in some of my hard times was "You Are My King" by Newsboys. The Lord wants us to praise Him in the middle of the storms and out of the storms. When you enter my house, all you hear is praise and worship songs. God even went so far as to tell me how to write my chapters. I am still amazed how everything just fell into place, just as God wanted it to. I have learned through this whole journey that when you hand it all over to God, He will take the wheel. I have family members and good friends that have all told me if they had not known me personally and lived through this journey with us, they would have never believed it. Faith and prayer got Katelyn and me to this point in life to be able to share God's miracles and never-failing love in our testimonies.

Let's begin this journey!

Chapter 2: "Word of God Speak"—MercyMe

My husband, Shane, and I were business-oriented individuals. Shane worked at Toyota Manufacturing and also had a custom cabinet shop at home. I owned Talk of the Town beauty salon in Lawrenceville, Illinois. Not only was I a hairdresser, but I also had four other hairdressers, three tanning beds, a nail tech, a massage therapist, a cleaning lady, and my assistant. I had worked for a few other hairdressers, but when the salon owner of my current employment approached me to buy her established business, I could not pass up the opportunity. I bought the salon, Talk of the Town, and the transition came easily. I would have, on average, twenty to twenty-five clients per day. I had worked very hard to make this dream of mine come true. *I could not be happier*, I thought.

We both had a lot going on at this time in our lives. Shane went in his direction all week, and I went in mine. He worked nights, and I worked days, so we did not have the opportunity to see much of one another. We typically only had family time on the weekends. It seemed, at this point and time in our lives, our main focus was financial gain. We were young and had the wrong priorities. It took me several years to figure out what God's ultimate plan was for me and my family, and making money was not it.

Shane and I also had a beautiful little two-year-old daughter named Shaelyn. She spent a lot of time with me at my beauty shop. We had set days for grandmas to be able to babysit since she was the first grandchild on Shane's side, and my mom thought she was pretty special too. To me, life was exactly how I wanted it.

Spontaneously one day, Shane asked if we could try for another child. I was a little shocked because that was not in my plans. In my mind, I thought our life was great! We had good jobs and had enough money to continue to fix up our home. I was doing what I had always dreamed of, and I thought there was no way I could handle a baby with my new shop ownership. I was content with having one child, but I could sense the sincerity in his voice.

Shane was blessed with a men's Bible study group at his place of employment. I was not aware that he had been talking to his close friends there about wanting another child. He said he had always wanted a boy to carry on his last name. After Shane and I had a serious conversation about growing our family, I felt condemned. How could I have such selfish thoughts? I was concerned about myself and what I wanted, not what was best for our family.

I was not only thinking of our financial situation or the practicality of not adding another child, but I was also thinking of all the complications of childbirth with Shaelyn. I didn't have confidence that I could handle another traumatic delivery. I loved being pregnant, and medically I felt wonderful. Shane loved it while I was pregnant. He said I had a special glow.

I realize my traumatic delivery was not common, but it still weighed heavy on my mind. On October 10, 1998, I delivered a beautiful 8 lb., 8 oz. baby girl, and we named her Shaelyn Erin Wilber. She was the start of our lifetime of miracles. My labor with her was twenty-five hours of contractions three minutes apart. She was stuck in my pelvis. The doctor attempted suction and forceps, but nothing seemed to work. She was too far down to do a cesarean section, and my only option was to "push!" The problem with this was I had already been pushing for close to twenty-five hours. The final moment when I knew God had to intervene was when the doctor got in my face and said, "You *have* to push this baby out, or you and this baby will die!" Her heart rate was crashing, and she was in distress. I did not realize it at the time, but my vitals were scaring the doctor as well. He told Shane later that he was afraid he was going to lose us both. I was exhausted from pushing for so long. But when the doctor told me this, I suddenly developed supernatural strength and pushed the baby out! I knew it had to be God because I was too weak to do it on my own.

Her stressful delivery left my body weak and torn up. I was small in structure, and Shaelyn was a very large baby for me to deliver naturally. Later I found out that her shoulders were too wide for my birth canal, and her head was tilted wrong, which in turn caused it to get caught in my pelvis. The anesthesiologist had administered three separate epidurals for delivery, and none of them took properly. So I felt every bit of the traumatic delivery with nothing to help with the pain. Not to mention all of my lower extremities tore immensely. It took the doctor two hours to sew me up before I could concentrate on my new baby girl. This delivery had my medical doctors and staff concerned for our well-being. We never received any type of medical bill for Shaelyn's delivery.

By the grace of God, she was beautiful and perfect! No signs of stress or brain damage. After her delivery, I promised God I would raise her in the church and His sight to the best of my ability.

Shaelyn's miracle was life-altering for Shane and me. We were active in church, but I don't think we took it seriously enough. Were we following God's will or just going through the motions? At the time I thought we were doing the "right" thing until later when we matured in our spiritual life.

My health was also a concern when deciding to have another child. When Shaelyn was two months old, I had a medical incident. I woke up one morning and could not move anything but my eyes. I was paralyzed. Shane picked me up and started walking me around the house. Eventually, I felt life come back into my body. I figured it was from the twenty-five hours of traumatic labor and delivery I had with Shaelyn. One month later, this incident happened again. This time, Shane made me go to the local doctor. After blood work and examination, the doctor sent me to a rheumatologist. He said he found something abnormal in my blood work but would not elaborate on the findings.

Months later, we went to a rheumatologist who diagnosed me with a disease called lupus. This is an autoimmune disease that attacks your internal organs. The doctor gave us a grim outlook. We were shocked by the diagnosis because I was young, felt great, and was in good health. I was very active and never sick, so it was hard to accept. Not to mention I was a new mother with a beautiful six-month-old daughter at home. We left and called our church family and my mom. My mom met us at our house to pray and ask for God's direction. We eventually went to a different rheumatologist for a second opinion, and he diagnosed me with Sjögren's syndrome. This disease does not attack your internal organs like lupus, but it is a sister disease. It affects your body fluids. So I could cry without tears and go out in midsummer and not sweat. The doctor did not have any idea how long I had had this disease. I do remember when I was in eighth grade and my grandfather passed away, I was crying and thinking to myself, *Why am I crying but no tears?* I think I had it for quite a few years before being diagnosed. It's an uncommon and rare disease.

When I lived at home, you didn't go to the doctor unless it was severe. We didn't have extra money for doctor visits. My mom was the queen of home remedies that she learned from my grandmother. Other than strange symptoms, I felt fine, so no need to draw attention.

Those two factors were the main reasons for my being hesitant to consider another child. Deep down I was scared of the outcome, and I also felt we were finally in a place where we could live comfortably financially. Shane and I grew up poor, and I finally felt satisfied with our finances, which we both worked diligently to accomplish. As I said earlier, I was thinking selfishly and not about what would be best for our family's growth.

After much discussion, we agreed to make an appointment with my rheumatologist to talk to him about having another child. Shane and I had looked on the internet about my health and pregnancy. According to the internet, another pregnancy did not look promising. We decided we would rather get a confirmation from my medical professional rather than the computer. My rheumatologist gave us some statistics on birth defects from mothers with Sjögren's syndrome. He assured us that through his years of a rheumatologist, he had never witnessed any of these birth defects in his patients. They were a one-in-a-million chance of happening is what he declared. He also informed us that most of the time with pregnancies my disease would go into remission. He explained it like cancer and how it does. I realized that was the reason why I felt exceptional during my last pregnancy. He then told us that most of the time if the disease goes into remission with one pregnancy, it will with another. I thought this was interesting information that I was not aware of previously.

Shane and I decided to pray for God's direction in our decision. Deep down, I was not yet comfortable with expanding our family. I was trying to trust God but be in control myself. My thoughts were that the cards were stacked against us with my health and my previous complications. Why press our luck because we already had one healthy child?

We were blessed with having Shaelyn as our first child. She was one of those babies that every parent dreamt of having. She slept all night from the first evening we brought her home. She rarely cried, and if she did, something was seriously wrong. Everyone loved her sweet personality. My mom always told me that no two children were alike. I was afraid to find out because my mom was always wise about raising children. She had a lot of experience with five of her own and countless grandchildren.

Shaelyn went to the beauty shop with me right after maternity leave. She would sit in her baby swing and be loved by everyone who came into the shop. To this day, she still remembers all my clients who would read to her and bring her gifts from their vacations. Most of my clients were teachers, so she learned a lot from them. I think the special attention made her mature for her age.

Our precious daughter was soon to be three years old, and we needed to decide on extending our family. Shane's heart was set on another child, and I didn't want to seem self-centered. My health was now my biggest concern in our decision-making process. I didn't want to risk bringing a sick baby into this world. I didn't know if mentally I could handle the responsibility. I was slowly feeling anxiety creep in, and I didn't want it to persuade me, but I slowly felt it control my

Never Will I Leave Thee...

thought process. I knew I had to contact my mom for divine intervention in the Lord.

I called my mother and asked her to come over for a conversation about Shane and me considering another child. She always gave great advice. She had a way of bringing peace to our conversations. It was her love for the Lord. She laid everything down to let Him guide her. I admired her obedience and longed to have a one-on-one connection with the Lord as she did. She was never at a loss for words when asked for advice. Mom reminded me of my promise to God with Shaelyn and that I was maybe being too self-centered. She then told me that Satan was using financial gain to overpower my divine responsibilities to our Lord. When Mom spoke, I listened! Everything she was saying was true, and her bringing it to my attention made all the difference to me. We then prayed, and I decided from that point on I was going to honor my promise to the Lord and start walking the correct spiritual life with Him. My focus was no longer on carnal things in this world. I was going to walk the spiritual life my mother prayed I would finally find to raise my family.

Fear is of Satan, and he is a liar. I was working hard to overcome the feelings of fear and put God first. I concluded that if God wanted us to have another child, He would provide. Little did I know the blessing God had in store for our future!

"'For I know the plans I have for you,' declares the Lord, 'plans to prosper you and not to harm you, plans to give you hope and a future'" (Jeremiah 29:11).

Honoring my promise to God was making my faith stronger. Our church family was becoming a big part of our lives. Church was becoming more of a priority. We started taking it more seriously, and in return, our lives were spiritually growing. Our marriage was getting stronger, and our priorities as a whole were changing for the good. God was working in ways that I never imagined.

I started trusting God more and what He wanted for our family. I was listening to praise and worship music continually. It was my quiet time with Him. I found myself wanting to be with the Lord more and more. Prayer became more desired. I could feel myself getting closer to God and looking more for His direction in our lives. I had no clue what our future held. The only thing I knew was that our future was now through Jesus Christ!

"Your beginnings will seem humble, so prosperous will your future be" (Job 8:7).

Chapter 3: "Above All"—Michael W. Smith

Our life of God's miracles and many blessings begins! Our life as we know it will soon change for the rest of our lives.

In January 2002 we found out we were going to welcome Wilber Baby #2! To answer your question, I'll say yes, I was excited! Truthfully, I loved being pregnant. Shane always told me I glowed and was so beautiful while pregnant. Needless to say, he was ecstatic about the news. Shaelyn turned three in October 2001 and wanted a baby sister for her birthday, but she got a new lab puppy instead. So when she found out she was going to be a big sister, it was all she could talk about. Shaelyn just knew she was going to get a baby sister to play Barbies with. Her favorite thing to do was play with her Barbies and all the accessories, such as a big house, cars, and a lot of other items. Shane and I took turns playing with her. I remember many times I played for three hours straight. I would do anything to have those special times back with her. Time flies by so quickly. We need to enjoy every moment and stage of their childhood.

Shane and I decided to find a new OB doctor. We did not anticipate complications with the pregnancy but were advised by my rheumatologist to do so as a precaution. We live in a very small town, and the more advanced hospitals were over one hour away. I began to search, and I found a wonderful female obstetrician, Dr. R, in Evansville, Indiana.

I went for an initial visit and exam. I told her about my diagnosis, and she didn't seem concerned. She said she'd like to watch me closely and have more frequent appointments.

While I was there, she had me visit a high-risk obstetrician down the hall. It was a precautionary procedure because of my medical diagnosis. Dr. R wanted to make sure everything was taken care of for the health of me and the unborn baby. I wasn't aware that Sjögren's put me at a high-risk factor for pregnancy. I felt blessed that I found a doctor who cared for her patients. Dr. R and I quickly became more friends than patient-doctor relations. She was one of a kind.

Shaelyn loved to go with me to doctor's appointments. We would go to the check-ups and then have some fun! Flat Rock and Lawrenceville are very small towns, and there's not much to do. We typically have to go to Evansville or Terre Haute, Indiana, to go shopping. In Evansville, there is a pizza and game place called Chuck E. Cheese. A lot of fun for a three-year-old. We frequented this place on our trips to the doctor. It was a fun mother-and-daughter time. I thought, *I better enjoy these one-on-one times because before long we won't have them. Shaelyn will have to share Mom and Dad with a new sibling.*

Everything was going very well. Dr. R even told me I needed to eat more ice cream because I wasn't gaining any weight. We took her advice and made sure we had ice cream! I felt so good. I felt the best I had since I was pregnant with Shaelyn. I continued to work full time and long hours.

We were busy trying to prepare our small house for our new addition to the family. We lived in a remodeled old farmhouse that Shane and I remodeled by ourselves. Anyone who knows about old houses knows that the rooms are tiny and there are no closets. In transitioning bedrooms, we decided we should start considering adding to the existing house. When we remodeled this old house, we added a kitchen, dining room, and utility room. But there was only one bathroom. It was clear to us that a house addition was short.

Shaelyn was the first grandchild on Shane's side and our first child, so you can only imagine her room. Yes, you are correct—anything she wanted. Shane's dad, Dave, was an artist. He could paint anything. We had her room decorated in Noah's ark. Dave painted on one whole wall a portrait of Noah's ark and all the animals. This mural was the attraction of the room. We decided to move Shaelyn into a big girl's room and move the new baby into the Noah's ark room. She was excited about this big move because she was going to be the "big" sister.

Around sixteen weeks, I felt a little different. I told Shane that I felt in my spirit that something was wrong with the baby. He asked me why I had those feelings. I told him the pregnancy seemed different. I believe God gives mothers a special "mother's intuition" sometimes to prepare us or to warn us. My mother was my "go-to" for spiritual advice, prayer, and support. I called my mom and told her that I felt in my spirit that something was wrong with the baby. My mother, a wonderful woman of God, said, "Then let's pray!" "Then hear from heaven their prayer and their plea, and uphold their cause" (1 Kings 8:45). I am truly blessed to have a praying mother. I learned from her to always pray and trust God's guidance. I tried not to focus on my feelings, but they continued in the back of my mind.

Dr. R was a wonderful, caring doctor. I told her on my twenty-week routine check-up that I was concerned that something might be wrong with the pregnancy. She checked everything and assured me that the baby looked normal. She asked me if I wanted to know the sex of the baby. She could see. I told her that we wanted the sex to be a surprise! We didn't find out with Shaelyn, and it was such a blessing to find out after you worked so hard to bring them into this world. It is just an amazing feeling.

I was blessed to find the best daycare/friend in Lawrenceville. Tammy and Trevor Seed became two good friends of ours. Shaelyn was Tammy's first little girl at daycare, and she stole Trevor's heart. Tammy and Trevor had two boys of their own, Jacob and Nate. Jacob and Shaelyn were the same age, and Nate was two years younger.

Tammy was one of those friends that I could call no matter what time of the night or day, and she would be there. Lord knows she got phone calls from me all hours of the day and night from me. Tammy and Trevor's house was Shaelyn's favorite place to go. Further along with my pregnancy, I started leaving her with them more often for doctor appointments.

My twenty-four-week check-up came quickly! We were so busy working and preparing the house that time slipped away. This appointment Shaelyn wanted to stay with Tammy, so I headed to the appointment by myself. This worked out perfectly because my beauty shop was so busy that I had to get back right after the appointment. No time to shop today. I remember that day so well; it was the end of May, and it was starting to warm up. The sun was shining, and all I could think about was that summer would soon be here! As I drove down the interstate, I saw all the landmarks that Shaelyn always yelled out at as we passed them. There was a huge strawberry out in the middle of a big field. I have no idea why it was even there, but she knew every time we were close to it. She would say, "Yummy, Mom, look at that huge strawberry! I love strawberries! I couldn't eat that strawberry in a week!" We would also pass a great, big Santa Claus statue. As soon as we passed it, she'd say, "Looky, Mom, there is Santa; we are almost to the doctor's office!" It amazed me how smart she was at such a young age. I then realized I was missing her on this trip.

Never Will I Leave Thee...

I arrived at my twenty-four-week appointment, and Dr. R began her routine exam. She got her medical Doppler to check the baby's heart rate. She asked if the baby had been very active. I was so busy, I had not paid much attention to the activity. She put the Doppler away and brought in a bigger device. Dr. R was very calm and asked me to lie on my left side and then my right. This was out of the normal for the routine checkup. I asked her if everything was okay, and she replied, "I am just having a hard time finding the heartbeat, but don't worry, I will find it!" As you can imagine, fear instantly hit me. My thoughts were, *I knew God was preparing me! Why did I not listen to the warning signs? I knew something was wrong with this pregnancy. I should not have ignored the maternal instincts.* All kinds of thoughts were running through my head. I then thought to myself, *Pray!* I instantly began to pray for the life of my child. I just lay there praying for what felt like an eternity. Forty minutes into looking for a heartbeat, Dr. R never gave up on finding it. Finally, she found a very faint heartbeat in my groin area. The baby's heart rate was only 24 bpm. But praise God there was a heartbeat!

"I will proclaim the name of the Lord. Oh, praise the greatness of our God!" (Deuteronomy 32:3).

Dr. R hugged me as we both cried. I thank God that she was such a caring and loving doctor. God was already working in my situation. I thought to myself how thankful I was that Shaelyn was not with me on this visit, but how I wished Shane was. After things calmed down, Dr. R called the high-risk OB doctor. I called Shane at work and explained what was going on. Then I called my mom, and her response was, "Sis, God has this!" She was such an encourager and prayer warrior. My mom always made things so much better. She always put situations into a different perspective for me. She knew there was nothing too big for God.

Dr. R quickly scheduled me with the high-risk doctor and walked me down the hallway to her office. She assured me that I was in good hands and to call her and let her know what the next steps were. I don't feel as if I should disclose the high-risk doctor's name, so I will just call her Dr. T. She took me to a little room in the back of her doctor's office. I still remember today the feeling of that room. The little room was so cold and uninviting. As I sat there alone waiting for her to come in, so many things were going through my mind. I knew my mom had already contacted our preacher and deacons of the church for prayer and started all kinds of prayer chains with local churches. At that time, we didn't have social media or Facebook. It was all by phone calls. I sat there by myself, scared and wondering what could be wrong with our baby. At that time, I never thought it would be a complication of my medical diagnosis. The rheumatologist told me pregnancy difficulty caused by Sjögren's was unheard of. One in a million were the statistics of something happening is what we were told. Once again I began to pray through my tears.

Dr. T entered the room after she evaluated the medical records that were available to her at this time. She sat down and told me that she wanted me to go see a pediatric cardiologist to confirm what she was thinking was wrong. She asked me if I knew that I was SSA and SSB positive. I had no idea what she was talking about, and needless to say, I wasn't thinking too clearly at this time. She explained that those were antibodies found in lupus. I told her that I knew that I had Sjögren's syndrome but was not fully diagnosed with lupus. She said she was going to look into the situation further, but meantime she had scheduled me with a pediatric cardiologist first thing in the morning. Dr. T said there was nothing they could do right now. She said she was going to get all my records from my rheumatologist and talk to the pediatric cardiologist. After seeing the pediatric cardiologist, I was to go back to her office, and they would have a game plan. I wasn't okay with that; I wanted a diagnosis and game plan now. I am one of those people who sees a problem and wants to attack it head-on! But I was not in control of this issue, so I had to do what the doctors advised at this point and time.

As I left the little cold room, I felt like I was in a fog or a dream. I drove home, and I listened to "Above All" by Michael W. Smith. When I felt myself struggling, I would use this song for inspiration. God is above anything in this world. God is above the doctor and their diagnosis. I prayed for God's mercy and healing power upon our baby. When I got home, my mom and Shane were there waiting on me. Shane held me as I stood there crying. The emotions I had were consuming. I was scared and blamed myself for this happening. I told Shane I should have listened when God was trying to tell me about the pregnancy. He said it was not my fault and we needed to have faith that God was protecting our baby. We all began to pray. I felt God's Spirit, and I believed that God had a bigger plan.

"For where two or three gather in my name, there am I with them" (Matthew 18:20).

That was a very long night, but as soon as dawn broke, Shane and I were on our way back to Evansville to see the pediatric cardiologist. Shane's parents only live three miles from us, and they were always willing to help with Shaelyn. After we dropped her off, Shane and I began the trip to the cardiologist. The car ride was very quiet. I remember staring out the window, and in my mind, I watched the landmarks that Shaelyn always looked for on our trips. I would play back what her little voice from the back seat would say every time we passed them. I caught myself starting to cry, and as I looked at Shane, I saw the sadness in his eyes. I also remember thinking, *How can this be happening? What am I going to tell Shaelyn if something happens to her new "baby sister"?* She was 100 percent sure this baby was a sister to play Barbies with her. Shane held my hand, and just his touch made me feel safe. Things felt so much better with his support. I thank God that He placed Shane in my life to weather this storm.

Shane and I reached the cardiologist, but before we entered the building, we sat in the car and prayed together. "Those who sow with tears will reap with songs of joy" (Psalm 126:5).

As soon as we were checked in with the pediatric cardiologist, we were sent down the hall to have an echocardiogram and ultrasound of the baby's heart. As we waited in the cardiologist's waiting room, there were multiple little kids there with heart conditions. They were playing with toys and seemed so happy. I thought to myself that these little kids looked perfectly normal. Surely our baby would also.

The nurse called our name, and my heart felt like it had jumped into my throat. I wanted to know, but yet I didn't. Different emotions started running through me. Shane looked at me with teary eyes and took my hand, and we both walked to the patient's room. As we entered, the cardiologist was already in the room with the results on the computer screen. The pediatric cardiologist proceeded to tell us the diagnosis. He told us that our baby had third-degree congenital complete heart block (CHD) and explained it to us. Congenital heart block is a rare disorder. One in 500,000 children is diagnosed with it. It is caused when a mother has SSA and SSB antibodies, and they cross the placenta and injure the previously normal fetal heart. This happens when the fetus is twenty-four weeks gestation. The antibodies attack the electrical system in the AV node. The AV node controls the extraction of blood to the body. So what this means is the blood will go into the heart, but the heart does not know to push it back out. He then told us that most fetuses with this degree of heart block do not make it to full term. But if the fetus does, it will have to have a pacemaker at birth, and the longevity of life is short. The doctor was very professional and caring. But as you can imagine, Shane and I were devastated. I felt numb. He then told us that the baby's heart rate was 24 bpm, and the baby could never survive with that low of a heart rate; it needed to be sixty or higher to survive to full term. If anything lower, the baby would have brain damage. The cardiologist did encourage us that the baby's heart structurally was perfect. The only problem was the electrical system in the AV node. It may not sound like much, but the perfect heart structure was a little glimmer of hope to Shane and me. The Lord always makes good out of the bad. Next, we had to go see Dr. T to see what the game plan was for treatment.

As Shane and I drove across town to go see Dr. T, I called my mom and gave her the diagnosis. My mom said, "I'll call Brother John (our preacher), and we will pray for the baby's heart rate to become 60 bpm!" As I said, she was my spiritual encouragement and prayer warrior. I quickly learned that when we are at a place where we don't know how to pray for ourselves, we need someone to be our spiritual support. My mom and our church family were exactly what we needed. Our preacher, Brother John, was very spiritual. When he would preach, you could feel God's Spirit in every message. His prayers, I felt, were sent straight to heaven with no hesitation. Wonderful man of God.

We reached Dr. T's office, and they took us to the little, cold, uninviting room. I was quickly learning to not like this room. It had a feeling of death and bad news. There were only bad feelings in this room. Dr. T entered and began to tell us her diagnosis and treatment plan. This was not at all what we anticipated. First of all, she gave me a lecture on getting pregnant with SSA and SSB antibodies. She told me I should not have thought about another pregnancy. We told her that we approved it first with our rheumatologist. She quickly told us the rheumatologist was wrong. Needless to say, this was a nightmare. I felt like I was a complete failure, and it was all my fault the baby was so sick. She then told us that the baby would more than likely not make it to full term. If the baby did survive, it would be a burden on Shane and me. It would have a lot of medical complications and surgeries. Babies who endure to birth, their life expectancy is short-term. I was sitting there listening to her, and I just couldn't believe my ears. She then said that we would have to go to pediatric cardiologist four times a week and visit with Dr. R three times a week to monitor the baby. The next thing we heard from Dr. T was, "You need to consider abortion." Shane and I looked at each other in total shock. I quickly said, "We are *not* aborting our baby! We believe *God* is in control and He has a bigger plan!" Shane and I left devastated and somewhat discouraged. We were in unbelief of what she said. Not only was the medical diagnosis horrible enough, but she also had to add to it with the suggestion of abortion. She was speaking so much negativity and death to our baby.

"The tongue has the power of life and death, and those who love it will eat its fruit" (Proverbs 18:21).

Brother John and my mom had anointed a cloth, and when we got home, she was waiting with it. We had intense spiritual prayer for our 60 bpm. I knew God could do this, but what if He didn't? What would I do? How could I live with myself knowing that I was the reason this baby's heart was not working properly? I knew God had complete control over our situation, but yet I let fear try to creep in. My mother and I held each other and cried. She said, "Sis, God has got this! We can't doubt God; we have to keep our hope in Him. Satan is not in control; our Lord and Savior is in complete control of this baby's life." I love her. She always made me feel so much better.

Our next cardiology appointment was the next morning. Luckily Shane's employer had family medical leave, and I had one of my hairdressers cover for me. My mom stayed at our house that night so she could entertain Shaelyn. It was a lot of juggling, but people were so willing to help. We were truly blessed with generous friends and family. Shane and I started our trip back down to the pediatric cardiologist. We were anxious but yet hesitant. We were still trying to digest all the bad news we got the day before, but yet trying to hold onto our faith that God was going to take care of us. We knew we had a huge support system at home praying as well. When we reached the cardiologist's office, they took us straight to the echocardiogram room for an echo of the baby's heart and then to the cardiology exam room. The cardiologist came into the room and asked, "Do you remember what I told you yesterday—what the heart rate had to be for this baby to survive?" We replied, "Yes, 60 bpm." He said, "You'll never believe this, but this baby's heart rate is exactly 60 bpm! Our baby's heart rate went from 24 bpm to 60 bpm overnight. Not one beat below or one beat above. Wonder how that happened. Could it be the power of prayer? Of course, it was! God answered our prayers about the 60 bpm. This is just the beginning of the multitude of miracles in our family. We knew from this point on that this baby was going to be a miracle from God.

"Ask and it will be given to you; seek and you will find, knock and the door will be opened to you" (Matthew 7:7).

Chapter 4: "God, You Are So Good"—Passion

Word traveled fast about our baby and our situation. As I tried to digest everything that was happening, Satan kept creeping in. Working on my mind and emotions. Fear, worry, and doubt were always on my mind. How did this happen? Why did it happen? Am I to blame for my baby's health? Did I put money before God and my family? Was this a punishment? So many questions and no answers. This heart condition was so rare that even the doctors had no hope or support for us. To make matters worse, Dr. T was trying to convince us to abort this pregnancy. I felt like the world was crashing down on top of me. I am the type who keeps everything locked inside and tries to deal with problems on my own and in my way. Is that healthy? No. Is that what God wants for us? No. You see, God performed a miracle with the baby's heart rate, and what did Satan do? Tried to distract me with all the negative thoughts and emotions instead of me praising God for the miracle. Satan only comes to steal, kill, and destroy. If he could steal my joy and distract me from God, then he would have won this battle. God came to give us life to the fullest! That was what I expected for our baby.

"The thief comes only to steal and kill and destroy; I have come that they may have life, and have it to the full" (John 10:10).

The next couple of weeks were pretty hectic with work and traveling back and forth to Evansville four times a week with a three-year-old and a very busy beauty shop. Every trip to Evansville I had to see our pediatric cardiologist and Dr. T. I would get an echocardiogram, ultrasound, and basic baby checkups. The trips were stressful, not knowing what to expect, but yet rewarding because the baby's heart rate was exactly 60 bpm every visit. Not one beat over or under but exactly 60 bpm. It was almost like God was saying, "Look at me! I got this!" How could I doubt that the heartbeat would be any different? After I had a pity party for myself, I decided to cast out all my fear! It was like a light bulb came on! Scripture says to cast all our fears on Him and He will take care of us.

"So do not fear, for I am with you; do not be dismayed, for I am your God. I will strengthen you and help you; I will uphold you with my righteous right hand" (Isaiah 41:10).

Two weeks after the diagnosis, Dr. T once again confronted me about abortion. She told me how much trouble all these trips to the doctor were. No guarantee that the baby would survive to full term. She had never seen one live past childbirth. It was my body that attacked the fetus, and did I want to prolong the inevitable? As I sat there, I started to fade out. Dr. T started sounding like the teacher of Charlie Brown. When she was finished, I looked at her and said, "I will *not* abort my baby! The Lord gave me this baby, and He will take care of us. We do not believe in abortion! It is against our religion, but I will tell you what I do believe in; I believe in Jesus Christ, and He is the Ultimate Healer!" She looked at me in shock and said, "I guess we are finished here." I replied, "Yes, we are, and I will have Dr. R take care of the rest of this pregnancy." As I walked out, I felt such relief. Once again I defeated Satan's tactics. I was not going to allow this doctor to speak death into my child. Faith is not believing God can, but God will!

Because of the critical nature of the baby's situation, Dr. R contacted a high-risk doctor at IU Med Center in Indianapolis, Indiana. IU Med Center was directly connected to Riley's Children's Hospital with an underground tunnel for emergencies. Our doctors informed us that the baby was living off of me and that when the baby was born, it would have to go directly into surgery and that Riley's would be the best option for us. We were also told the baby would not survive natural delivery. We would have to plan a cesarean section delivery. In July, we went to Indianapolis to get established with our new high-risk obstetrician. She was very nice and informative. She explained what to expect at delivery and after. We also had to meet with a pediatric cardiologist who would perform the surgery and an electrophysiologist who would take care of the pacemaker. It was going to take a lot of professionals to bring this baby into the world. During delivery, we would have a surgical team, high-risk OB physician's team, pediatric cardiologist team, electrophysiologist team, pediatrician team, anesthesiologist team, and an emergency team to transport the baby underground to Riley's Children's Hospital. If you noticed, I said "team" because each specialist has a team of nurses and doctors they work with individually. I thought to myself, *Where am I going to be? Will there be any room for me?* As Shane and I left Indianapolis, I was overwhelmed and exhausted. So much information in such a little time. I continued my trips to Evansville to our pediatric cardiologist. I now had to travel to Indianapolis to see my new high-risk OB physician. At this point and time, I didn't care. All I focused on was the health of our unborn child. I would travel anywhere to get the best doctors for our care.

I'm sure you are wondering, with all the traveling to doctor's appointments, how I had time for anything. I still made time to play Barbies with Shaelyn and work at my beauty shop. I had to cut back hours at the shop for appointments, but the hairdressers who worked for me were great to take up the extra load. Our support from our friends and family was humbling. Our church was great to help with extra prayer or anything else we needed.

Shane couldn't take time off for appointments because he knew he would have to take off for the delivery and unknown time we would be at the hospital. My mom and Shaelyn were my travel buddies a lot of the time. Everything was going well; the baby's heart rate was staying at 60 bpm and was developing normally. The baby was a little small, but they told us that heart babies are typically smaller in size. I felt great and felt myself growing closer to God. I believe God allows these trials to draw us closer to him. Looking back, Shane and I went to church but were just going through the motions and not taking God seriously. We loved God and believed in him but never really relied on Him or had a real relationship with Him until our circumstances with our unborn child. He wants us to rely on Him. With everything going on, I was quickly learning to rely completely on God.

"Trust in the Lord with all your heart, and do not lean on your own understanding. In all your ways acknowledge him, and he will make straight your paths" (Proverbs 3:5–6).

On the morning of August 1, 2002, Shaelyn and I opened the sunroof and turned on her favorite song, and headed to Tammy's. It was such a beautiful morning! Shaelyn and I loved our time alone together in our morning car rides. Lord knows we spent much time in the car, but mornings were special to us. We were only three blocks from Tammy's house when a car ran a stop sign and hit me at the driver's door. After the car hit me, my first concern was Shaelyn! She always sat right behind me in her car seat. I heard her crying, and I could see her in my rearview mirror, so I knew she was okay. I had to crawl out the passenger side door because my door was smashed. I ran over and tried to get her out and had to pull her out of the passenger door because her door was smashed too. I called Tammy first because the accident happened right down the road from their house. Trevor was there before the ambulance or police officers. The accident happened in the front yard of one of my clients. She came out and welcomed us to her home while we waited for the ambulance.

When the ambulance arrived, they were more concerned about me. All I cared about was getting Shaelyn examined for injuries. The EMTs saw that I was pretty far along in my pregnancy and wanted me to get evaluated first. I assured them I was fine but would go to the hospital and get Shaelyn evaluated. I'm sure you are noticing that I am a little stubborn.

As we were in the emergency room, the doctor asked me how I was feeling. I told him I was fine and just had a little mark on my stomach from what I was guessing was the steering wheel. He then advised me to let him make sure everything was fine with the baby. I figured it wouldn't hurt by this time because Shaelyn was doing fine. With the doctor's evaluation, he discovered I was in active labor. I was so concerned about Shaelyn I didn't pay attention to myself. This opened a whole new situation.

We live in a very rural area. I learned quickly that the small hospital had no idea about heart block. Not to mention they were not knowledgeable on how to treat me or the baby. The longer I lay there, the harder the contractions got. They did an ultrasound and told me the baby's lungs were not developed, and with the heart condition, delivery was not an option. The nurse came in to give me a shot to stop the labor. I told her, "In no way, shape, or form are you going to give me a shot!" I insisted they contact my high-risk doctor in Indianapolis.

I told them I had worked way too hard to get this baby this far, and I was not comfortable with an injection without the high-risk doctor's approval. They got the doctor on the phone, and she asked to talk to me. My doctor told me that if they had given me the shot to stop the labor, the baby would have instantly died and that I needed to go by ambulance to IU Med Center. She would be waiting for me with the team of doctors to prepare for delivery. Meantime, my mom made it to the hospital to pick up Shaelyn and left to prepare to head to Indianapolis to meet me at the hospital. Shane was at work, and my mother-in-law finally got through to him to tell him what was going on and to head to IU Med Center ASAP. We had a whole lot of things going on in a short amount of time.

They quickly got me in an ambulance to start the trip to Indianapolis. This was around a three-hour trip from the hospital. As I was lying in the back of the ambulance, the EMT informed me that they were both new to the job and had never delivered a baby before. I thought to myself, *You have got to be kidding me. This really can't be happening right now.* I do have to say after the EMTs got the info about the baby's heart condition, they were as scared as I was. Needless to say, that was a very quick trip to Indianapolis. I remember the interstate was blocked because of a wreck, and the ambulance driver drove down in the median to pass the wreck. I heard him say, "Hang on," and I just started bouncing all over. I told the EMT he was going to bounce this baby out. What a trip!

Back home, a lot was going on behind the scenes. There were multiple prayer chains. I always knew our preacher, Brother John, was in his shed praying every time we called him for prayer. My in-laws were so great at keeping Shaelyn and keeping her calm. She was so scared and worried about her mom and baby. One of the hardest things to deal with was

Shane's workplace. They would take their time giving messages to their workers even if they were told it was an emergency. I was worried Shane was not going to make it to Indianapolis in time. My four sisters were awesome too. They were always there to help with whatever we needed. Many times, they would rotate and keep Shaelyn for us. Then there's my mom. My wonderful mom. My best friend, spiritual adviser, and prayer warrior. She was on her way to Indianapolis to meet the ambulance. I seriously don't know what I would have done without my mother.

As we arrived at the Emergency room at IU Med Center, one of the EMTs said to me, "Thank goodness we made it!" They were as relieved as I was. When they opened the door to the ambulance, there was my high-risk doctor and all these other doctors rushing me inside. In Indianapolis, the EMTs were communicating on the phone with the hospital. They took me to the OB floor and got me settled in a room and started running tests. I was scared and all by myself. I knew my mom and Shane were on their way, but I was worried they wouldn't make it in time. The doctor came in and told me that I was in active labor and that the baby was not ready. She told me the baby did not have developed lungs, the heart was too weak, and the baby was too little to survive. She said that if I delivered right now, the chance of survival was very slim. As she left the room, I just began to weep. I thought, *How could this be happening?* The next thing I knew, my mom and Shane walked in. I began to cry even harder as I told them what the doctor had just told me. I will never forget this. My mom looked at me with teary eyes and said, "We will pray in the Spirit that this labor stops!" Shane, Mom, and I began to pray, and as soon as we started praying, the contractions stopped instantly! It was another amazing miracle! Shane went out and got the doctor, and to her amazement, the contractions had instantly stopped! She was confused because she was convinced we were having a baby that day. We told her about our prayers and how God once again answered them. She said, "Whatever you did worked! Keep it up!" This unborn child had already had two miracles performed in my womb. I was exhausted but energized by God's unfailing love. Four hours later, we were released from the hospital. The only thing the doctor did was give me a steroid shot to help the baby's lungs develop more quickly.

God is just that good. Mom explained that, once again, we defeated Satan. She said, "God has something big in store for this baby."

With each miracle, our faith grew stronger. We knew that day that God was in control. Two miracles happened that day. The Lord told me in my spirit not to take the shot from the nurse and the instant stop of the contractions. How could you argue that God was not in control? That Sunday, when we went to church, we had the whole congregation wanting to know the entire story. It was such a pleasure to tell them about the greatness of God and the miracles He performed that day. After church, Brother John pulled Shane and me to the side and told us that God gave him a word when he was praying in his shed that day for us. The Lord told him, "That baby is going to be just fine." Brother John said he knew in his spirit that the Lord was going to heal this baby. I will never forget the word that Brother John gave us because I knew his relationship with God was very powerful. I thank God for surrounding us with such spiritual family and friends.

On August 20, 2002, my mom and I traveled to Indianapolis for a routine doctor's appointment. After the emergency trip, my mom wouldn't let me go by myself to the doctor. That was perfectly fine for me. I enjoyed the extra time with her. When the doctor hooked me up to the heart monitor, she quickly saw that something was not right. The baby's heart rate was dropping slightly. The longer I lay there, the heart rate just kept changing. She said, "It doesn't look like the baby is in distress, but I don't want to take any chances. I think we need to start planning to have this baby." I quickly told her that I couldn't have this baby without Shane, and I had to go home to make sure I got Shaelyn settled while I was gone. She told me I should not leave the hospital because she thought they should call all the teams and get me ready to deliver. For some reason, I wasn't concerned. I just knew I needed to go home first. So that is what I did. I couldn't understand why she let me leave, but she did. I called Shane and told him that we were going to have a baby tomorrow, and I was on my way home to get him and our bags. While I was driving home, my mom once again called all the prayer warriors and family members and told them the news. After I got home, I got Shaelyn settled, picked up Shane and our bags, and headed back to Indianapolis to get ready to welcome our little miracle baby to this world!

On August 21, 2002, at 6:00 a.m., the nurses took Shane and me back to the surgical delivery room. As we entered, it was exactly how the doctor explained. There were doctors and nurses everywhere. There was just enough room for me to be on the table, and they allowed Shane to stand right by me. At 7:15 a.m. I delivered a beautiful little girl by C-section. Yes, a little girl. She was so tiny and had the most beautiful complexion. She didn't look like a newborn baby. She looked like a little angel. Shane got to cut the umbilical cord and hold her briefly. They held her up for me to see her, and then they whisked her away to Riley's Children's Hospital through the underground tunnel from IU Med Center. I had so many emotions going on at that time. I told Shane to go with them and be with our daughter, but he wouldn't leave me. I was stuck, and because of the C-section, I couldn't leave. It was torture lying there and not knowing what was going on or how she was doing. After Shane knew I was okay, they took him to see our daughter. They gave her some medication to see if her heart would beat without surgery. But the medication did not work. They put an external pacemaker on her until they could prepare her for heart surgery.

The doctor assured me that everything looked good and she was holding her own. I just remember lying there thanking God for this little miracle baby. Shane wasn't gone long before he came back to tell me how perfect she was. Her surgery was scheduled for later that day. The doctor advised me not to go because I had just had a C-Section. I told her I appreciated all she had done, but I was going to my daughter's heart surgery. She told me that we would talk more about it later. Later that day the doctor came into the room and told me again that she advised me not to go because it was too much with the surgery I had just had. Shane said, "You don't know my wife too well. If you don't bring a wheelchair, she will be walking out of here to go to our daughter's heart surgery. You are not going to keep her from going. One way or the other, she will be at that surgery." You guessed it—I got the wheelchair.

I could not wait to go see our beautiful daughter. Shane pushed me to the surgical area, but by the time we got there, she was already in surgery. I still did not get to see her or hold her, and it was eating me up inside. Shane and I sat there in silence waiting for our daughter to come out of surgery. I began thinking of the scripture that God did not give us a spirit of fear. Fear was Satan, and faith was Jesus Christ. From day one, it seemed like the deck was stacked against us. But, as I look back, it wasn't. God had His hand in all of this. He was

Never Will I Leave Thee...

just waiting for Shane and me to realize it and depend 100 percent on Him. We were getting stronger in Christ. I saw our lives had changed drastically for the better. God was working in our lives and everyone around us. I saw my family's faith grow. God was bringing all of us together in Spirit. It was so amazing. Fear comes from unbelief, and we believed God was in control.

"So do not fear, for I am with you; do not be dismayed, for I am your God. I will strengthen you and help you; I will uphold you with my righteous right hand" (Isaiah 41:10).

After four hours of surgery, our daughter was taken to the Neonatal Intensive Care Unit at Riley's Children's Hospital. Shane and I had to wait another hour before we were allowed to go see our new, precious baby girl. The pediatric cardiologist and electrophysiologist came and talked to Shane and me in the waiting room. They told us that she was one strong baby. She had the will to live, and she was very special. They said the surgery went well, but she was weak and was going to be in the neonatal intensive care unit or NICU until she got stronger. I asked if we could hold her and if I was able to breastfeed her. I was raised to know that breastfeeding was the healthiest for babies. I breastfed Shealyn, and she was never sick. Still to this day, she is the healthiest person ever. The doctors told me I could pump right now, and as she got stronger, they encouraged breastfeeding for intensive-care babies. That may not seem like much to some people, but to me, it was some of the best news they could have given us. I believe it also creates a wonderful bond between a mother and her child. The doctors said she would be monitored closely in an incubator, and we could touch her but not hold her. We were okay with that; we were just ready to see her.

One hour later, a nurse came to find us. She told us the baby was settled in, and we could go see her now! I can't explain how excited I was. It was almost sixteen hours after delivery that I finally got to see my new daughter. Before we could enter the cubical, we had to scrub and put on gowns. A cubical in the NICU is a room where the babies have special illnesses. Many like ours were heart babies. As we entered, there were five incubators on the north wall and five on the south wall, and a room in the back with the very intensive care heart baby. As Shane pushed me into the room in the wheelchair, I was just in shock with all the incubators, wires, and sensors going off. It is overwhelming, to say the least. Our daughter was the fifth incubator on the north side. As we approached the incubator, I was so excited to finally get to meet her. She was so tiny and had so many wires and monitors hooked up to her. I just felt myself weep uncontrollably. It was so much to take in. I don't think I was prepared for it.

The NICU nurse came and gave us instructions. We could touch her through the incubator but couldn't hold her yet. As soon as we put our hands in the incubator, her little hand grabbed our finger and just held on. It was so powerful and emotional. The nurse told us that it was proven that critically ill babies heal faster with their parents' touch. That wasn't a problem for us because all we wanted to do was to touch her. I remember her little feet were like monkey feet. She would grab those wires with her toes and yank them off then the alarms would sound off. She was so beautiful and angelic. God had His hands on her. She was our miracle baby.

I had been sitting in that wheelchair for quite a few hours, so Shane took me to the waiting room to try and stretch out and rest for a little bit. As we sat there, Shane said, "You realize we have not named our daughter yet." We hadn't named her because we couldn't decide on a name. We decided on a boy's name but not a girl's name. I told him he could name her whatever he decided, but I wanted her middle name to be "Grace." I wanted Grace because it was by the grace of God that she made it into this world. We agreed on Katelyn Grace Wilber. Now our miracle baby had a perfect name.

It was amazing how each day made a difference in Katelyn's recovery. Each day she got stronger and healthier. We got the opportunity to meet the other parents in our cubicle and hear their stories. Amazing stories they had too. We found out that NICU parents are kind of like their own little community. We were all so supportive of one another. Do you remember me mentioning the individual room in the back of the heart cubicle with the critically ill baby? When you have a critically ill baby in the NICU, they are not always happy stories. We learned a lot there. The baby in the back room's parents never came to see him. They just left him. It was so sad. I couldn't imagine a parent leaving their baby because it was ill. Every day I would watch and pray for his parents to change their hearts. Another thing we discovered was that out of the ten heart babies in the cubicle, eight of the baby's mothers were hairdressers. Yes, that is right. What are the odds of that? We never did find out why—just assumed it was chemicals that we used every day. There was one baby who had been in there for over a year, and he was finally going home. These parents and babies quickly became part of our everyday life too.

After a week in the NICU, Katelyn could have visitors, but it was limited to grandparents. My in-laws (Grammy and Pappy) finally got to see their new granddaughter. My mom finally got to see her too. There were so many tears of joy. Shaelyn was having a hard time understanding why she couldn't see her new baby sister, but my sisters were trying to keep her entertained.

I wouldn't take any pictures because I didn't want to remember Katelyn this way. It was hard for people to understand, but it was just my way of dealing with the circumstances. So nobody knew what she looked like.

After about two weeks of pumping breast milk and feeding her through a feeding tube, I finally got the opportunity to breastfeed Katelyn. That little stinker latched right on and went to town. I couldn't believe it because, typically, you have to teach babies right out of the womb. She was just improving so much. It was encouraging to watch her improvements. She was still so tiny and had so many wires, but I could see her getting stronger. She responded so much when Shane and I could hold her. She loved it. She also loved having her arms and hands rubbed. We got a room at Ronald McDonald House, and Shane would walk over there late at night to sleep a couple of hours, but I would not leave her side. I was there with her twenty-four seven. I didn't have time to let myself heal from the C-section. I think I was running on adrenaline. Mothers just do that for their children. My only focus was getting Katelyn better and home.

Day by day, improvements kept coming. She would lose different monitors and wires as she improved. It came to a point where I started missing Shaelyn. I had never been away from her this long. I would have given anything to play Barbies with her. I missed her so much but knew at that point and time I needed to focus on Katelyn and getting her home. I knew Shaelyn was getting spoiled and probably didn't even know I was gone. I later found out that all the stress was very hard on Shaelyn too.

I could feel the presence of God, and I knew that the prayer warriors were covering us. Daily we could see the work of the Lord in Katelyn. If it wasn't for His presence, I don't know if

Shane and I could have made it through. The stress was unreal. Having a sick child is unexplainable. Watching that baby lay there while you are completely helpless. There is nothing you can do. It is out of our hands. That is where faith and trust in the Lord come in. Without faith you have nothing. I knew God had gotten her this far, and He would continue. There were too many miracles already to doubt. He was visibly showing us that He was working in this baby's life.

"Now faith is confidence in what we hope for and assurance about what we do not see" (Hebrews 11:1).

After seven weeks of being in the NICU, Katelyn was moved to the pediatric cardiology floor of the hospital. You can only imagine our excitement! That was a major step for Katelyn. She was no longer going to be in that incubator, and we could hold her as much as we wanted. We had covered so much ground from twenty-four weeks gestation to moving to our room. It was just amazing. As soon as we got this update, my mom brought Shaelyn up to see us. We had not seen Shaelyn for seven weeks, and my heart was just breaking. I will never forget the look on her face when she saw us. It was priceless. And you guessed it—she had her Barbies. And yes, I was excited to sit down and play with her. I missed her so much. We had such a great time, and Shaelyn thought the hospital was really neat! They brought her toys and food and made her feel special too. We only had to stay in the hospital for one more week, and then we were on our way home! It was the best feeling in the world. It seemed like we had been there forever. As I look back, I think about how blessed we were that we were only there for two months. There were a lot of babies and kids that were there a lot longer or never got to leave. The Lord always gives us something to be thankful for—don't miss the opportunity to see it.

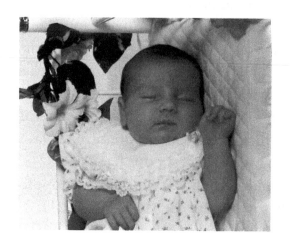

Never Will I Leave Thee...

Chapter 5: "Always"—Chris Tomlin

Shane and I were exhausted mentally and physically. I had not had time to let myself heal from the C-section, and I was still pretty sore. My main concern was Katelyn getting stronger to come home. We were ready to get home and start our lives with our new little addition. Shaelyn was very excited to be able to hold and play with the new baby, whom she nicknamed "poodoos." I have no idea where that nickname came from, but we went with it.

Katelyn was so tiny and looked so fragile. She had the smallest features. I know I said this before, but she looked just like an angel. My dad always said that when a baby was born with a disability or abnormality, God always blessed them differently. I thought of that often when I looked at Katelyn. There was no doubt in my mind that God had her wrapped in his arms. God's protection was on her, and it was obvious to anyone who met her.

The doctors placed me on steroids after the wreck, so Katelyn weighed seven pounds at birth. Her features were so petite, and her body was so little; she did not look seven pounds. Shaelyn was a very big baby and so healthy. She weighed 8 lbs. and 8 ozs. and looked like a sumo wrestler. From Shaelyn to Katelyn, it was a big difference in babies.

Shane and I were just amazed at all the love and support we had for Katelyn. When we finally made it home, our family was so elated to see this beautiful miracle baby. We were ecstatic to show her off too! Needless to say, we had a lot of company.

My mom was one of the first visitors. I remember my mom holding her and just crying. She sat there holding Katelyn and thanking God for the healing miracle in her body. This was when Katelyn received her nickname from my mom, "Tiny Tutu." This nickname was shortened a little to "Tiny."

After family and friends, all came to visit, we finally had the chance to settle in and enjoy being home. It was delightful to see our little family together and full of love for one another. Shaelyn was so excited that all she wanted to do was hold her new baby. She was a good big sister.

My mother came to stay with us for a couple of days. She knew that I was exhausted and wanted me to rest and heal from my C-section. Shaelyn was excited to have Meemaw stay a couple of nights with us. Mom was the best cook, too, so Shane knew he was going to get well-fed while she was here. I don't care what anyone says—you never get too old to have your mom come and comfort you. I needed her there with me mentally and physically. I felt at peace and could rest with her watching over me and my family. I knew we were in good hands.

Katelyn was the smallest baby at Riley's Children's Hospital to receive a pacemaker. They had to implant the pacemaker at the base of her sternum because that was the only area big enough for the pacemaker. Katelyn came home with a little opening in the top of her incision at her sternum. I was concerned about it and watched it closely.

In my family, we had a little crib that was handed down for generations. That little crib was just the right size to put by my bedside so I could roll over and check on her. I remember finding myself just lying there and making sure she was breathing. The doctors gave me signs to watch just in case her pacemaker quit working. I caught myself watching her constantly to make sure I didn't see any of the indications the doctors informed us about. Katelyn is 100 percent dependent on her pacemaker.

Most people who have pacemakers only use them if their heart rate goes too low. The pacemaker will kick in and bring their heart rate back up to normal. Not Katelyn—her pacemaker makes her heart beat all the time. Without the pacemaker, her heart rate would plummet to 24 beats per minute. It would then continue to slow until it stopped beating altogether. So, with all this being new to me, of course, I just wanted to sit and watch her make sure her heart continued to beat. I was trying to depend on God, but I also wanted to be a mom and take care of her by myself. I would be lying if I said I wasn't scared to death because I was. All I knew was this baby was fragile, and I was praying that I did not mess something up.

We were home one week, and Katelyn began to get fussy one morning. Shane had gone back to work, and Mom had gone home, so I was there alone with the girls. I felt Katelyn, and she was clammy, and it was evident that she was not feeling well. I went to change her diaper and looked at her incision. As I looked at the incision, I touched it, and out of the open area, puss began to ooze out. I looked closer, and the area around the incision was starting to look red. I then knew exactly what was going on! I called Riley's and spoke to her electrophysiologist, and she told me to get her back to Indianapolis as soon as possible. There was a problem: I didn't have a vehicle. We didn't have time to get one since I wrecked my car on August 1st. I quickly called my mom to come and stay with Shaelyn, and then I called my sister Sarah to see if she could take us back up to Riley's. I thank God for my family. They didn't hesitate and were here in no time. I packed a bag for Katelyn and me. I knew we would be having another hospital stay. I left a message for Shane at work and told him I would let him know what was going on once we got to the hospital. I knew he could not leave work and get home quickly enough to get us to the hospital. We were quite a distance from Indianapolis, and Shane was an hour in the opposite direction.

Sarah did not waste any time getting to our house. She is a nurse, and I had her look at the incision. She didn't have to say anything because her facial expressions said it all. I then knew this was not good. We loaded up and headed to Riley's once again. On the trip up there, Katelyn got quiet. She started running a fever and slept most of the way. I was already mentally and physically exhausted from our last hospital stay. Mental exhaustion is worse than physical. Satan likes to play games in your mind when you are tired and weak. I had all kinds of thoughts and fears. I looked over at my beautiful miracle and her weak little body. Satan was telling me that this was it and she would not survive. I had fear creeping in once again. I was scared, but I found a little faith the size of a mustard seed, and I began to pray. We had made it this far, and I was not about to let Satan take her now.

"[Jesus] replied, 'Because you have so little faith. Truly I tell you, if you have faith as small as a mustard seed, you can say to this mountain, "Move from here to there," and it will move. Nothing will be impossible for you'" (Matthew 17:20).

When we arrived at the emergency room at Riley's, Katelyn's cardiologist and electrophysiologist were waiting on us. They quickly took us up to the cardiology floor to be examined. They soon determined that Katelyn had staph infection. Staphylococcus bacteremia infection is very serious. If it gets into the blood, it can lead to sepsis or death. People are at higher risk for staph infection when they have surgery or stay in healthcare facilities or have medical devices in their bodies. Katelyn had all of the above-mentioned.

The doctors and nurses quickly started working. The doctor informed me that Katelyn needed surgery to remove her pacemaker and lead. They explained to us how serious this infection was, and they called in the surgical team to prepare for surgery as soon as possible. The nurse came in to prep Katelyn for surgery and put in an IV. She instantly saw that little Katelyn did not have any veins left from recently staying in the hospital. Her arms, legs, feet, and head were all bruised, and all the veins big enough to use were not accessible. The nurse told us that she would have to call in a surgical team to put an arterial line in Katelyn. After the nurse left, I had to ask Sarah what an arterial line was. I was clueless. She explained that when there are no veins for an IV, they would come in and put a catheter in the artery. The only good thing about that was they could use the arterial line for taking blood, IV meds, blood pressure, and anything else they needed for surgery. They wouldn't need to poke her again. Katelyn's little body had nothing more to give. When the surgical team came in to put in the arterial line, they told me I could stay. When they looked at her, they decided to put it in her groin. I'm not sure what happened, but when Katelyn began to cry hysterically, I began to cry and got light headed. My sister rushed in and told me to go out and wait in the waiting room and that she would stay with Katelyn. I felt so weak and helpless. My baby had been through so much, and now she was going to go through it all again. I just began crying and praying. *Please, God, save my baby!*

By the time I walked to the waiting room and called Shane, the surgical team was already finished. I returned to Katelyn's room, and Aunt Sarah was holding her. She was ready for her next surgery. I sat beside Sarah and Katelyn and began to pray for her surgery. As soon as I was done praying, the nurse came into the room to take her back to the surgical room. We were able to carry Katelyn to the surgery door and then hand her off to the nurse. It was all I could do to hand her back over to the doctor. I knew I had to and couldn't treat her on my own. I kissed Katelyn and gave her to the surgical nurse. All this happened so fast; I am just thankful that Sarah was there with me. Sarah and I went down to the waiting room and waited for Shane to arrive.

As we sat in the waiting room, I had time to process the urgency of Katelyn's condition. I broke down and began to weep. I was trying to understand what had just happened and how it happened. I trusted my medical doctors to give my baby the best medical care, and she got a severe infection while they were caring for her. Satan was putting doubt and blame in my mind. Satan attacks at your weakest moment. This was a weak moment, as I was tired and worn out. I was looking at the negative side of this infection instead of the saving of Jesus Christ. He saved her by the motherly instinct that the Lord gave me to act fast on getting her to the hospital. Without that discerning spirit, Katelyn would not have made it. God was once again looking after His miracle child.

Shane arrived about twenty minutes after they took Katelyn back for surgery. He was in shock over the whole situation because it came on so suddenly. While she was in surgery, Sarah and I explained what had happened. Because of work, he was not able to be with us during this stressful time. I know Shane felt like he let us down. I encouraged him because I knew he was with us in prayer and spirit. Katelyn was under the knife for five hours. The surgeon came in to talk to us. He told us that she for sure had a staph infection, and it had gone up her lead and was within millimeters of her heart. He told Shane and me that it was a good thing we were watching her closely and got her to the hospital as soon as we did. If it had reached her heart, it would have instantly killed her. We could not comprehend what he was telling us. It was just too surreal. After all we had just gone through, now this. They took her pacemaker and lead out, and she was on an external pacemaker. He told us she would be in the hospital for another two weeks on intense IV antibiotics. He also said that the wound would have to heal from the inside out, so they were going to leave it open for the air to heal the wound. After the staph was cleared up, they would implant another pacer but down behind her stomach muscle on the left side of her abdomen. We were overwhelmed by all this information. They had no answers about how she got staph or why they sent us home with an open wound that they were concerned about. I was certain that God listened to all of our loved ones who were home praying continuously for this little miracle baby. In our eyes, this situation looked bad, but we were also thankful that the staph infection did not reach Katelyn's heart. There is always something to be thankful for.

"Rejoice always, pray continually, give thanks in all circumstances, for this is God's will for you in Christ Jesus" (1 Thessalonians 5:16–18).

After two weeks of intense antibiotics, Katelyn was ready for another pacemaker and lead placement. The nurse came in to get her prepped for surgery, and we began to converse about the antibiotics. I was asking questions because my sister said they might cause organ damage or other side effects. She told me that some, but not all, do have long-term adverse effects later in life. Some may have liver damage, but one of the most common was the enamel on their teeth. She said intense antibiotics make the enamel on the teeth very thin. This causes tooth decay in young children's baby teeth. That information was very interesting. I wasn't concerned; I was being inquisitive.

Katelyn once again went back into surgery for her second pacemaker and lead. At this time, Katelyn was only ten weeks old and was getting ready for her third big surgery. Our precious baby was in surgery for three hours this time. The cardiologist and electrophysiologist came to the waiting room to explain what they had done. They had to avoid any area that had the staph infection. So the pacemaker was placed on her left side behind her abdomen muscle. They then took the lead up the left side through her ribs to her heart. They told us the surgery was a success, but she would be in ICU for a couple of days and then back up to the heart floor. The cardiologist said they wanted to see how she healed and reacted to the new pacemaker before they sent her home. Even though Katelyn was petite, she was a fighter. She had the will and determination to survive. Our Lord continued to wrap her up and carry her through. I thank God for His saving grace.

The Lord is so faithful! His mercy is mighty! I believe in His healing and never-failing love. God can't deliver us if we are not in trouble. How could we know if God is our physician if we aren't sick? Without trouble, we would not see God's greatness and proclaim it. God is the light in our darkness. It is up to us to find His light and tell the world of His glory. What better way than through His miracles of children?

"And call on me in the day of trouble; I will deliver you, and you will honor me" (Psalm 50:15).

Chapter 6: "Here in the Presence" —Elevation Worship

After we came home, we tried to transition back into our normal routine. It was a little harder because we had spent quite a bit of time in the hospital with Katelyn. I still had my beauty shop and our four-year-old daughter, who was missing her mom and dad like crazy. During all the hospital stays, I had left my beauty shop thinking it was in good hands with one of my hairdressers. Little did I know she was stealing from me and the beauty shop. I had good friends watching over the shop and reporting back to me. She was stealing products, giving free tans, and ruining my customer's hair. It was a mess! The business that I worked so hard to build was being destroyed in less than three months. Ever hear the old saying, "Kick 'em when they are down"? That is exactly what was happening to me. I trusted this individual. She knew what our family was enduring and the stress I was under, yet she took advantage of me. Was God trying to show me something? I believe He was. You see, it doesn't matter how much money you have or make or what possessions you own. No earthly treasures matter. The only thing that matters is your faith in God and His never-failing love for us. My dad always said, "You can't take it to heaven with you!"

"For everyone born of God overcomes the world. This is the victory that has overcome the world, even our faith" (1 John 5:4).

"Who it that overcomes the world? Only the one who believes that Jesus is the Son of God" (1 John 5:5).

Shane and I had discussed selling the shop when Katelyn was a newborn in the NICU. When all this happened at the beauty shop, our minds were made up. It was time to sell and concentrate on my family. Money was not a priority to us anymore. We prayed and believed God would provide. The Lord sent us a reputable buyer, and the process of selling my beauty shop went very smoothly. I worked very hard to make my beauty shop a success, but not one time did I question the sale. There, too, it was all God leading the way.

God blessed me with the opportunity to be able to stay home and be a full-time mom to our two beautiful daughters. The ability to stay home and raise our girls has been my biggest blessing through all of this. The Lord knew what was in our future and how much I needed to be home with our children. I also thank God for an understanding and supportive husband. He has worked with great love and devotion to provide for our family for the last twenty years.

Shaelyn was such a big help with her baby "poodoos." If Baby Sis needed anything at all, Big Sis was there in an instant. She was in love with her new baby sister and couldn't wait for her to play with her Barbies. Don't get me wrong—somehow the Barbies always found a way to lay beside Katelyn. Our girls were such a joy to our lives.

Typically after you have a baby, you get newborn baby pictures. Well, Katelyn's life was so abnormal that we didn't get them until she was out of the hospital the second time. As you can tell, nothing so far has been what any mother would call normal. Even the littlest thing, like newborn photos, may not seem big, but to me, it was just another abnormal thing in our life. I was starting to realize that I just needed to be thankful for every day that I had with Katelyn. Normal or not, we were just thankful for all God had blessed us with.

"Give thanks to the Lord, for he is good; his love endures forever" (Psalm 118:1).

Katelyn was growing but still so tiny. She seemed so fragile. I found myself watching her continuously. I wanted to make sure she was breathing properly. I caught myself interrogating her for all the symptoms the doctor told me to watch for. Before Katelyn was sent home, her electrophysiologist gave us a crash course on symptoms that her pacemaker was not working or that something needed to be attended to. The symptoms included blue lips, palish blue complexion, vomiting, lethargy, loss of energy, or anything abnormal. The previous emergency trip to the hospital had me on the alert for symptoms. I trusted God, yet I was the mom. Motherly instincts seemed to kick in. Brother John always told me to give it all to God, but it was so hard to let go and give it all to God. I wanted to hang on to some of it. I am a very determined individual, and I was always a very independent woman. I never wanted to rely on anyone. So handing it all over to God was a big step for me. It was something I was working on. All these major adjustments to my life were very hard on me, to say the least. But I was learning to let go.

In January 2003, Katelyn was almost six months old. We started the day with our normal routine. It was snowy and icy that day. Katelyn started to get a little fussy, but I figured it was Shaelyn smothering her a little bit. Shaelyn always had to touch her, and it would make Katelyn upset. I went in to check on her, and her face was a little pale. I picked her up, and her lips started to turn blue in color. Those are two of the most important signs that something is wrong with the pacemaker. Those symptoms warned us that Katelyn's heart was not getting the correct blood supply and she was losing oxygen. I knew as long as she was crying, I had time to get her somewhere to a hospital. But what I didn't know was how much time I had to get her to the emergency room. I called Katelyn's electrophysiologist, and she said to get her to the nearest hospital ASAP! I once again called my sister Sarah to tell her what was going on. She knew how upset I was and told me to hold tight and that she would be right over. The roads were starting to get pretty slick. I tried to call Shane at work, but he could only check his phone at certain times of the day. I then contacted my mother and father-in-law to come over and sit with Shaelyn. After I set everything in motion, I sat down and comforted Katelyn. Shaelyn and I began to pray and ask the Lord to please watch over us and let us get her to the hospital quickly and safely.

When my sister arrived, we quickly traveled to the closest hospital, which was twenty miles away in a town called Vincennes, Indiana. Those twenty miles seemed like a hundred miles by the time we got there. The roads were getting treacherous. I knew we needed to get to Riley's Children's Hospital, but it was not possible to drive that distance on these slick roads at this time. As Sarah and I rushed her into the emergency room, I noticed Katelyn was starting to get inaudible and was still blue in color.

As we entered the ER, the admitting nurse could see right away the seriousness of Katelyn's condition. She rushed us back to an examination room and called for a cardiologist STAT. As all of this was happening, I was giving them Katelyn's health history. This was a very small hospital, and I knew they were not equipped to take care of her properly. Katelyn's condition was so rare in our small rural area that our local hospitals didn't know about treatment. I was hoping they could get her stabilized for us to get her transferred to Riley's. This was the same hospital I went to after the car accident. I don't know who was more alarmed, them or me.

In the ER examination room, they put heart monitors on Katelyn to watch her heart rate closer. Here's the thing—her heart is not normal, and the monitors could not pick up a good reading because of her heart block condition. As I sat there with my sister, cardiologists kept coming in and looking at her but doing nothing. I felt like I was in the movie *ET*. They would just look at her and touch her now and then, but that was it. It was like she was an alien. If you have seen the movie, you know exactly what I meant. The sad truth was they had no idea how to treat her because they had never treated a child with complete heart block. I sat there and watched life leave my daughter. She got to the desperation of no body movement. All she could move was her eyes. She was so weak that her crying stopped. It was the scariest thing I had ever encountered in my life. I was watching my daughter die right in front of my eyes. I looked at my sister and said, "Is this really how it's going to end? Are they seriously going to let her lie here and die because they are clueless about how to treat her?" My sister looked at me with big tears running down her cheeks. I then felt a surge of energy run through my body. I now know it was the Holy Spirit! I thought to myself, *Not on my watch!* I called Katelyn's electrophysiologist and told her exactly what was going on and that we could not get to Riley's because of the snowstorm we were currently having. I explained how this small hospital was not equipped to treat Katelyn and that we needed help! Our electrophysiologist contacted the hospital and gave them instructions. She wanted them to connect Katelyn to a pacemaker machine and turn her pacer up as far as it would go. Well, guess what? They did not have the proper equipment to do so. The next step was to fly a pacemaker tech into the hospital to get Katelyn stabilized. This was such a disaster and complete chaos. While all this was happening, Katelyn's little body just lay there limp and helpless. I kept going over to her and talking to her and trying to keep her looking at me. I felt if she was looking at me, she knew I was there and was never going to leave her. I was not giving up!

Finally, the helicopter came with the pacemaker tech from St. Jude's pacemaker company. There are so many different models of pacemakers available. St. Jude's is the pacemaker company that made a pacemaker small enough to fit into Katelyn's little chest. So that company was the pacemaker our electrophysiologist decided was the best for Katelyn. I was never so relieved to see someone in my whole life.

The pacemaker tech hooked Katelyn up to the pacemaker machine and turned her pacemaker up as far as it would go. I sat there and watched life go right back into my daughter. It was the most amazing thing I had ever witnessed. I was elated, yet sad. My daughter's life is controlled by a machine. I knew that in a way, yet it hit me hard when I sat there and watched life return to her little body from near death. No words can even explain how I felt at that time. I knew then who was in control, and it wasn't me.

The electrophysiologist was constantly communicating with the tech. The pacemaker machine can also run tests that sometimes show what is wrong with the pacemaker. Thank goodness this time it did show the problem. The machine showed that the lead to the heart from the pacemaker had a fracture in it. When there is a fracture in the lead, the pacemaker is not receiving the electrical pulse to the heart. The heart didn't know to beat. What this meant was we needed to get to Riley's Hospital for another surgery. The adjustment would last temporarily, but we didn't know for how long. With all the energy going to the pacemaker to keep the heart beating, the pacemaker's battery would run down quickly. We would need a complete pacemaker system again. She was almost six months old, and we were preparing for surgery number three.

After the tech was finished with all the adjustments and had Katelyn stabilized, we were getting prepared to transfer her to Riley's Children's Hospital. I thought to myself, *What has just happened?* This was all a whirlwind of chaos. After this experience, I knew that the local hospital was not a place we could take Katelyn for help. Sometimes living in a rural area does not have favorable benefits. As soon as Shane could get to the hospital with his four-wheel drive truck to combat the hazardous roads, we took off to Indianapolis.

After I got into the truck with Shane, I broke down. I was trying to explain to him what had just happened, but I couldn't. All I wanted to do was hold my daughter and thank God for His mercies once again. No words could explain what we had just endured. I saw my daughter dying, and then God restored her lifeless body to a smiling and happy baby again. Right in front of my eyes. I knew without a shadow of a doubt that my mom and Brother John were praying their hearts out once again for Katelyn Grace.

"'Have faith in God,' Jesus answered" (Mark 11:22).

"Truly I tell you, if anyone says to this mountain, 'Go, throw yourself into the sea,' and does not doubt in their heart but believes that what they say will happen, it will be done for them" (Mark 11:23).

"Therefore I tell you, whatever you ask for in prayer, believe that you have received it, and it will be yours" (Mark 11:24).

We arrived safely at Riley's hospital and prepared for yet another surgery. We were sent to the cardiac floor, and they hooked her up to heart monitors. Believe it or not, it was a relief for me because I felt like I could rest there. Only because I knew that they were watching her closely and I didn't have to be on alert. I sat there looking at her as she was playing with the monitor wires. She looked so peaceful and full of life, but three short hours before, she was lifeless, and I didn't know if she was going to live or die. That is how fragile her life is. It was hard for me to grasp that concept. Little did she know that she had another surgery coming up shortly. I wondered then if that is what God means when He says we need to have faith like a child. "And said, Verily I say unto you, Except ye be converted, and become as little children, ye shall not enter into the kingdom of heaven" (Matthew 18:3). I just know that I am so blessed to be Katelyn's mom.

It was time for surgery, and they came to prep Katelyn. This time, they waited to put an IV in until they had her in the surgical room. I was thankful for that because IVs are so painful and hard to get successfully into her little veins that are already overused. Shane and I carried her to the surgery door once again. This was starting to feel like a horrible routine now. As the nurse took Katelyn, she was all smiles and was clueless about what was behind those doors. It was so hard to hand her over because I knew what was about to happen. Shane and I went to the waiting room, and neither one of us said a word to the other. We both just sat in silence. I was playing back in my mind what had happened the past two days. I think until that point in time I was still running on adrenaline.

Katelyn's surgery lasted only three hours this time. The cardiologist came to the waiting room and spoke to Shane and me again. The doctor said it all went well and they were sending her to ICU just to be monitored closely. He did tell us that her lead was broken. We had no clue how that happened.

I just know now by experience how critical it is when there is a fracture in her pacemaker lead.

Shane had run out of days that he could take off work, and he was our only income at this time, so I told him to go home and get some sleep for work. I assured him that Katelyn and I would be just fine. My mom offered to come and pick us up when it was time to come home. Shane hated to have to leave, but we knew it was for the best, and Shaelyn needed her dad too. We were only in the hospital for ten days this time. Shortest stay so far!

With all the excitement, I forgot that the day we were released from the hospital was my thirtieth birthday! Nobody said a word about my birthday, but when Katelyn and I walked through the door, Shaelyn and Shane had made me a birthday cake. Shane knew that I was not excited about turning thirty. I didn't like the idea of getting older. My mom told me it was better than the alternative. She was right about that! Shane and Shaelyn were trying to make it special for me since I had just gone through all this trauma with Katelyn. I do have to say this was the prettiest birthday cake I was ever given! Coming home was the best present I could have ever hoped for. We were home, and we could be a family once again.

"May the God of Hope fill you with all joy and peace as you trust in him, so that you may overflow with hope by the power of the Holy Spirit" (Romans 15:13).

Chapter 7: "Who Am I"—Casting Crowns

Katelyn recovered in a timely matter from her third surgery. From February to May, we had trips to Riley's Children's Hospital once a month. We were on a personal level with the electrophysiologist, cardiologist, and their nurses. Everyone knew Katelyn Wilber. She was still young and didn't understand what all these appointments consisted of. On every visit, we had chest X-rays and an overall examination. The worst part of the appointments was the interrogation of the pacemaker. Since Katelyn's heart rate is only twenty-four beats per minute on its own, they had to check her threshold to make sure it was at a safe place. They did this by turning her pacemaker as low as it would go to see if her heart would beat on its own. That test would make her sick every time. She would always vomit and take a deep breath like she was going to pass out. They were taking the life out of her little body to see if her heart would spontaneously start beating. Every time they did that analysis, I sat there praying, "Please, God, answer our prayers and heal our baby." That process was so scary to her and me. I had such a hard time with this test. I sat and watched with such hope as they took the life out of my baby and then put it back in. Most of the time I couldn't hold my tears back but tried to be strong and not let Katelyn see me upset. But sometimes I failed and couldn't stop crying. It was too traumatizing to watch your baby look at you for help, but you were helpless. I was supposed to be her protector, but I felt like I was letting her down. I knew that until God healed Katelyn, her life was in the hands of the little electronic device in her tiny little body. It was hard coming to terms with this process. I knew for now that it had to be done and God would be right there beside us through all of this. We had to keep our hope in Jesus Christ.

Riley's Children's Hospital was a hospital that centered around making patients comfortable and less afraid to be at a hospital. They had little red wagons by the entrance, and Katelyn loved riding in them. There were toys and stuffed animals all over. After each appointment, I would take Katelyn for a ride around the hospital looking at all the neat things. She loved that! They worked to make it fun for all the sick little kids. During every stay we had there, the volunteers always tried to make us as comfortable as possible. Anything we needed, they always tried to accommodate. That is a blessing, especially if you are in the hospital for any length of time. It was incredible how all these people donated time and money to try and help make sick kids' hospital stays as comfortable as possible. I knew that God was working through many of those individuals and some unknowingly.

When we were in the hospital, it amazed me how many parents left their babies because they were sick. Sick babies were considered a hardship to some. It broke my heart. I decided when I retired, I was going to be the lady that volunteers to just hold babies and give them the love they miss out on from loving parents.

Life was kind of crazy, and yet it didn't seem real. I was still trying to figure out our new life. It seemed like so much was thrown at us at one time. Not only Katelyn's health issues but life in general at home too. I was adjusting to becoming a full-time mom. Shane had a custom cabinet and countertop background for twenty years, so he decided to put a cabinet shop of his own here at the house. He also worked full-time at his regular job. We did need the extra money because all the doctor's bills and the trips back and forth to Riley's were very expensive. We joked and said that Katelyn was our million-dollar baby, but she was. I didn't worry about the money so much but found out later that Shane did. Men typically are the providers and feel unworthy if the amount is not enough. Shane worked twelve-hour days and drove an hour one way to work. He then came home to work in his cabinet shop until ten or eleven at night, just in time to shower and go to bed. Having a sick child and financial stress sometimes took a toll on our marriage. A friend of mine told me it was considered normal. She said that 75 percent of parents with critically ill children end up in divorce. I didn't want Shane and me to be part of those statistics. We just had to dig in and grow closer to God to put us back on track sometimes. We were in agreement that God had to be our foundation for our marriage to survive.

Before I knew it, Katelyn was nine months old. I was too caught up in doctor's visits and making sure Katelyn "looked" fine to realize that she had not rolled over yet. At our electrophysiologist appointment in May, I asked her if she thought it was strange that Katelyn had made no effort to roll over. The doctor told me she thought because of all her surgeries on her belly and chest area, she had never been put on her belly, so she probably didn't know how to roll over. Besides, her incisions were probably still sore and uncomfortable. I thought it was a natural thing for babies, but what she told me made sense. Then I had to remind myself that our normal is different. We don't have anything normal.

I decided to find an occupational and physical therapist to work with Katelyn. They were available through the state and would come into the house and work with her. I was amazed by all the information they had for Katelyn. I had no clue that babies have to roll over and lay on their bellies to be able to push up to crawl and then walk. It all goes hand in hand. Here we were, almost ten months, and Katelyn couldn't do any of those things. We quickly found out that Katelyn had no desire to roll over onto her stomach. She would cry and resist. We concluded that tummy time was not going to happen. Katelyn was very smart but behind in her motor skills and strength. She began therapy three times a week throughout the summer.

We saw progression in her motor skills. Sometimes the way we think things should be is not at all the way it ends up. Katelyn was not going to roll over. By the end of the summer, Katelyn had learned to adapt. Since she wouldn't roll over, she had no idea how to crawl. She went from laying on her back to scooting on her rear end. She didn't struggle to scoot; this girl could race her sister on her rear end! Most of the time

I had her wear her diaper only because she ruined her pant bottoms. From that point on, I knew that nothing was going to stop this girl. She had the determination to succeed. She was not going to be singled out.

On August 21, 2003, our baby was one year old. I looked at that miracle and all her little scars and thanked God for giving us a whole year with her. I thought back to all the near-death experiences in one short year and was just in awe of God. What if our faith in God hadn't been so strong that He was going to take care of us and we had aborted this precious baby? She had already brought us so much joy, love, and faith in one year. I couldn't wait to see what joy her whole life would bring to us. Needless to say, we had a wonderful first birthday celebration!

Shaelyn started preschool in August at a local Christian school. The preschool was at a church in Robinson, Illinois. Once a week during preschool, they had a Christian moms group. The moms would meet for devotions and prayer. I wasn't acquaintances with many local Christian mothers, so I thought it would be good for me to reach out and make some new friends. Little did I know one lady in the group would have such an impact on Katelyn and my life. Lynda Vaughn and I quickly became best friends. Katelyn stayed with me through the mom's group, and Lynda was so fun and loving. She instantly gravitated toward Katelyn. Katelyn was not sure of her in the beginning, but Lynda said, "This little girl will love me." I didn't realize Lynda was prophetic, but sure enough, Katelyn ended up loving Lynda and her husband, David. They were a huge part of our lives for many years.

Katelyn didn't like a lot of people, and she did not warm up very fast. My mom always said that it was because every stranger she met was always poking her or making her sick. She associated strangers with pain. Katelyn was not a happy baby. She was always sad or crying. When I look back at her pictures, I realize how sickly and sad she looked in them. In almost every picture, she is crying or has been crying. The only people she got close to was Shaelyn, my mom, and me. I knew she loved her aunts and Shane's parents, but she just didn't bond with them.

She loved her dad, but he was always at work providing for us. Shane had a hard time dealing with Katelyn's illness. I believe he buried himself in work, and that was his way of coping with everything. I almost wondered if he was afraid to get too close because her life was so fragile and uncertain. Don't get me wrong—he loves her dearly, but I always thought he couldn't deal as easily with her life uncertainty.

Her big sis was her world, and she loved being around her. She loved watching her sister at tumbling and dance class. I could see on her face that she wanted to tumble and dance like her sister. I knew the time would eventually come when she would want to take classes. I was just concerned with her tumbling and stretching her lead too much. Shane and I never wanted to keep her from doing things. We never wanted her singled out in any way, but tumbling was a little concerning.

This little girl had so much determination. I believe that God allows obstacles in life to give us strength in Him. Katelyn's obstacles were strengthening her, but I think they strengthened Shane and me more. All of these trials made us rely more on God. Our faith was growing abundantly. I got to where I didn't listen to any secular songs; it was only praise and worship. I found myself praying randomly all day. Our home was transforming into a home of faith and praise. A song that played constantly in my car and home was "Who Am I" by Casting Crowns. It helped me have faith and reminded me that I was God's child. Not because of who I was but because of who

God is. No fear because I am God's child, and He will always take care of us.

"Now faith is confidence in what we hope for and assurance about what we do not see" (Hebrews 11:1).

It was fun watching Katelyn acquire her little personality. She wasn't anything like her big sis. Nothing ever bothered Shaelyn. She was easygoing and went with the flow. Katelyn, on the other hand, was not the case. She could talk with her expressions. Katelyn did not like to be bothered or be around strangers. She was happy to do her own thing in her own house. I believe she felt her home was a haven.

Shane and I needed some alone time together to rekindle our relationship, but I couldn't make myself leave Katelyn with anyone. I felt like I was her protector. I was afraid nobody else knew what symptoms to look for in case she had another complication with her heart. Katelyn didn't like to stay with family members for any length of time. With all she had been through, I couldn't make her stay where she was uncomfortable. The doctors told me I needed to keep her as calm as possible to keep the stress off of her heart. That alone caused more stress on me, but I was willing to do whatever it took to keep her here on earth with us.

I was still breastfeeding Katelyn, and every time I thought I would wean her off, the heart doctor told me to continue because she wasn't strong enough yet. He informed me that mother's milk had the nutritional value that Katelyn still needed. She was still fragile, and he advised me to continue breastfeeding. That was fine with me. Anything to help her I was willing to do.

All of the factors mentioned above led to Katelyn being so attached to me. She was always under my feet. I would back up in the kitchen and trip over her because she was on her bottom right behind me. If I was missing in the house for five minutes, it was grounds for a search party. There were times I would go to the bathroom, and she would sit right in front of me watching. I could not get out of her sight. Sometimes I miss those days. Later Katelyn told me the reason why she could never leave my side was that she only felt safe around me. She knew that I was going to take care of her. I told her that it wasn't me that took care of her, but I believe she could sense my faith and God's presence. God's presence gave her comfort.

"Praise be to the God and Father of our Lord Jesus Christ, the Father of compassion and the God of all comfort, who comforts us in all our troubles so that we can comfort those in any trouble with the comfort we ourselves receive from God" (2 Corinthians 1:3–4).

Our church family was a saving grace for us during this time in our lives. They constantly prayed for us, and if we ever needed anything, they were there. We had such a wonderful support group, and everyone loved Katelyn so much. It amazed me how one little miracle baby could pull so many people close to God. People are drawn to signs and wonders. Katelyn is a sign and wonder from God. I always had people ask me how I could do what I have done, and my answer was the same every time. Only through Christ could I ever make it. Christ strengthens me daily. Not just weekly at church but daily. I have to keep my focus on Him and only Him.

"I can do all things through him who gives me strength" (Philippians 4:13).

Chapter 8: "How Great Is Our God" —Chris Tomlin

The Lord references "fear not" 365 times in the Bible. That is for every day of the year. It took me a few years to realize this fact. But once I realized it, I looked at life differently. You have to have faith out of your heart, not your mouth. Faith in Jesus Christ overcomes fear.

One morning in January 2004, Katelyn woke up vomiting. I instantly was alarmed. When you have a child with a life-threatening illness, you are constantly on alert. I thought to myself, *This is what happens when they shut her pacemaker off at her doctor's appointments.* I looked at her, and she was a little pale, but her lips were still pretty pink. Shane observed her and thought she possibly had a virus. I felt in my spirit this was not the case. I was with her all day and the one who took care of her most of the time. So I felt this was abnormal behavior. She was very tired and just wanted to lie around. That was not Katelyn's nature. In the back of my mind, I knew something was not right but did not want to overreact. The history of emergencies with her made me want to contact the doctor immediately but decided to monitor her instead. That night when I went to check on her, Katelyn had thrown up in her sleep. She was covered with vomit and was dead asleep. I had to shake her to wake her up, and this was not normal because she was a very light sleeper. After she awoke and realized she had vomited, she began to cry. I cleaned her up and settled her down. I decided to sleep the rest of the night in the recliner with her on my chest. I am not sure about her security or my peace of mind. Either way, I was concerned.

The next morning I called her electrophysiologist and told her all the symptoms I had noticed. I believed that the doctor respected me and knew that I was not one of those moms that overreacted. I always assessed Katelyn thoroughly before I called the doctors. She knew our distance from the hospital and the issues we'd had in the past with Katelyn's pacemaker. She asked us to please come up to the hospital to let her interrogate Katelyn. I called my mom, and she once again went with us on another road trip to Indianapolis. I called my mother-in-law to please come and get Shaelyn. I wasn't sure if we were in for another surgery, so I thought it was best for her to stay at home. My mother-in-law, or "Grammy," never hesitated to come over when I called. She was a lifesaver a lot of the time for us. We were blessed to have Grammy and Paps only three miles away.

On our way to the hospital, my mom looked at me and said, "Are you okay, Sis? You look so tired. I worry about you." I am a person who never wants attention, and I didn't want my mom to worry about me. I responded that I was fine and to not worry. I was only concerned with Katelyn's health, so I never paid any attention to myself. I was exhausted mentally and physically. It was like I lived on a constant alert. Not fear because I knew that God was taking care of Katelyn. I just knew that God gave her to me for a purpose, and it was my job to watch after her. I felt like I was her protector here on earth to help God groom her for His glory. I know that our children are a gift from God, and we only have them for a short time, and we must take care of them to the best of our ability through Christ. That was exactly what I was going to do!

Never Will I Leave Thee...

"Start children off on the way they should go, and even when they are old they will not turn from it" (Proverbs 22:6).

My mom and I made it to Riley's safely and found the little red wagon for Katelyn to ride in. Believe it or not, the red wagon was a highlight for her, and it kind of kept her mind off of things. As we reached the electrophysiologist, the nurses were so happy to see us. As I said before, the nurses had an instant attraction to Katelyn. We were on a first-name basis, and they were comforting to us.

The doctor hooked Katelyn up to her pacemaker machine to interrogate it. Katelyn was seventeen months old at this time and was starting to know what her doctor's appointments consisted of. It was getting harder for me to keep her still for the tests. She associated the doctor with making her sick. In a way she was correct. The doctor would lower her pacemaker to see if her heart would beat on its own and to see if there were any irregularities. When she did this, Katelyn would instantly take a deep breath, begin to cry, and then vomit. She did this with every interrogation. It would scare her and me to death. I kept thinking to myself, *There has to be an easier way to see if the pacemaker is working properly*. The stress of this test on her and me was a lot to handle. My mom was allowed to watch the pacemaker interrogation during this visit. It was a lot for my mom too. She sat there and cried with Katelyn and me. Later she told me, "That was one of the worst things I had to witness and don't care to watch it again. It was too sad to watch them take the life out of my little 'Tiny Tutu.'" My mom told me later on the drive home that I was the strongest mother she had ever seen and was very proud of me and my strength. I told her I got my faith and strength from watching her rely on God all the years of my life.

The doctor was amazed at Katelyn being so symptomatic. She did not have any other patients who had the same reactions to interrogations or pacemaker malfunctions. I look back now and thank God that her symptoms were so apparent. Sometimes God watches over us differently than we expect. I believe this was God's way of warning us to get Katelyn to the hospital in a life-saving time.

After the interrogation, the doctor told me that there was nothing wrong with the pacemaker. Everything checked out accurately. I was not convinced this was the case and questioned her about all the symptoms. She told me that with her symptoms she was wondering if there was a possible break in her lead. The lead to the heart from the pacemaker is so small that physically finding a break is almost impossible unless you catch it at the exact time when it is not making contact. The doctor then ordered a twenty-four-hour halter monitor. A halter monitor is a device that has wires that stick to Katelyn's chest and records her heart activity. If something is abnormal, it will record it and send the results to the doctor. After they put the halter monitor on Katelyn, we hit the road back to Illinois. On our three-hour trip home, the song "How Great Is Our God" by Chris Tomlin kept coming to my mind. How great is our God? He is the name above all names and worthy of my praise. My heart sings, "How great is my God!" Thank You, Jesus, for Your never-failing love for my family and me.

The next day, Katelyn had an appointment with her physical therapist. I thought this worked out perfectly because we could see if activity changed her heart rate. I also thought that maybe she would be active enough that the lead might separate, and they could see it on the monitor. Katelyn went through her physical therapy session just fine and without any symptoms. After her session, we boxed the monitor up and mailed it back to the doctor. Now, we had to wait for it to be examined to see if the doctor had seen any abnormalities.

Katelyn was just a sign and wonder. Although she was behind in her motor skills, she was super smart. She was very self-driven. When she set her mind on something, she was going to do it! We have a big patio door, and she would scoot and sit in front of the door and just look outside. We took our shoes off inside the patio door when we entered the house. One day I was in the kitchen, which is beside the big door, and looked over at her. She had a tennis shoe and was playing with the shoestrings. I kept watching her and realized she was trying to figure out how to tie the shoes. She never liked anyone to help her; she always wanted to do things on her own. I just continued with my chores and left her alone. She sat fiddling with the shoestrings for two hours. Yes, you guessed it—she figured it out! She taught herself how to tie her shoes at seventeen months old. Katelyn couldn't walk yet, but she could tie her shoes. A couple of days later, my sister Kristin and her son Grayson came to visit. Grayson was five years old at this time, and Kristin had been battling him to learn how to tie his shoes. I have found out that most boys want to do things on their own time. He was energetic and didn't want to sit long enough to learn. When he saw Katelyn could tie her shoes, he couldn't have a "baby" tie her shoes and he couldn't! He went home and learned how to tie his shoes. It was pretty funny! I still remind him of it to this day, and he is now twenty-one years old.

It was about a week before we got the results from the halter monitor, and everything checked out fine. I still felt in my spirit that something was wrong. I thought, *How in the world could we be battling this again already?* We just had a replacement surgery almost exactly a year ago. Katelyn was making good progress with the physical therapist, and now she was faced with another surgery. It seemed every time Katelyn would start to get a somewhat normal life, Satan would throw another wrench in her progress. I had so many questions for the doctors, but even the specialists couldn't answer them. I knew God was in control, but of course, I am human. I had times when I would just break down and cry in private. I tried to keep my sorrow locked inside of me so the girls wouldn't see me upset. I only wanted the girls to be encouraged and never have fear of the future.

"There is no fear in love. But perfect love drives out fear because fear has to do with punishment. The one who fears is not made perfect in love" (1 John 4:18).

After Katelyn's first pacemaker placement, they sent us home with a home monitor from the pacemaker company. This monitor is a fast and easy way to send pacemaker readings to her heart doctor. Most of the time, if I called the doctor with concerns, she would have me send a pacemaker reading before we would travel the distance to the hospital. It was an easy process. I would attach the monitor to Katelyn with heart sticky pads. After that, I would call the 800 number on the monitor, and it would contact a tech. Then I would set the monitor by our landline and place the phone in the monitor's phone holster. They would walk me through step by step how to send the transmission. The transmission would then go straight to our heart doctor. If there was a problem, the doctor would call us. It was about two weeks after we got the test results that Katelyn had another episode of bluish lip color and vomiting. I quickly sent a transmission through our home monitor. Within thirty minutes the heart doctor contacted us and said that she saw a little episode in the transmission but did not think it looked dangerous but a little concerning. She told me she thought it would be a good idea to come in to have her pacemaker replaced because the battery had depleted. I asked her about the lead, but she said she wouldn't know until they went in for surgery to see if there was a break. She said they would not replace the lead unless they saw a break in it during surgery. I had learned from past issues that if the pacemaker battery depletes quickly, then there has to be a break in the lead. There was no logical reason that the pacemaker battery should be depleted in one year. These batteries are supposed to last for many years, sometimes twenty years. Another concern I had was if they did not replace the lead during this surgery and she continued to have the same problems, then Katelyn would have to have yet another surgery later. To me, it just made sense to replace it all in one surgery. I knew in my spirit that she had a fractured lead, but I could not get the doctor to listen to me. I began to pray for the doctors to have discernment in this situation. I also prayed that the Lord would show them the actual problem with the pacemaker's complete system.

Surgery was set up for the following week. On Sunday at church, we had special anointing and prayer for Katelyn and our family. Much to our surprise, the church took up a love offering to help pay for hotel, gas, and food. We also had two couples that were good friends of ours from church that booked us all hotel rooms close to the hospital. They had been with us since the beginning and knew what kind of stress it put on us. They wanted to help lessen the burden. This was such a pleasant surprise. With everything we had been through, we had never asked anyone for financial help. The financial aspect of the frequent travel, hotel, and food weighed on our family. Shane worked twelve to fourteen hours a day for seven days a week to provide enough for me to be able to run to doctors and stay home with the girls. I always felt bad for him because he missed out on a lot because of working and providing for us. All we ever asked for was prayer, and sometimes it was a lot of prayers. I just thank God for all of the blessings that He so graciously blessed us with.

"Therefore, since we are surrounded by such a great cloud of witnesses, let us throw off everything that hinders and the sin that so easily entangles. And let us run with perseverance the race marked out for us" (Hebrews 12:1).

Shane and I got everything prepared to leave for Katelyn's surgery number four. This surgery was different because it was scheduled and not an emergency like the last three surgeries. We once again had to leave Shaelyn at home. I had it set up where Shaelyn was staying with different family members to keep her busy and having fun. I never wanted her to feel left out or resentful of her sister taking her parents away from her all the time. That was always a concern of mine. Shaelyn was my first and always held a special place in my heart. We said our goodbyes and traveled to Indianapolis for our early morning procedure.

Once we got to the hotel, we met up with our friends from church. We had a nice dinner and a special prayer for us and the surgery. Prayer always eased our minds and comforted us. We set up a time to meet in the morning before we all headed to the hospital for prayer once again. We took Katelyn to the pool, and she and Shane had a good father-and-daughter time playing in the pool before bed. I sat there watching them play and just thanked God for the time He had given us with Katelyn. Our time with her was so valuable to us because we didn't know how long God would allow us to keep her here on earth. As I sat there, I still felt in my spirit that the lead had a fracture, and I could not get it out of my mind. I knew the importance of a properly functioning lead to keep from another surgery, hospital emergency, or possible death because of the distance to get to the hospital. It was very critical to have the lead intact and not fractured.

It was time to say our good nights and prayers, but of course, I was not able to sleep. I stayed up all night praying and watching my baby sleep. As I prayed, I asked the Lord to please guide the doctors with the proper decision about the lead. If the lead was fractured to please show the doctors so it could be replaced. It seemed like that night took forever to end. I had faith that God was in control once again, and whatever we pray in faith and believe in our hearts the Lord will hear our cries and answer our prayers. I knew my strength had to come from the Lord because I could not handle the stress on my own.

Morning came, and we gathered in our hotel room with our friends to pray before we went to the hospital. We circled up, anointed one another, and held hands to pray. We all started to pray, and Katelyn was standing up holding my leg. As we began to pray and ask the Lord to please show the doctors the fractured lead without any question, Katelyn began pulling at my leg. The next thing I heard was her taking a deep breath and falling onto the floor. I looked down, and she was passed out and blue. I picked her up and called her name to wake her up. She woke up but vomited. She was very weak. Shane and I instantly knew what had just happened. I felt myself go weak, and I started to weep. I began to cry out to God, asking for Him to save our miracle baby. We picked her up and ran to the car without hesitation. We knew we had to get her to the hospital as soon as possible. It was a matter of life or death.

We put her in the car seat and took off to the hospital. Shane and I knew exactly what God was doing. God answered our prayers about the lead. The lead completely broke during prayer. We left our friends praying in our room to meet with them later at the hospital.

Katelyn's electrophysiologist had given me her cell phone number in case of emergencies. I called the doctor and told her what had just happened, and she said she'd meet us at the emergency room. We were only twenty minutes from the hospital. As Shane was speeding there, Katelyn kept going in and out. I sat in the back with her trying to keep her awake. By the time we reached the emergency room, she was incoherent. I could no longer wake her up. I was so scared. She was breathing shallowly, and lips were blue, and her complexion was pale. She was lifeless. After we pulled up to the emergency room door, Shane grabbed Katelyn's lifeless body and went running into the hospital. Our doctor met us and showed us where to take Katelyn. We carried Katelyn to the operating room door. Our doctor took Katelyn from us and rushed her through the doors. Shane and I stood there crying and praying. I was the most scared I had ever been to this point and time in our lives.

In about ten minutes, our doctor came out of the operating room crying. I had never seen our doctor that upset. When I saw her crying, I automatically thought the worst. I then broke down and began to weep even harder. I was so scared because I knew when Shane handed Katelyn to her, she was unresponsive. She told us that they had to stabilize Katelyn before they could consider doing surgery. She was in a critical state right now and too dangerous to try to perform surgery. She then said that once Katelyn was stabilized enough, they would proceed with her surgery, and the nurses would give us updates. I worried. I cried and was anxious. I then remembered this powerful scripture, "Cast all your anxiety on him because he cares for you" (1 Peter 5:7).

Within thirty minutes Katelyn was stable enough for surgery. Katelyn's surgery lasted five hours. The surgery went well, and they replaced her pacemaker and lead. Yes, it was fractured. It had broken in half. I guess you can say the Lord made it so there was no question if it was fractured or not. God answered our prayers and took care of Katelyn but not at all how we thought He'd answer them. It's not for us to question but to be thankful for God's graces and unfailing love for us.

Shane and I sat and waited in the waiting room for the nurse to contact us to go see Katelyn in the recovery room. As we sat there waiting, I once again was trying to process what had just happened. I was thankful that God showed the doctors the broken lead, yet I was wondering if it could have been less dramatic. We went from a scheduled surgery to an emergency very quickly. After about thirty minutes, the nurse called us back to see Katelyn in recovery. By the time we got back there, she was crying and asking for us. I was never so happy to see her. I couldn't pick her up and hold her. All I wanted to do was hold her and let her know that I wasn't going to leave her. She had too many wires hooked up to her, and all I could do was hold her little hand and give her reassurance that I was there. It was very traumatizing for all three of us.

Katelyn was sent to ICU so they could keep close watch over her since she had been through so much trauma. We were blessed because Shane was able to stay with us this whole hospital stay. I was drained and not feeling the best, so it was good that he was there. I felt physically and mentally exhausted. The doctor told us that our hospital stay would be longer this time because of the stress on Katelyn's body and they wanted to keep a close watch on her before they let us leave the hospital.

Riley's Children's Hospital always tried to be as accommodating as they could to the sick child's family. Shane and I were able to stay in the room with Katelyn. They always welcomed the parents to interact with the patients, and I appreciated that. I always wanted to be hands-on as much as I could with her.

One day as Katelyn was sleeping peacefully, I decided to take some time to myself. Shane was napping, and I was feeling pretty down. I had all kinds of thoughts going through my mind. I know it was Satan working on my mind. Satan always attacks when you are at a weak point. I wanted to go outside for a little walk and get some fresh air. I wanted to clear my mind.

I got on the elevator and pushed the button for the bottom floor. The elevator went two floors and then stopped. As the elevator door opened, a mother and her little boy in a red wagon entered the elevator with me. The little boy was probably three years old and was wrapped from head to toe in gauze wrap. As I stood there watching this little three-year-old baby and his mother, I knew he was badly burned from head to toe. As the elevator reached the bottom floor, the three-year-old and his mother got off the elevator. I couldn't leave. I waited as the door shut, and I stayed on the elevator and just cried. I then realized we didn't have it that bad. God showed me at that moment some mothers were dealing with children who had problems that were worse than we had. I realized at that time I needed to straighten up and be thankful for the blessings that God had blessed us with!

"Out of his fullness we have all received grace in place of grace already given" (John 1:16).

I was ready to get home and see Shaelyn. She knew that Katelyn had to have surgeries, but she was still so young that she had no idea the extent of the seriousness of her baby sister's health. She was always excited when her baby "poodoos" got to come home. I knew one day we would have to explain to her the extent of her sister's heart condition. For now, we wanted to enjoy the time that we had together as a family. When the time was right, God would open the doors.

Jesus reassures us with this message. "Therefore do not worry about tomorrow, for tomorrow will worry about itself. Each day has enough trouble of its own" (Matthew 6:34).

Chapter 9: "I Can Only Imagine"—MercyMe

"Children are a heritage from the Lord, offspring a reward from him. Like arrows in the hands of a warrior are children born in one's youth. Blessed is the man whose quiver is full of them. They will not be put to shame when they contend with their opponents in court" (Psalm 127:3–5).

As I explained before, Katelyn's heart condition was caused by my body attacking her heart because of the lupus antibodies. There was a point and time when I blamed myself for Katelyn's heart block. After a lot of prayers, I realized Katelyn is exactly who God wanted her to be. My doctors advised me to not have any more children because the chances of another child having a heart block were very high. Shane and I concluded that our quiver was full. We were okay with that. Shane always wanted to have a boy to carry on his name, but he understood the risks. I didn't want to take the chance of putting another child through what Katelyn had been through in her short little life so far. My mom once told me to be happy with the blessings the Lord had already given us.

We traveled home from the hospital, but I still wasn't feeling myself and was afraid I had caught some sort of a bug at the hospital. Katelyn was very sore after this surgery, so she was pretty restless. We were ready to get home. These trips were starting to wear on our emotions and health. When we got home, my mom was there to greet us with Shaelyn. I was so glad to see both of them. After we got settled in, my mom left, and Shane had to go to church to do some construction work.

The girls got snacks and curled up together in the recliner to watch their favorite cartoons. They loved cuddling together.

The longer I was home, the more I questioned why I felt so terrible. I wasn't running a fever or any other symptoms. I just felt weak and sick to my stomach. I just wrote it off as an effect of the stress I had gone through with Katelyn's emergency and figured my body just needed rest. When I went to the bathroom, there were two old pregnancy tests from when I tested with Katelyn. In the back of my mind, I thought I did feel like I did when I was pregnant with the girls. I decided to take one just to weigh that option out. I said, "Oh please, Lord, don't let me be pregnant!" Pregnancy was not even an option. I took the first test, and instantly it was "positive." My thought was, *No way, this can't be right!* So I took the second test. "Positive." My thought was they were bad tests because they were old. I called Shane in hysterics. He answered, and I was crying so hard he could not hear me. Shane said, "Calm down! I can't understand you! Is Katelyn okay?" I said, "*Yes*! But I'm pregnant!" He said, "Whew, I thought something was wrong." I said, "There is! I'm not supposed to get pregnant again!" I'll never forget what he said. "It's okay. God has a reason for this. God doesn't make mistakes." I told him to please stop and get a couple of tests on his way home because these had to be wrong.

When Shane got home, he brought me two more pregnancy tests. He said, "Why are you so upset?" I told him through tears that I couldn't go through this again. I couldn't do to another baby what I did to Katelyn.

I took the pregnancy tests, and both were positive. Shane held me as I cried. He knew I just needed him to hold me, and nothing he would say at this point and time would matter.

I knew I needed to contact my obstetrician as soon as possible. I called Dr. R the next morning, and through my tears, I told her I was pregnant. She agreed to see me that afternoon. When I got to her office, she greeted me with a hug as I stood there and cried. Dr. R was more of a friend than a doctor to me. She told me that she knew of a medication that was still being tested but not 100 percent proven to work. If taken early in pregnancy, it would block the antibodies from attacking the baby's heart. She thought it was a good idea to get started on it as soon as possible. She assured me that she would watch me closely, but I also needed to see the high-risk obstetrician again. Dr. T was the only local high-risk obstetrician. If the baby was healthy, I thought I'd only have to see her a few times. She had been angry with the last pregnancy and told me to never get pregnant again. I was upset with myself, and the thought of an appointment with her made me sick to my stomach with nerves.

As I traveled back home, so many thoughts were going through my mind. My first thought was, *There is no way I can tell my mom and in-laws!* I knew they would not be very understanding. I kept thinking, *What are people going to say? How can I do this again?* How could I be so stupid as to put another child at risk? But my biggest question was: How in the world did this happen?

I realized we would soon have our third child, but getting pregnant was a miracle in itself. I was on birth control and still nursing Katelyn. Both of those are supposed to lessen your chances of pregnancy. Not to mention I was never home because of all the hospital stays and doctor visits. To this day, I still can't wrap my mind around how it happened except that it was God's will.

On my way home from the doctor, I called my best friend and asked if we could meet to talk. I had to talk to someone, and I knew my mom was not an option at this point. Lynda and I had been best friends for a couple of years, and she knew me better than anyone else. When I called, she could tell something was wrong. As soon as I got to her house, I broke down and began to cry. She instantly thought something was wrong with Katelyn. I proceeded to tell her that I was pregnant and that I was to never get pregnant again! She just stood and hugged me. At that point, that was all I needed. When I calmed down, we were able to sit and talk about it. I'll never forget what she said to me. She said, "Why are you so upset? This is another miracle from God. You will see this baby will be such a blessing!" I know God was talking through her because it then made sense to me. As we prayed, I felt such peace. I knew it would be okay.

"Give thanks in all circumstances, for this is God's will for you in Christ Jesus" (1 Thessalonians 5:18).

I decided it was time to head home and see my beautiful family. When I got home, I was greeted with hugs and kisses. I'm pretty sure they missed me! That was all I needed to make this day better.

Shane told me that Katelyn was a little fussy most of the day. I figured it was because she was still sore from the surgery. We had only been home one day from her big surgery. That night, she started to run a low-grade fever. She and I slept in the recliner. When we woke up the next morning, she had red spots all over her face. I changed her diaper, and low and behold, they were all over her chest, back, and bottom. You guessed it—she had chicken pox! The only place she could have contracted them was at the children's hospital when she had her surgery. Here is the kicker: Shaelyn had to get the chickenpox vaccine before she was allowed in the children's hospital to see her sister. What are the chances?

The next day when I took Shaelyn to school, one of my favorite songs came on. I drove just listening to this song and thinking how perfect God's timing was. A few short months before this, I had rededicated my life to Jesus Christ at a Joyce Meyers Women's Convention to this song. As this song came on at the conference, I had a vision of my father. My father had been gone for several years, and he had such a huge impact on my life. After my father passed away, I fell away from the faith. I had a time running a little wild. But when I saw the vision of my father at the conference, I knew it was time to rededicate my life and live 100 percent for Jesus Christ. I was trying to live for Christ, but I was not completely dedicated to living for Him. The Spirit working through the song overcame me, and all I could do was stand in God's presence. I was surrounded by His glory. All I wanted to do was to forever worship Him and sing hallelujah. As that song came on in the car, I felt God's presence once again, and I knew that everything was going to be just fine. "I Can Only Imagine" by MercyMe will always hold a special place in my heart.

"Sing to the Lord a new song; sing to the Lord, all the earth. Sing to the Lord, praise his name; proclaim his salvation day after day. Declare his glory among the nations, his marvelous deeds among all people. For great is the Lord and most worthy of praise" (Psalm 96:1–4).

It was time for me to travel to the high-risk obstetrician once again. As I entered the office, I felt a big lump in my throat, and I felt sick to my stomach. This visit was not going to be a pleasant one. As I sat there waiting my turn, I tried to concentrate on my precious girls at home and the miracles God had blessed us with. My thought was, *Why would this be any different?* I finally had peace with this pregnancy. I knew I had to have faith.

"He replied, 'Because you have so little faith. Truly I tell you, if you have faith as small as a mustard seed, you can say to this mountain, "Move from here to there," and it will move. Nothing will be impossible for you'" (Matthew 17:20).

The nurse called my name and led me down a dark hallway that was all too familiar to me. Next, she led me into the same cold, dimly lit little room where I was when she gave me the bad news about Katelyn. I sat there for at least twenty minutes by myself. The discomfort I felt in that room was indescribable. As the doctor entered the room, I could tell she was not happy about my pregnancy. She looked at me and began to scold me. She reminded me of the talk we had earlier about never getting pregnant again! Then she proceeded with, "Do you actually want to bring another baby into this world with another heart condition?" I told her that I had started on the medication to help prevent a complete heart block. She argued and said that it was not a guarantee and not proven. The next words out of her mouth were "abortion." I couldn't believe I was hearing that horrible word again. At this point, she once again started sounding like the teacher in the Charlie Brown cartoon. I blocked her out and began praying for strength. As I looked her straight in the eyes and once again voiced, "I will *not* get an abortion! God will take care of my baby!" I got up and walked myself out of the room, knowing I would never step foot in that doctor's office again!

Looking back now, I have matured enough in my walk with God that I realize why the room was so uncomfortable and cold. That room was Satan's room. Lord only knows how many mothers were talked into an abortion in that room. Abortion is murder. No matter how dark and grim she tried to make my situation look, I knew who the ultimate healer was. No matter what anyone says, that is a baby, and God knew him before he was formed in my womb. God had big plans for this child that He had so graciously blessed me with.

"Before I formed you in the womb I knew you, before you were born I set you apart; I appointed you as a prophet to the nations" (Jeremiah 1:5).

As I had mentioned before, my OB doctors are in a town one hour and forty-five minutes from our house. Typically, on my way home was when I had the opportunity to listen to my praise and worship music and pray. As I traveled home this time, all I could think about was the pressure she tried to put on me to abort this precious child. At first, I was traumatized that I was pregnant, but I believe I was upset because of fear. I was afraid of the possible outcome of the health of our unborn child. All the doctor ever did was put negative and morbid thoughts into our minds. As I prayed, the Lord put peace into my heart. I knew these were just ways to try and scare us into aborting this unborn gift from God. Abortion is Satan, and life is Jesus Christ! Satan only comes to steal, kill, and destroy, and that is exactly what abortion is. Abortion steals your peace, kills your baby, and destroys your life. I was not going to bow to Satan's schemes. This child was a blessing from our Lord Jesus Christ, and we chose to give this baby *life*!

"Children are a heritage from the Lord, offspring a reward from him" (Psalm 127:3).

When I finally made it home, Shane was there and wanted to talk to me about the doctor's appointment. We were so busy that we had little time for each other. I could tell that something was on his mind, and he was anxiously waiting to tell me. After we sat down to talk, Shane opened up to me, "I've been wanting to talk to you, but we haven't had the chance. Some time ago, I was talking to one of my Christian coworkers about how badly I wanted a son to carry on my name." He asked me, "Have you prayed for one?" I told him, "I have not." He then replied, "You have to pray a specific prayer for a son. How does God know what you want if you don't ask specifically?" Shane then told me, "That hit home with me, and I began praying specifically for a son. I believe the baby you are carrying is the son that I have prayed so hard for."

"And pray in the Spirit on all occasions with all kinds of prayers and requests" (Ephesians 6:18).

As I sat there listening to Shane pour his heart out to me, I knew without a shadow of a doubt this child was of God. This baby was not a mistake but a perfect miracle from Jesus Christ, and I knew that "he" would be perfect.

"For you created my inmost being; you knit me together in my mother's womb. I praise you because I am fearfully and wonderfully made; your works are wonderful, I know that full well" (Psalm 139:13–14).

Chapter 10: "Here with Me"—MercyMe

"Trust in the Lord with all your heart, and lean not on your own understanding; In all your ways submit to him, and he will make your paths straight" (Proverbs 3:5–6).

Bring your decisions to God, use the Bible as your guide, and then follow God's paths set for you. He will make your paths straight by leading and guiding you. Sometimes it's hard because our flesh tries to get involved, but I have learned to solely lean on God. Above all else, He wants us to seek Him. Let God guide you so you can witness all the amazing miracles and blessings He has in store for you.

Katelyn always amazed me with how quickly she bounced back after each surgery. Each day she got stronger and healthier. I would just sit back and watch her in amazement. Her strength and courage were so encouraging. When I had bad days, my girls were my encouragement to keep pushing through. I knew we had to live day by day through Christ.

A week had passed since we came home from her surgery and my last OB appointment. It was time for me to once again travel to see my doctor and friend, Dr. R. As I entered her office, she took me right back to a room. She did an ultrasound and saw that I was only four weeks gestation. She put me on a prescription called dexamethasone. It was an experimental drug to block my antibodies from attacking the baby's electrical system in its heart. It was proven to work better if used in the very early stages of pregnancy. Dr. R was so supportive and encouraging. She told me that she would be with me every step of the way. I knew she meant what she said.

Shane and I still hadn't told anyone but my friend Lynda about the pregnancy. We were waiting until we couldn't wait any longer. Little did I know, but that day was rapidly approaching. It was almost overnight that I started gaining weight. Dexamethasone is a steroid treatment that makes you gain weight. When I was pregnant with the girls, all I had was a little belly. With this baby, I started gaining all over. With this rapid change in my body, I knew the time had come we had to tell my mom and in-laws. Once we told them, everyone would find out quickly…you know what I mean.

My mom came over to check on the girls. I fixed lunch, and over lunch, we began to talk. I told her I had something I needed to tell her and to pray about. As I told her I was pregnant, her response was, "I already knew that." My response was, "How did you know?" She said, "Moms just know things." I use this comment today on my kids.

When you have a connection with God, He guides you and prepares you for trials. The Lord often wakes me up in the middle of the night to prepare me for something coming down the pike. I know that one day when I get to heaven to see my mom again, I am going to tell her that I now know how she knew.

After we told the inlaws, then we could tell the girls about the new baby. The girls were so excited! Guess what they wanted? You guessed it, a baby brother. This baby was already loved so much, and we were just starting the journey.

"For no word from God will ever fail" (Luke 1:37).

As the weeks went by, I could tell this pregnancy was not at all like it was with the girls. When I was pregnant with the girls, I didn't gain much weight, and I felt so good! I had already added a lot of weight during this pregnancy and was miserable. Dr. R told me that this medication would cause excessive weight gain. I hated to see what extent the excessive would go to.

At twelve weeks gestation, I went in to have the standard blood work done. At this time, I had already gained 50 lbs. I went from 128 pounds to 178 pounds in eight weeks. There are two funny stories I have to tell about my weight gain. At church one Sunday, we had the normal seats we sat in every Sunday. A lady behind me leaned up and said, "Boy, you weren't this *'fat'* with your girls!" Yes, she said fat. Shane and I laughed about that for years. In another instance, I had the girls at a local pizza restaurant named Mr. Gatti's. In one of the rooms, there was a birthday attended by a guy I had grown up with and knew very well. I hadn't seen him for a couple of months. I walked up to him and hit him with my shoulder. He looked at me and said, "Sorry, excuse me." He then moved over. I walked over and bumped into him again. He again said, "Sorry, excuse me." He then walked away. After he walked away, I went up to him and tapped him on the shoulder. He said, "Can I help you?" I replied, "You seriously don't know who I am?" He said, "I'm sorry, but I do not." When I finally told him who I was, he apologized a thousand times. To this day, we still laugh about that one as well. Needless to say, I was getting to a point where I did not look like myself.

I got a phone call from my doctor that the blood test results were in. She wouldn't give me the results over the phone and asked me to please come to the office. I called Lynda, and she came down and got Katelyn and was going to pick Shaelyn up from school for me. The girls loved going to Lynda's house. Lynda was one of the few people Katelyn would stay with.

Once again, Satan started creeping in and putting different thoughts into my head. I just started praying and rejecting any negative thoughts. When I reached the office, Dr. R took me into a private room. There she proceeded to tell me that the test results showed that the baby had trisomy 18. She was so upset and hated to give me this news. Dr. R knew that I would rather have the truth than be kept in the dark. Trisomy 18 is a condition in which the baby has one extra chromosome. The condition is very rare, and the mortality rate is high. She proceeded to tell me that the baby would probably not make it to birth. If the baby did make it to birth, it typically only lived six months and would never leave the hospital. The baby would be on feeding tubes and would never breathe on its own, and the baby would be abnormally small and underdeveloped. Trisomy 18 is worse than Down's syndrome. As she gave me this horrible news, I sat there in disbelief. Dr. R asked if it was okay to set me up with an amniocentesis test for the next morning. She informed me that the risks of miscarrying were high with the test, but it was the best way to find out to what extent the severity of the trisomy 18. I agreed to the test, got the appointment, and left the office. I remember walking down that hallway again in a fog. I thought to myself, *How much more can one person take?* When I got to my car, I called Lynda to see if she would meet me at the house and told her the bad news. She assured me she would be there when I got home. I tried to call Shane at work, but once again he would not receive his message. I sat in the car in disbelief at what I was just informed. I remember thinking, *How could this even be happening?* I was first in shock over the pregnancy and now over this horrible medical diagnosis. All I could physically feel was hurt. My heart and chest were tight. I sat and wept uncontrollably. At this point and time, I felt as if I was all alone.

My stress levels were extremely high. I was not doubting God, but I found myself trying to figure out what He was trying to show me. I felt as if I was loyal in following Him with Katelyn, but why the trials with my new baby? I felt doubt creeping in and questioned if I was truly as loyal as God required of me. I let Satan try to convince me that I was not worthy and that I had failed God. I knew I had to go home, but I did not want to face my family.

I got home, and Lynda and Katelyn were waiting for me. As I walked into the house and saw Katelyn, I broke down. I told Lynda, "I'm only human. How can I go through this trial?" She responded, "You don't have to go through this alone! We are here for you, but most importantly, God is here with you!" I walked in and sat in the recliner. Lynda anointed me and my belly. Katelyn scooted over and pulled herself up to me, and as Lynda started praying, Katelyn put her little hand on my belly. As we were praying, I felt my stomach get "hot!" Lynda pulled her hand away and said, "Do you feel the heat off of your stomach?" I could feel the heat radiating through my body. I looked at Katelyn's little innocent face, and she was beaming. I believe at that moment God used Katelyn's childlike faith to show me how my faith needs to be. I knew at that moment that God had just healed our precious baby. Why did I ever doubt that God would not be with us? He had not failed us yet. I prayed, "God, please change me to be the loyal vessel You need me to be to raise these miracle children in Your sight."

He called a little child to him, and placed the child among them. And he said: "Truly I tell you, unless you change and become like little children, you will never enter the kingdom of heaven. Therefore, whoever takes the lowly position of this child is the greatest in the kingdom of heaven."

Matthew 18:2–4

Shane could not leave work to go with me the next day for the amniocentesis test, so Lynda said she'd go. Lynda had two girls, and the youngest, Amelia, was Shaelyn's best friend. So we took the girls out of school, and we all went to the doctor's appointment. Anytime Lynda was involved, it was a good time. She knew how to liven things up.

As we traveled to Evansville, Lynda and I could not stop talking about the prayer the night before. We both knew in our hearts the baby was now healed of trisomy 18. Neither of us had witnessed healing to this extent. We were standing on our faith that God had this baby wrapped in His arms and would not let harm intrude.

"May your unfailing love be my comfort, according to your promise to your servant" (Psalm 119:76).

I went into the room for the test as Lynda sat in the waiting room with the four girls. During the test, I felt complete peace. I didn't have any doubt in my mind that the Lord was in complete control at this point. How could I doubt since we had just witnessed God's presence the night before as we were praying for the child I was carrying? The test went smoothly, and Dr. R told me she'd call me later with the results. I told Dr. R about our prayer the night before. I don't believe she was a believer, but she told me she hoped it was true for our sake. I knew it was true! God healed my baby with our faith in our prayers and the touch of his miracle sister.

During this time, Shane and I finally bought a new car. It was a Toyota Sequoia. We needed something big enough to travel with our expanding family. Evansville had the closest dealership to service the vehicle. While waiting for the doctor to call with the test results, we had my vehicle serviced. As we were waiting for my car to get finished, Dr. R called. She proceeded to tell me that the tests came back and the baby did *not* have trisomy 18! I hung up and started screaming, "Thank You, Jesus!" We were all so excited, and the girls started jumping and screaming too! We made a huge scene at the service center, and we didn't care. Jesus healed our baby!

"Is anyone among you sick? Let them call the elders of the church to pray over them and anoint them with oil in the name of the Lord. And the prayer offered in faith will make the sick person well; the Lord will raise them up. If they have sinned, they will be forgiven" (James 5:14–15).

The next few months were a whirlwind and hard. Every prenatal test that was performed came back positive. Gestational diabetes, high blood pressure, excessive weight gain, and any other routine test. I knew it was Satan trying to break us down. I finally told my OB doctor that I was no longer taking any prenatal tests. She knew I had been through enough. She did abide by my wishes but told me not to hesitate to contact her if I had any concerns. Sometimes in life, we have to stand by what we believe. Some people will agree, and some will disapprove. After witnessing all the miracles in our children, how could we question that God did not have a bigger plan? We were having this baby, and the Lord was taking care of everything. Faith is not believing God can, but God will!

I know there isn't a day that goes by that I don't need God's presence. I know He is everywhere I go. Sometimes I just get caught up in His grace for my family and all the miracles He has performed. I am humbled and know that we are loved eternally.

"But when you ask, you must believe and not doubt, because the one who doubts is like a wave of the sea, blown and tossed by the wind" (James 1:6).

Chapter 11: "The Blessing"—Kari Jobe

The months seemed to fly by so quickly. Before I knew it, I was twenty-four weeks along with our third child. It was time to go and check this baby for complete heart block. If you remember, the heart block showed up at twenty-four weeks with Katelyn. This is when the body decides to attack the baby's heart. My flesh was a little concerned because of the history with Katelyn, but I knew in my spirit that God would not forsake us. He had already healed this baby from trisomy 18. So how could I doubt Him?

My mom decided to make the trip with Katelyn and me this time. She didn't want me to do this alone. We took Shaelyn to school and headed out. I have always loved road trips with my mom. She and I used to always take off on random trips. You never knew where we would end up. She loved to look at fall leaves. That was one special thing we always did together. After we visited the doctor, we were going to take a detour to go and see how pretty the fall leaves were this year. She would always say, "I wonder if the leaves look this beautiful in heaven. Someday I will see for myself."

Before we entered the doctor's office, we sat in the car and prayed. I owe a lot of my spiritual growth to my mom. I watched her struggle in life, but she would hold fast to Jesus Christ. Life was not easy for my parents. They had many battles in life. But they held fast and endured. Their faith in God was their witness. The older I got, the more I wanted to have their faith. Mom's anointed prayers were nothing as I had ever witnessed.

When Mom prayed, the Holy Spirit showed up. I knew with this prayer that this baby was heart-healthy.

Dr. R greeted us with a smile. She was always so welcoming and comforting during my visits. She was truly a blessing to have as a doctor. She knew the struggles we had, and her bedside manner was exactly what we needed at this time. When she asked how I was feeling, I was very truthful. I felt horrible! I had gained so much weight that I was miserable. She told me that after the test today, she was hoping I could scale back on the dexamethasone medication. Katelyn was so excited to be able to see her new baby on the ultrasound machine. As we watched this miracle baby on the monitor, I began to cry. God entrusted me with another blessing. As I watched the baby move, I looked at the heart rate. The baby's heart rate was 120 bpm! No sign of complete heart block! Out of nowhere, my mom loudly said, "Thank You, Jesus!" "Therefore I tell you, whatever you ask for in prayer, believe that you have received it, and it will be yours" (Mark 11:24).

After this awesome news, I couldn't wait to tell Shane, our family, and the church family. I knew many prayers were going up for this doctor's visit. What an awesome way to witness it once again. God was trusting me now with not one but two miracle children. I felt like I was walking around in the clouds. It was like the Holy Spirit was lifting me off the floor. I love walking in His presence.

It seemed like every time we had victories, Satan would throw more struggles in. If Satan couldn't destroy us with health issues, he seemed to try in other ways. Just as I felt like things were starting to be somewhat normal, Shane told me that he applied and got a job closer to home. I tried to be understanding because he had a two-hour drive every day for his job, and he did not like his place of employment. They were lax about getting him emergency messages—often Shane didn't know until he got off work about emergencies with Katelyn or anyone in the family. The opportunity in the long term was good, but the short term and timing were by no means ideal.

I was dealing with so much at this point and time. My due date was in three months, and there was uncertainty about the baby's outcome. Katelyn's health was always up in the air. Now was not a good time to make such a big decision that affected our whole family. His current job had excellent pay and great insurance benefits. With this new job, his pay was cut in half, and the insurance didn't begin to compare to our current insurance policy. We were struggling financially, and medical bills continued to accumulate. The thought of cutting his wages in half kept me up at night. I didn't know how in the world we could ever make it financially. I was not happy about this decision. Truthfully, I was extremely upset and stressed beyond belief. I distanced myself from Shane. In my mind, I thought there was no way I could handle one more thing at this point and time. We had too much going on right now for this big of an adjustment in our lives. I had to do a lot of soul-searching. To be truthful, I was so upset that I thought about leaving Shane. To me, it was a very selfish move. With all that we were going through, why add unnecessary stress? Satan was accomplishing exactly what he had set out to do. He was destroying our marriage. The divorce rate of parents with chronically ill children is ten times higher than parents with normal children. I did not want to be part of those statistics, but I was weak at this point.

My mom sat me down and gave me a lecture about forgiving. She had a way of putting things into a godly perspective. I had to realize that I was not in this alone. God had been with us from the beginning, and why would He leave us now? Shane was supportive of me, so why could I not be supportive of his decision? Then my stubborn faith came in! I knew it was Satan trying to destroy my family. He knew his schemes for our children were not working, so he had to try elsewhere. I told Satan to get beneath me, and he would once again fail.

> Finally be strong in the Lord and in his mighty power. Put on the full armor of God, so that you can take your stand against the devil's schemes. For our struggle is not against flesh and blood, but against the rulers, against the authorities, against the powers of the dark world and against the spiritual forces of evil in the heavenly realms.
>
> Ephesians 6:10–12

December came, and I was as big as a barn! Dr. R finally took me completely off the medication because it was soon time for delivery. As the due date approached, Shane and I prepared to bring our new baby boy into this world. Yes, I said a baby boy. We didn't need an ultrasound to tell us what we were having because Shane and I just knew it was a male. We were so certain that we only picked out a boy's name and only purchased a boy outfit to bring him home. We both believed this was the boy that he so fervently prayed for.

On December 29, 2004, it was time to welcome our baby into this world. I told Dr. R previously that if at all possible, I'd like to have this baby naturally. Shaelyn was a natural birth, but Katelyn was a C-section. This is almost unheard of after a C-section. Dr. R needed to monitor closely from the beginning of contractions with an internal monitor. She told me the process was not invasive. Dr. R assured me that she would stay with me from the start to the end. She also wanted me to have this last child naturally. Did I mention before that Dr. R was amazing? My sister Kristin was blessed to watch this little miracle enter the world. After eight hours of labor, we brought forth our new baby boy naturally! He weighed eight pounds six ounces and was twenty-one inches long.

After delivery, he was taken to the neonatal intensive care unit because he had some sort of trauma in the womb. This trauma was evidence, too, that he was healed of trisomy 18. He was only in the NICU for one week before we could bring him home. Shane agreed to let me name him because he named the girls. I named him Chance because it was Shane's "*last* chance" to have a boy. Michael is Shane's first name, and of course, Wilber carries on Shane's last name. Shane's prayers were answered when he got his healthy son, Chance Michael Wilber. "You then, my son, be strong in the grace that is in Christ Jesus. And the things you have heard me say in the presence of many witnesses entrust to reliable people who will also be qualified to teach others. Join with me in suffering, like a good soldier of Christ Jesus" (2 Timothy 2:1–3).

Shane and I were excited to bring this new baby brother home to his two anxiously awaiting big sisters. When they heard we were bringing them home a new baby brother, they squealed with excitement! Shaelyn said, "Well, no Barbie for him. We now have to buy trucks and boy stuff." Her little mind was already working. She was correct. All we had was girls' toys and dress-up clothes. I told her I figured Daddy would take care of the boy's stuff and not to worry about it.

Bringing a new baby home was a little on the stressful side for me. I was excited yet wondering how I was going to take care of everything. Katelyn wasn't even walking yet, and all the doctor visits and hospital stays. I thought I needed help before; I was going to need assistance now.

When we walked into our home with Chance for the first time, the love on the girl's faces was priceless. Shaelyn, of course, being the big sister, had already figured everything out and had prepared Katelyn. The girls instantly fell in love with their new baby brother. Shaelyn and Katelyn were always willing to help Mom with their new baby.

I would catch Katelyn staring at her brother. She always found a way to be right beside him. I would breastfeed him, and Katelyn had to sit beside me with her hand on his head. I don't know why, but she always had to be touching the new baby.

Shaelyn always wanted to hold him. She was my hands and feet helper. If I needed anything, she would always go and get it for me. There were times when I needed four hands and four feet. I had two of the best helpers a mom could pray for!

I believe we transitioned into a family of five pretty well. Chance was a blessing to our family, and God had His hand in every aspect. I look back now, and it wasn't as hard juggling everything as I had first anticipated. I don't know what I would have done without my three beautiful children. God's plan is always better than our own.

The last two years were such a struggle. Satan threw everything at us so that he could break us down. Sometimes our flesh got in the way, but our faith would bring us out. God never said things would be easy, but He did say He would be there to take us through. I believe that Katelyn and Chance have a mark of God on them. Satan tried to kill them, but God said, "Not My children!" I do not doubt that they are highly favored and God has big plans for their futures.

As we welcomed this new little warrior for God into our lives, I prayed for strength over him to be able to endure like a good soldier the call that God has placed on this child. As trials come, I know that my children are chosen for God's work and to glorify Him. We will continue to pray fervently for protection over them and to raise them to the best of our ability in Jesus Christ. "Fear not, for I am with you; be not dismayed, for I am your God; I will strengthen you, I will help you, I will uphold you with my righteous right hand" (Isaiah 41:10).

I look back at the past three years at all the trials, but all I can focus on is all the blessings.

We overcame death, trials, and tribulations. Whatever Satan decided to throw at us, we overcame in God's favor. His favor is upon our family and our glorious children. His presence is before us, behind us, and all around us. God is with us in the morning, the evening, and in the night. What do we have to fear?

"What, then, shall we say in response to these things? If God is for us, who can be against us?" (Romans 8:31).

Chapter 12: "Same God"—Elevation Worship

Therefore, since we have been justified through faith, we have peace with God through our Lord Jesus Christ, through whom we have gained access by faith into this grace we now stand. And we boast in the hope of the glory of God. Not only so, but we also glory in our sufferings, because we know that suffering produces perseverance; perseverance, character; and character, hope. And hope does not put us to shame, because God's love has been poured out into our hearts through the Holy Spirit, who has been given to us.

Romans 5:1–5

Shane's and my sufferings were sometimes unbearable. I was constantly humbled that God had given us these precious miracles that were our children. These wonderful gifts from God were entrusted to us. We had faith and hope through Christ that we would take care of and raise these miracles the best way we knew how through Christ. I couldn't see how we deserved them because life here on earth was always a struggle. Shane and I dealt with our sufferings differently, but God's love poured out onto us, and we knew we could persevere through all our trials.

I asked Shane to write out his view on our struggles. Sadly through these years, I did not pay attention to how Shane was handling our strife. Because of this, it caused recurring problems in our marriage. I later came to realize that our marriage had to be held to a higher level than we were holding it. The Lord blessed us with a covenant to Him in marriage. It was our duty to take care of this sacred covenant with the Lord.

Below is Shane's testimony of how he saw the struggles in our lives. I thank God that He chose Shane to be the father of our three beautiful children. God chose us to be His vessels to glorify Him. We learned that the battles we endured were only to strengthen us to withstand the future obstacles that we would have to overcome. Without Christ we are nothing.

Through a father's eyes:

"I guess I will start by saying I was raised as a fix-it kind of guy. We never had the money to pay someone to do things for us, so my dad and I would fix anything we ever had problems with. I would say that by the age of ten or so, I was a professional Snapper mower mechanic. Those were the only mowers we owned, and we seemed to work on them weekly. Anything from belts to clutches to a different motor, you name it, we fixed it. By thirteen I was riding my bike to a local turkey farm and working there after school and on the weekends. I had also picked up work at a local farm working in the hog barns as well. Through my teenage years, it seemed all the local farmers wanted me to work for them because I could take on any chore, big or small, and be productive at anything they needed to be done. I guess you could say my parents instilled a good work ethic in me from a young age.

"Fast forward through life to my early twenties when I would meet a young lady who would capture my heart and change my life forever. This beautiful young lady would become my wife just a little over a year later. Heather and I started our life together and just seemed to take life by the horns. Once again, my fix-it-and-get-it-done life skill set would come into play when we bought our first house. We bought an old farmhouse that most people thought we were going to bulldoze down and build a new home. We proved them wrong by taking on a yearlong project of totally remolding the house. We worked countless hours that year with family and friends and turned an old abandoned farmhouse into our new home.

"Less than a year later, Heather was turning our new home into our little nest with a new baby on the way. On October 10, 1998, Shaelyn was born. It wasn't long until we realized what work was all about raising our new baby girl. The next three years would turn us into adults learning the ins and outs of raising a child. Heather would soon make the next announcement that we had another baby on the way. Wow, one was tough, and now we'd soon be raising two. I wondered what God would give us this time. Excited but nervous again, I couldn't wait to see what we'd be getting. Deep down inside I wanted a boy this time so I could teach him all the things I had been taught; you know, the guy's stuff you couldn't teach your little girl.

"Little did we know what God had in store for us when Heather had her twenty-four-week checkup. Heather had gone by herself to the doctor that day while I was at work. I worked for Toyota in Indiana during this time and had no access to phone calls—only during a break or at lunch. During my afternoon break, I checked my phone and had a message to call her when I could. This message was one that I could tell she was full of anxiety, and something was not right. I called her, and she gave me the news that the doctor could not find the baby's heartbeat, and when she finally did, it was only twenty-four beats per minute. This was way too low for a baby in the womb, and we were scheduled to see a specialist the next day. I spoke with my boss and was able to take off the next day to go with her to talk with our new doctor.

"During the visit, the doctor did an ultrasound and took several pictures of the baby's heart. I remember like it was yesterday how quiet and not a word was said to us by the doctor during the exam. She completed her duties, and we were taken to a room down the hall that I remember all so well. The sign on the right side of the door said, 'Private Consultation.' I had never been in this type of room before, but deep down I knew what the sign meant. This is where they take families to give them the bad news. I wasn't wrong. She entered and sat down to tell us the prognosis. The baby had complete heart block, and if this baby made it to term, it probably would not live long. She encouraged us to think about abortion at this point. The appointment was short, and she gave us only one other option, which was to put Heather on a steroid and try to get the heart rate up.

"The drive home was tearful and full of conversation between Heather and me. The first thing we both agreed on was that in no way, shape, or form would we go against God and His plan for our baby. Heather started making phone calls to get as many people praying as we could get. For the first time in my life, I was faced with something I could not fix. This was not my style, and I felt like the weight of my family was all on my shoulders, and there was nothing I could do. I did know deep down that I was going to have to get closer to God in my prayer life.

"Through the next three months, I seemed to get as close to God as I had ever experienced. I would work all day on the assembly line and just pray constantly. Heather and I would pray together and cry together all the time. As hard as this was to think your baby would be born with a lifelong challenge, it seemed to make our relationship so strong between each other. Little Shaelyn, at the age of three, never understood what was going on inside Mommy's belly; she just knew we had taught her to pray for Mommy and the baby. The Bible says in Psalm 8:2, 'Through the praise of children and infants you have established a stronghold against your enemies, to silence the foe and the avenger.' Our enemy was Satan trying to take our unborn baby.

"On August 21, 2002, Katelyn Grace was born. This was the little girl the doctor had encouraged us to abort. To this day I cannot fathom the beautiful babies who never made it to life on earth. Our beautiful 7 lb., 13 oz. baby looked as healthy as you could imagine. One small problem was she had a complete heart block. The bottom two chambers of her heart had no electrical function. Life was really about to change for the Wilber family. We honestly had no clue what the road ahead had in store for us. Once we made it home with Katelyn, we decided it would be best for Heather and the babies to be able to stay at home and not have to face daycare outside of Mom's care. This decision was hard for Heather because she had worked so hard to build her salon business and felt we couldn't make it without two incomes. Maybe God knew again what He had in store for us because two years later when that baby boy 'Chance' came along, we definitely couldn't afford daycare. I reflect and think how blessed I am with a wife who gave up her career to raise our children. My prayer is someday the kids will know how blessed they were to have a mom to run after them and make our house the home it is today. I think we both agree that twenty years later we made a great decision and God provided all our needs.

"As I write this short story through the eyes of my life, there's nothing I could or would want to change. We have taken every challenge God has brought us through looking forward, never turning our heads or taking our eyes off Him. This life has been very humbling to me and has made me understand that we, as human flesh, cannot fix everything, and God is actually in charge of all things. The beat of the heart is one of the first things He creates in the baby. He made Katelyn special for His purpose, not ours. I don't know why and have never questioned Him why. I just know that was His plan and I'm also part of it. God has truly blessed Heather and me, and I thank Him every day for our life together. I am so glad I was raised in a Christian family and have Jesus as my Savior and can proudly say Heather and my kids know Him as well.

"Thank You, God, for everything You've done in my life and blessed me with upon this earth. I long for the day to see Your face, take Your hand, and hear Your words, 'Well done, my good and faithful servant.' Amen."

CHAPTER 13: "THERE'S NOTHING THAT OUR GOD CAN'T DO"—PASSION

Restoration in the Bible is abundance. When something is restored, it is always better than how it started. God promises a restored life and future for us and our loved ones. I believe God was healing our family to glorify Him. I always go back to God never saying it would be easy but that He would always be there for us. I am a firm believer that His promise is true.

"'But I will restore you to health and heal your wounds,' declares the Lord, 'because you are called an outcast, Zion for whom no one cares'" (Jeremiah 30:17).

As the days ran into months and our family was being restored, our faith in Christ continued to grow. God put such wonderful godly mentors in our lives. From friends and family to pastors to teach self-discipline, God was in every part of our lives.

Shane was settling into his new job, and God was blessing us with cabinet jobs to make up for the wages that were lost from the change in jobs. I believed that God would provide because it was out of my hands. God said to give it all to Him, not partially but all.

The kids were growing up so quickly. Katelyn continued to get stronger and improve every day. She was finally walking on her own and loved to play dress up with her sister. Shaelyn was in dance and gymnastics classes, and Katelyn loved to go and watch. She always told me she wanted to do it too and couldn't understand why Sissy could and she couldn't. She didn't understand that she had to walk first. As soon as Katelyn was walking and strong enough, I put her into the classes too. That was one of the best things I could have done for her. It was almost like it gave her a boost of confidence, and she was no longer the little sick one with limitations. After that, she thought she could do anything that Sissy could do, and I wasn't going to stop her. Every day that we had with Katelyn was a blessing from God, and I was not going to be the one to hold her back. I always told her she could do anything she set her mind to, and that's what she did!

Katelyn always thought she was a princess and liked to play dress up. We had countless dresses for her and Shaelyn to play with. Dressing up was a big thing at our house. My niece Mykala was the same age as Shaelyn. She would come to our house a lot to play with the girls. As soon as Mykala hit the door, she was running straight to the dress-up box. Those three spent hours playing with those clothes. I am guessing we had all the cool dresses.

My older niece Jerin was to be married the next year and asked if Katelyn could be her flower girl at her wedding. Jerin is my sister Sarah's daughter. Katelyn has always held a special place in Sarah's heart. In emergencies, she was the one I would call when Shane was not available to take Katelyn and me to hospitals. Sarah told me that Katelyn was special to her and we never knew how long we would have with her. She said this was Katelyn's opportunity to be a "real" princess. This gesture meant a lot to all of us. Katelyn had touched their lives too.

It was soon time for Katelyn to start preschool. She was also old enough to play t-ball. She always watched her sister play softball and wanted to play just like Shaelyn. People who knew Katelyn's story could not believe that I let her do all these things with her "health" condition. I had people ask me,

"Aren't you afraid she'll get hit by the ball and die?" "How can you let her do these things? I'd be scared to death to let her out of my sight!" "What is her life expectancy?" "Can she get a heart transplant?" People never ceased to amaze me with their unfaithfulness. I usually responded with, "God's got this, and we are not treating her any differently than any other child."

The girls went to a local Christian school, and it was a very close-knit family. The principal, Mrs. Wassell, was an amazing woman of God. When Katelyn started school there, she already knew about Katelyn's health. She welcomed Katelyn with open arms and watched her closely for me. I felt very safe sending Katelyn to this school. I knew they would take excellent care of her. Mrs. Wassell and the whole school were such a blessing to our family for many years.

Pre-school was half days, but kindergarten was full days, and that was a big step for Katelyn. Katelyn was extremely attached to me. She would not stay at anyone's house except my friend Lynda. She wouldn't even stay at Grammy and Papa's house. Katelyn and I were never apart. It seemed like we spent most of our time traveling to and from doctors' visits and hospitals. If Katelyn needed anything at all, I was the one there to take care of it. I never went anywhere without her. All-day kindergarten was hard at first, but she quickly got used to it, and I believe it was because of the loving teachers and staff. We thank God for New Hebron Christian School and Mrs. Wassell.

In 2007 we had Shaelyn's ninth birthday party! Her birthday is in the fall, and we have a huge fall birthday celebration! We always had a big wiener roast, hay ride, and games, and all our family and friends came over to celebrate. Shaelyn got a trampoline on her third birthday, and that was the "hit" at all our parties. The kids would even have campouts on the trampoline. Katelyn didn't do a whole lot of jumping on the trampoline but would sit on the side and let everyone else bounce her.

Later that evening, Katelyn started feeling unwell. She had an issue a month before of being sick to her stomach and feeling "funny and sicky" as she described it. We took her to her electrophysiologist to have her checked out. At this appointment, her doctor said her battery was running low but not to a point of replacement yet. I questioned her because the pacemaker was only three years old, and it shouldn't be running low already. Once again she could not answer my questions. I kept a close watch on Katelyn, and she seemed to not have any more episodes until the morning after the birthday party. When she woke up, her face was very pale. She kept telling me she felt "funny and sicky" again. I contacted her doctor, and she asked me to bring her back up to get interrogated again.

The older Katelyn got, the more vocal she was about how she felt. When she was a baby, I just had to keep a close watch on her symptoms. On the way to her doctor, she got sick once again. This time she told me her "heart hurt." This was a new one. She had never said that before. So, of course, I got a little concerned. As we got to the hospital and got the little red wagon, Katelyn instantly knew where we were going and began to cry. She begged me to take her back home because they made her sick there. That ripped my heart out. Her becoming older had a downside as well. It got harder to take her to the doctor without her realizing where we were going. I had to carry her to the doctor this time because she was heading back out the door.

The doctor checked the function of the pacemaker and told me everything was just fine. I proceeded to tell her that something was not right. There had to be some reason why she kept getting sick. Not to mention her pacemaker had dropped six months in life expectancy in only three short weeks. I'm not a doctor, but I know that is not normal. As we sat there discussing symptoms and the quick loss of battery life, she agreed it was time to replace the pacemaker. She thought the battery had dropped low enough now that it would be in our best interest to replace it. Katelyn was so symptomatic that when the battery got this low, it would affect her more than most patients. The electrophysiologist set her up for surgery the next day.

Katelyn and I left the hospital and went home to pick up Shane. I also contacted my in-laws to take care of Chance and Shaelyn. After we got home, Katelyn got very sick. She turned pale, her lips were blue, and she started to vomit. I was afraid her lead had broken again, and we were three hours from her doctor. I packed our overnight bags and made a few phone calls, and we headed back to the hospital. On the way up, I called her doctor and explained what happened, and she agreed we should bring her back to the hospital that night. She said she'd put all the orders in and they'd be waiting for us. I think the last emergency with Katelyn made a believer out of her electrophysiologist.

My sisters and mom always came to Katelyn's surgeries. We always filled the waiting room with family and friends. I look back at all our love and support, and I am just humbled. My mom's health had started to fail in the past couple of years; she had to walk with a walker. It made it harder for Mom to come with me because of her inability to get around freely. When my sisters heard about Katelyn, they decided to all come up to the hospital for the surgery. They also brought Mom and my friend Lynda.

Shane and I arrived at the hospital and got settled. Katelyn was resting peacefully. The pediatric cardiologist was keeping a close watch on her. I felt safer and more at peace at the hospital because I knew if the lead happened to break completely, they could take care of it promptly. I decided to lie beside her in her hospital bed. I was amazed by her strength and beauty. *Why is this baby going through this once again? God, please just heal her!* I lay beside her and just held her as she slept. I didn't want to leave her side. I prayed for strength and healing.

"I can do all this through him who gives me strength" (Philippians 4:13).

As I lay there with Katelyn, I felt myself drift off. Then I was awakened by the sounds of fire trucks and sirens. Shane looked out the window and saw all kinds of medical people

Never Will I Leave Thee...

outside. It looked as if there were some kind of accident. About thirty minutes later, our room door opened, and there stood Lynda and one of my sisters. They had awful looks on their faces. I knew something was up when they started with, "We don't want you to worry; you don't need any added stress, but…Mom had an accident coming into the hospital." I said, "Please tell me that is not what the sirens are all about!" You guessed it—the sirens were for my mom. They proceeded with the story, and what a story it was!

The walk to the hospital was quite long from the parking garage. Mom walked for a while and then got tired. Her walker had a seat on it, so she could sit when she got tired. Lynda told Mom to just sit there and she would push her the rest of the way to the hospital door. Lynda was clueless about how steep the hill was from the parking garage to the front door of the hospital. My mom was a bigger lady, and the seated walker was too small for Mom, but it was all we had at the time. Lynda began to push Mom backward and lost control of Mom and the walker. As Lynda was running with Mom, trying to slow the walker down, the walker hit a ledge in the sidewalk right in front of the front entrance of the hospital. Mom fell backward with Lynda on top of her and hit her head on the concrete. The hospital personnel saw the whole thing and quickly called for help. We weren't sure why they called the fire department, but they did. Unconscious Mom lay on the ground. Lynda fell on Mom so hard that she had a bruise on her forehead from Lynda's chin. To top it off, Mom ended up in the hospital with bleeding in her brain. We had Katelyn in the heart department, and Mom was in the ICU. It was a complete train wreck, to say the least. At the time, it was not funny. As time went on, it became a big conversation piece and a good laugh!

The nurses came to get Katelyn, but this time was different. Katelyn cried and clung to me. She was five years old and about to have her fifth pacemaker and lead replacement. This was the first time she realized what was going on. In the past, she was too young, and it was easier to make the transition. The nurses then decided to give Katelyn some "happy juice." It was a medication to make her relax. After they took her back, Shane and I discussed how hard it was to let her go this time since she knew more about what to expect.

The look on Katelyn's face when they took her was unexplainable. At five years old, she didn't understand why Mommy would let the doctors hurt her again. I was supposed to be her protector. Not the person to hand her over willingly to be hurt again. With her being so young, there was no way to reason with her. I just prayed that someday she would understand that Mommy had to do this for the time being until God healed her little heart.

"Jesus turned and saw her, 'Take heart, daughter,' he said, 'your faith has healed you.' And the woman was healed at that moment" (Matthew 9:22).

Even though Katelyn received a pacemaker and lead with each surgery, none were routine replacement surgery. Each surgery was a special one, and each one always held a miracle and a blessing from God. After six hours of surgery, the doctor came out to talk to Shane and me about the procedure. As I mentioned before, Katelyn was a sign and wonder. She was a special case. Her doctors had never had such a small baby get a pacemaker, and they had never had a child require so many replacement surgeries. When the surgery started, they concluded that Katelyn's body was producing excessive scar tissue. This was the body's way of rejecting the leads and pacemaker. They needed to figure out how to prevent it. Their only resolution was to go intravenous with the lead. Katelyn's last leads were attached to the outside of the heart. Intravenous meant to go through one of her arteries to the heart, and that would be less exposure and fewer chances for rejection. The only problem with this procedure was they prefer to implant the intravenous leads when a child is in their teens or later. Katelyn was only five and would have multiple pacemakers for the rest of her life. They also had to move the pacemaker to the left side of her chest and out of her abdomen. The cardiologist would implant the pacemaker behind her breast muscle. He thought this would add a little more protection in case of injury. They didn't want to risk damaging one of the arteries but felt there was no other way to extend the longevity of the pacemakers and leads. The doctors also informed us that they were advising Katelyn to no longer take gymnastics and to stay off the trampoline. They were afraid that the scar tissue and the extra pulling on the lead from gymnastics played a part in the lead breaking this last time. The doctors also thought the trampoline was too much jerking and was bad on the lead as well. They wanted to take extra precautions to save the intravenous lead for as long as possible. We knew this news would be devastating to Katelyn. She loved gymnastics and participating in activities that most children do. She was finally able to lead a normal life. Now it will all come to an abrupt stop. As we said before, we never wanted her to be singled out, but we decided this was the best decision to make for her health. This news was not great news, but we were just trusting the doctors to do what they believed was the best for Katelyn.

Katelyn was now five, and Shaelyn had just turned nine. I didn't realize how Katelyn's health and frequent hospital visits affected Shaelyn. She was getting old enough now to understand the severity of Katelyn's heart condition. I always tried hard to keep her life as normal as possible. I didn't want her to worry about anything and just lead a normal life. Little did I know she was wise beyond her age. She was my first child and will always hold a special place in my heart. I believe she had to mature earlier because of being tossed around by friends and family so frequently. I asked Shaelyn for a testimony of how she saw her sister and living the life we lived for so many years. This is what Shaelyn composed to share with you all:

"Growing up, I never really thought any differently of my sister. I remember she could never jump on the trampoline with my brother and me. I would get really upset because she would cry, and I wanted her to be able to join in on the fun. I don't remember much of when she was a baby. My mom would say how I was so excited to finally be getting a baby sister. I remember the yellow shirt my mom had made for me to wear to the hospital the day I could finally see her. She was so little and fragile when I saw her. I'm sure it was very hard to try and explain to me that she was sick. When I looked at her, all I saw were pretty features and a bald head that I loved to rub.

"I always kind of knew when she would start to feel bad or if something was wrong with the pacemaker. Tiny always got up so early, especially on the weekends. She would sit in the living room and watch her cartoons with her blanket and crazy hair from sleeping so hard the night before. When something was wrong, she would sleep half the day away. You could see it in her face and eyes that she was not feeling great. She was also very grouchy and would cry more than usual. Then I would know it would only be a matter of time before I was rushed away to a relative or close friend's house. When I stayed there, it felt like years. Everyone was always so welcoming and always made sure I had more than I needed while I stayed. It just wasn't home. As I got older, I became more aware of just how serious things were when my family was gone. The people I would stay with would ask me to pray with them for my sister. I remember standing in a circle and joining hands and praying for her many times. One of the stays I remember the most was when my brother and I stayed with my aunt Sarah. As soon as we got to her house, we went to the local grocery store in Oblong and got groceries for our lunches, breakfast, and, of course, some sweet treats. She let us get these new orange cream sodas, and they were delicious! I'm not exactly sure how long we stayed, but I was glad we were safe and loved while our parents were gone.

"I feel, as the big sister, I am so blessed to be able to witness all the many miracles our family has received over the years. Was it hard? Absolutely! We all went through our hardships on our way. Do I wish my life was different? No, not even a little. How many people can say their sister is living, breathing proof that God is still the miracle-working God that He was thousands of years ago? If anything, I think my life is better! Learning at a young age that life is precious and to never take for granted anything God has given you is tough. I believe God does everything for a reason and in His timing. We, as a family, are the blessed ones. Most people would look at me and think I was crazy for saying that, but I'm telling you, we can get up every day and praise God that He has brought us out of some of the deepest and darkest pits. Thank You, Jesus, for my sister!"

CHAPTER 14: "BATTLE BELONGS"—PHIL WICKHAM

"Adjust and adapt." Whenever we live a life with difficulties, but yet we are content, that is pleasing to God. When we can adapt to circumstances and still praise God for His goodness, that is pleasing to God. When we are discontent with our circumstances and do not adapt, that is telling God we are not satisfied with Him. I try not to let our circumstances rob me of my joy. My joy isn't from what I have in life, whether good or bad. It's based on what Jesus Christ has done in our lives. He has blessed us so much, I have to praise Him.

> I am not saying this because I am in need, for I have learned to be content whatever the circumstances. I know what it is to be in need, and I know what it is to have plenty. I have learned the secret of being content in any and every situation, whether well fed or hungry, whether living in plenty or want.
>
> Philippians 4:11–12

Katelyn's fifth surgery went okay but not as well as the last four. Katelyn had an unusual amount of discomfort with this pacemaker. From strange twitches to constant throbbing pain. She could only lay a certain way to sleep because of the pain in the pacemaker's site. We made quite a few trips back to the doctor to try and see what was happening, but they did not come up with any solutions. Katelyn once again had to learn to adapt. She tried not to let this stop her from her activities and school. She amazed me, but this was her life. All she knew was to adapt.

Shaelyn was now in sixth grade, Katelyn in second grade, and Chance was in kindergarten. Aside from all of Katelyn's health problems, at this point and time, we had more than just health issues. It was a vicious pattern. It seemed every time I was distracted by Katelyn's health Satan used it as an opportunity to try and enter in different ways. Satan always knows our weakest points. He knows exactly when and where to attack. I believe he knew that Katelyn was safeguarded and chosen by God and he couldn't touch her. So, in turn, he attacked when he had other opportunities. I think I was so consumed with prayer for Katelyn that I let my guard down in other areas of my life, especially my marriage. Where I seemed to fail the most was that I was too concerned at this point in my life with my children's well-being. I worried so much about Shaelyn and Chance feeling left out because of all the attention I had to give to Katelyn that I spent my free time making them feel loved. I neglected my husband. Shane would work his twelve-hour work shift, then come home and work another four or five hours in his cabinet shop. A lot of the time, I slept where I could hear Katelyn if she needed me and not with my husband. Our marriage started to struggle. I saw Shane draw away from me and our family and was blaming myself for his ungodly decisions. I was stretched so thin that I didn't think I had any more to give to anyone. Satan found the little crack to put his foot in to try and destroy our family that God put together. This was a very trying time, and we were concerned that our marriage would not survive. We both had to do a lot of soul-searching and even tried a Christian counselor. I had to work on forgiveness before the Lord would heal our marriage. Shane and I decided to study the Bible. We knew only

God could heal our marriage. After a few months, we worked through another time of hardship but only through Christ.

Along with this, my mom's health began to deteriorate. We had to decide to put her into a nursing home. My mom had a bad heart and had a pacemaker/defibrillator implanted five years prior. I could see her getting tired and her health fading gradually. At the time of her device implant, the doctors didn't see her living for more than a couple of years. Once again, the doctors were not accurate. At this time she had been given another five years.

Putting my mom in the nursing home was such a hard decision, and I knew she would hate it there. At this time, it was our only choice for Mom to get the medical help she needed. At this point in my life, I was not able to take care of her, and my sisters all worked full time and could not do it either.

My best friend, biggest supporter, and prayer warrior was now battling her illness. I felt like I was now in Katelyn's battle alone because my mom was not able to help me this time. But I knew she would still be there for prayer. My faith was starting to fade as my flesh was rising again. It seemed like it was one battle after another. Satan was trying his hardest to wear me down. He wanted my children and my family. Little did he know I am a fighter, and I was not going to let Satan have any of them! He was picking on the wrong family of Christ.

Resist him, standing firm in the faith, because you know that the family of believers throughout the world is undergoing the same kind of suffering. And the God of all grace, who called you to His eternal glory in Christ, and after you have suffered a little while, will Himself restore you and make you strong, firm, and steadfast. To Him be the power forever and ever, Amen.

1 Peter 5:9–11

Katelyn began having more symptoms. In my spirit, I knew something was wrong, but I could not figure it out. The doctors did not help figure it out either. Katelyn and I made yet another trip to her electrophysiologist. In an interrogation, the doctor said that, once again, her pacemaker battery was running low. Here it was, only two years later, and after multiple trips to the doctor. Did I ask why? *Why is this pacemaker losing energy like this? Are we going to have to do this every two years? What is going on? Why did we have issues with this pacemaker from day one of implantation?* The doctors could not answer any of my questions. I began to think that maybe they were not equipped to take care of Katelyn properly with her rare case. The doctor then told me that she would like to put Katelyn on the heart floor to watch her overnight and see if their monitors would catch something. I was relieved because it seemed that they were, at last, making an effort to try and figure it out.

Typically when we stay on the heart floor, we get a private room. This time since it wasn't an emergency, we had to share a room with another patient. This patient was a three-year-old girl. She made me think of Katelyn when she was three years old. Over the years, I learned that babies with heart conditions all looked the same. I started talking to her mother and quickly found out that they were struggling financially and spiritually. As I said before, God always puts someone in front of us that has it worse than we do. They were trying to find out what was wrong with this little girl. She was so petite. She looked just like a cardiac baby. Heart babies all had the same look. This tiny girl would just lie and cry. Her mother was in and out a lot, so I would try to talk to her and comfort her. There was even one time when I went over and picked her up to hold her to comfort her. I couldn't handle her being so upset and crying all the time. The nurse came in and scolded me because she was not my child to comfort and it was against hospital policies to hold other children. That didn't do any good because I am a mother, and I comforted the little girl. I remember sitting there holding her and praying over her just like I did Katelyn. Later that evening, I went down to the gift shop. There was a little pair of glitter slippers that I knew Katelyn would love, so I picked them up for her and also for the three-year-old. I also found a soft teddy bear for the three-year-old. When I took those special gifts to her, her little face was priceless. She loved them! It filled my heart with joy just to see her so happy with her little gifts. That sweet girl never cried the rest of the night. I believe my prayers and the love I showed her gave her peace.

The next morning, the nurse entered the room. I asked if they found anything abnormal overnight. I was not prepared for her response. She said, "We think this is all in Katelyn's head. We think she is making it up for attention." I will never forget those words. Why would a chronically ill six-year-old child make this up? The last thing she wanted was another hospital stay or surgery. I was proud of myself because I held my composure. I was already having doubts about the care we were getting, and this just "sealed the deal." I looked at the nurse and just said, "Okay, we are ready to leave." The nurse asked if I was taking it upon myself to leave. I told her, "If it is all in Katelyn's head, then it's time to go back home." I knew our time here was over. I had no clue what we were going to do from here, but I knew God had a plan. I was solely using my motherly instincts, which I believe were guided by my Lord, Jesus Christ. The nurse brought the release papers for me to sign. We left and never looked back. Our season there was over. It was time to find a new doctor.

Shane was supportive of my decision to leave her old doctor. Now I had to find a new pediatric cardiologist because something was surely wrong with Katelyn. Her case was so abnormal that finding another doctor was going to be very hard. I knew I had to solely rely on God to guide me in the right direction. I didn't even know where to begin the search. I firmly believe that God gives us these obstacles to strengthen our faith and to solely rely on Him.

"Be joyful in hope, patient in affliction, faithful in prayer" (Romans 12:12).

I started searching on the internet for pediatric electrophysiologists in St. Louis, Missouri, which was about three hours away. This city was known for its good hospitals and doctors. I was also faced with finding a doctor that accepted Katelyn's rare heart condition. With God's guidance, I found a well-known pediatric electrophysiologist who was willing to take a look at Katelyn. We were home for one week then we were off to see the new doctor.

I had Katelyn's records sent to the new doctor. I was worried because her case was so abnormal but continued praying that this new doctor knew how to take care of her. We were starting from square one again. Once we got there, Katelyn had to get evaluated all over again. This included everything from blood work, echo, X-rays, and EKG to pacemaker interrogation. I told the pacemaker tech about Katelyn being so symptomatic with her pacemaker interrogations, but she soon saw for herself. As she shut the pacemaker off, Katelyn took a deep breath to pass out and then began to vomit and cry. This scared the tech—she had never seen that happen before. I reminded her that Katelyn was not a typical pacemaker patient. I remember sitting there crying with Katelyn but also trying to be strong for her. She was so scared, and so was I.

After all the tests, we finally got to see the doctor. I told him about all her symptoms and her past. He said he would watch her closely because the battery should not have run down so fast. He was leaning toward another lead fracture but couldn't tell for sure unless the surgery was performed. For now, he thought she would be okay to go home if we watched her closely. Katelyn was released from the hospital.

All of this was so exhausting. When we left the hospital, I just had to take a little nap before we went home. We both took a catnap in the car before we drove our three hours back home. Katelyn just kept telling me on the drive home that she felt sick. I figured it was from them adjusting her pacemaker. We were about forty-five minutes from home, and Katelyn yelled, "*Mom*!" I looked at her, and she was white as a sheet, and her lips were bright blue. She took a deep breath and passed out. I slammed the car into park and jumped out to go back to her. Grabbing her lifeless body, I began to shake her. She took another deep breath and began to cry. I just sat down at the door of the SUV and started sobbing. I was so scared. I just had my baby die and come back to life. I just started crying out to God, "What do You want me to do? I can't do this anymore! I'm tired, and I'm weak. Please, God, help me!" In a bold voice, I heard God say to me, "Never will I leave thee, and never will I forsake thee!" I knew at that point that God was with us and was not going to leave us! He had big plans for Katelyn Grace.

"Be strong and courageous. Do not be afraid or terrified, because of them, for the Lord your God goes with you; He will never leave you nor forsake you" (Deuteronomy 31:6).

I called Shane and told him what had just happened, and he said, "Turn around and take her back!" That is exactly what I did! I turned that SUV around, and back we went to the hospital. When we got there, the doctor was gone, so I took her to the emergency room. I explained to them what had just happened, and they admitted her. As I sat there watching the monitor, her heart rate was going crazy. It was going all over the charts. She would say, "Mom, I don't feel good!" as her heart rate would drop to 40 bpm and then shoot up to 120 bpm. If her pacemaker was working properly, her heart rate would not go below 60 bpm. It just continued to fluctuate like that. I called the nurse in, and she told me that since she was pacemaker dependent, the monitors never picked up the heart rate properly. I knew that was not correct. I just sat there watching and comforting her.

We were at the emergency room for around four hours, and she was getting tired. I told her to just rest. I was there with her. Katelyn said, "No, Mom, I'm afraid to go to sleep because I may never wake up." You can't imagine how those words ripped my heart out, but I was trying to be strong for her. Then she said, "Mommy, am I going to die?" I couldn't believe my ears. My baby had to think about dying. She was too young to have to think about these things. I can't imagine how my baby was feeling. I knew she was scared to death, and to be truthful, so was I. I assured her God was there with us. She replied, "Please, pray with me, Mom." Katelyn was wise beyond her years. She knew where our strength came from, Jesus Christ, our Savior. Shortly after she asked for prayer, she had another incident. She told me she felt sick. When I looked at her, I heard her monitor start to beep, and her heart rate dropped to 26 bpm. She turned as white as a sheet again, and her lips turned blue. She took a big deep breath and once again passed out. As all of this was happening, I already knew what was going on and was already springing into action. I ran over and started shaking her. She took a deep breath and came back to me. I just sat there and held her as we both were crying. Soon the doctor and nurse came in and asked what had just happened. They heard the monitors going off. I explained to them and asked them to please contact her pediatric cardiologist. They informed me he was out of town and that they didn't see anything on the alarming monitors. I couldn't believe what they were saying! I asked them if 26 bpm was not alarming, and I explained to them how she just took a deep breath and passed out and I had to shake her to make her come back. Then I asked them what would have happened if I were not there to shake her back to life. Was that not alarming? They told me that sometimes their monitors were not accurate. All I can say is Mamma Bear came out! I demanded to see a pediatric cardiologist and informed them that we were *not* leaving the hospital! They knew I meant business and they had better do something! Shockingly it wasn't very long after that our cardiologist came into the emergency room. He looked at me and said, "Let's get her up to the heart floor and replace this pacemaker." Those were wonderful words to my ears. I thanked God that somebody finally listened to me.

It was now time for Katelyn to get her sixth pacemaker in her seven years. I've learned the battle belongs to God and there is nothing I can do. Nothing is impossible for my God. I've learned that when I have to fight, I have to fight on my knees, and God wins every battle. Nothing can stand against the power of my God! I lay every fear at His feet. Because every battle belongs to my Lord, Jesus Christ.

As I sat in Katelyn's hospital room waiting on Shane, all I could think about was the Lord speaking to me in my SUV. It was proof that when we are at our lowest, the Lord is there to pick us up. When I heard those words, I knew without a shadow of a doubt that the Lord was taking care of Katelyn and me. He was just reassuring me that He was right there by our side, guiding us.

Shane arrived in time for the surgery. Here we were, preparing for yet another surgery. I knew God was with us, but I couldn't understand what I was doing that was not pleasing for Him to not completely heal Katelyn. I wondered why He did not hear my prayers. Was He trying to teach me something? As time went on, I realized He was pruning us and preparing us for His bigger plan for our lives.

"He cuts off every branch in me that bears no fruit, while every branch that does bear fruit he prunes so that it will be even more fruitful" (John 15:2).

Katelyn's surgery went very well, and we were home within three days. I was ready to be home with my other two babies. It was time to work on God's fruit.

Chapter 15: "Graves into Gardens" —Elevation Worship

"But if a widow has children or grandchildren, these should learn first of all to put their religion into practice by caring for their own family and so repaying their parents and grandparents for this is pleasing to God" (1 Timothy 5:4).

Not long after we were home from the hospital, Shane and I decided to move my mom home with us. She had gotten better and was so miserable in the nursing home. I could not leave her there. Once again, we learned to adapt. Chance stayed in Katelyn's room, and we turned his room into my mom's room. I knew it would be a lot of work, but I could no longer see her so sad in the nursing home. This move caused a lot of separation between my sisters and me. They were concerned because I already had so much going on with my kids and my health. It was going to take a lot to care for our mom. I was up for the challenge, though!

Those seven months were some of the best times that I had with my mom. The kids loved having Meemaw at our house. Mom loved watching the kids get ready for school. She told me one time that she enjoyed the hustle and bustle of the mornings with the kids. Mom loved sitting in the beauty shop doorway and talking to all my customers. Anyone who knew my mom would tell you that she did not know a stranger. She would talk to anyone. We would go for random car rides, and we once again got to look at fall leaves. I would never change anything about it, and I would do it all over again for my "best friend."

In the middle of the night, my mom woke me up in severe pain. I called 911, and the ambulance came to take my mom to the hospital. My mom was diagnosed with cellulitis in her legs. Cellulitis is a potentially serious bacterial skin infection and is very painful. She had problems walking anyway, and this made it impossible for her to be ambulatory. After her medical treatment, we decided to send her to a nursing home for physical therapy so she could come back home with us.

My mom was transitioning to the nursing home very well. The physical therapy program was working and rehabbing her very quickly. My mom was one of those people who did not know a stranger, and people were drawn to her just like Katelyn. One day I went to the nursing home, and all the aides that were on break were in Mom's room laughing and having a great time. I asked them, "Is this the hangout room?" They responded with, "We love your mom! She is an inspiration to all of us!" Mom was an inspiration to anyone who met her.

About a month into rehab, I went to see Mom, and we once again had a heart-to-heart talk. Mom said, "Sis, I think it is time for me to stay here. I appreciate you opening your home to me and taking care of me, but I believe it is time for you to concentrate on your family. I am fine here. Just promise me that you will still come and get me and take me to your house on Christmas Eve." Christmas Eve and Christmas morning was our special tradition that I was not about to break! After Shane and I had Shaelyn, my mom would come every Christmas Eve and stay the night with us. She loved being there when Shaelyn woke up to see her gifts from Santa Claus. We would open gifts, have a big breakfast, and spend Christmas Day together. We would continue this special tradition with our other children too. My heart broke when Mom told me to leave her at the nursing home. Of course, I wanted to argue and take her home with me, but I had peace with it, and I believe the comfort was from God.

On December 24, 2010, it began to snow. We received a lot of snow in a short amount of time. It was very slick, and I questioned how in the world I was going to get Mom in the car to bring her home. I told Shane no matter what, Mom was coming home for Christmas! I would find a way! As I left to get Mom, Shane was building a ramp to get her into the house. We both knew how important Christmas was for all of us. I will never forget because when I arrived at the nursing home to get Mom, she was sitting at the door in her wheelchair crying and waiting on me. As I walked in, she said, "I thought for sure you would not come and get me with all this snow." Through my tears, I told her no amount of snow would keep me from coming to get her. No matter what, I would be there! As I loaded her up to come home, I had no clue that would be our last Christmas together.

On February 21, 2011, my beautiful mom went to heaven to see our dad. That was by far the hardest day of my life. My mom's heart was failing, and there wasn't anything they could do. My sisters and our husbands were all at the hospital. Mom's heart would stop, and the defibrillator would shock her back to life. This went on for almost two days. My mom would laugh and be her normal self. She didn't know what was going on, or if she did, she never let us know. She'd just say, "Back up, girls. I'm having another spell." She had her mind and acted normal. Her heart just couldn't take anymore. It was worn out.

My sisters decided to go out for a break, but I would not leave. As they went down the hallway, my mom looked at me and said, "Sister, I love you so, so much." I believe that time is when Mom handed me her spiritual mantle. Mom's heart stopped, and the defibrillator no longer shocked her back to life. As I stood in the hallway watching them try to revive her, my sister Sarah said, "Heather, we can't do this. Mom would not want this. We have to let her go." I was the one who had to make the decision. My sister was right. Mom would not want that. She was ready to go see our dad. I was just selfish and not ready for my best friend to leave me. I told the doctors to let her go. After my sisters said their "goodbyes" to our mom, I stayed longer. I couldn't make myself leave. The nurse made a mistake by telling me to take my time. I knew she was gone, but I couldn't bring myself to let go of her hand. I knew that when I did, that would be the last time. She looked so peaceful lying there. I knew it was time to let her go because she was in a better place. There was no doubt by the peace on her face that she was no longer in pain and in heaven with our heavenly Father, Jesus Christ. I kissed her goodbye. The walk down the hospital hallway was the longest walk I'd ever had to make. I wanted to just run back in there and shake her like I did to Katelyn and wake her up, but I knew I couldn't. She was gone. I felt indescribable grief for the loss of my "best friend."

I don't remember much of the funeral. I believe I was in shock. To this day, I still want to pick up my phone to call her when I'm having a bad day or need some "mom" advice. I am so thankful for so many things with my mom. Most of all, I'm grateful that she never gave up on me. She loved me unconditionally. Her prayers and faith made me the godly woman I am today. I want to be that foundation for my children. Thank you, Mom.

After her passing, I felt a shift in my spiritual life. As I mentioned, I believe Mom gave me her spiritual mantle as she passed. The mantle in the Bible represents a person's spiritual gifts or the call of God in their lives. My mom had been the spiritual leader in our family since my father's passing. I was prepared to take that role. I proudly picked up the mantle from my mom, and I could feel it in my spiritual life. "There are different kinds of gifts, but the same Spirit distributes them" (1 Corinthians 12:4).

> Now to each one, the manifestation of the Spirit is given for the common good. To one there is given through the Spirit a message of wisdom, to another a message of knowledge using the same Spirit, to another faith by the same Spirit, to another gift of healing by that one Spirit, to another miraculous power, to another prophecy, to another distinguishing between spirits, to another speaking in different kinds of tongues, and to still another the interpretation of tongues. All these are the work of one and the same Spirit, and he distributes them to each one, just as he determines.
>
> 1 Corinthians 12:7–11

David, the husband of my best friend Lynda, is a preacher. Our families were very close. David taught me so much about gifts of the Spirit, forgiveness, demons, and God's love in general. I owe a lot of my spiritual growth to him too. My mom was very close to David as well. David told me, after her passing, that she had sat him down one day. She hit her fist on the table and said, "When I am gone, you have to take care of my Heather!" He assured her that he would take on the task. Little did he know I was not an easy project.

The Lord gave my mom the gift of prophecy through dreams. When I was growing up, I remember Mom dreaming things and warning our family about future events. We always joked and told her not to dream about us. Back then, we had no clue that it was a spiritual gift. After I matured in my faith and my walk with God, I realized Mom's gift was a blessing. Three years before Mom's passing, she had a dream and a warning for David. I will never forget it. It made a believer out of anyone who questioned her gift.

One morning, Mom called me. She was frantic. She said, "I have to get a hold of David! Something bad is going to happen to him!" At this time, Lynda and David had moved two hours away. David was not allowed to take electronic devices into his employment, so it was almost impossible to contact him. He was a chaplain at a prison. Mom had already tried calling him. Lynda could not contact him either. Mom said, "Heather, this is serious. I have to get a hold of him. I saw that he was going to be in a serious accident and not survive." I finally got in touch with Lynda and told her about Mom's dream. Later that evening, David called my mom and gave her a testimony. That day at work, David had a coworker check on him. He told David that he felt moved to pray for him. He felt uneasy about something with David. That afternoon, David, who was a creature of habit and always took the same way home every day, decided to take an alternate route. David's coworker called him on the way home and told him that there was a serious accident on the interstate involving a semi with fatalities. That was the same route that David took every day except for that day. As David got home, he was eager to tell Lynda, but little did he know she was anxious to tell him about Mom's dream. After they told each other their stories, David called my mom. Mom was so relieved to hear that he was safe. Mom and I had prayed all day for David. We knew God had told her to warn him. This is just another story of divine intervention and the power of prayer.

"For if you forgive other people when they sin against you, your heavenly father will also forgive you. But if you do not forgive others their sins, your Father will not forgive your sins" (Matthew 6:14–15). To carry out Mom's mantle, I had to learn to forgive. The Lord teaches us that there is no limit to forgiveness. We have to absolve everyone who has hurt us and ask for forgiveness from everyone we hurt. There should be no limit to forgiveness. I was not aware of all the bitterness I had from my past. I also had to swallow my pride and ask individuals for forgiveness. David was there to lead me on this journey.

The first issue I believed I had to take care of was asking my ex-husband for forgiveness. This was very big for me. I married my high school sweetheart one month after high school graduation. I always felt convicted because I believe I only married him because of money. My family was very poor, and his family had money. I fell in love with the idea of having what I thought would be a better life. I was unhappy and unfaithful to him. I was not a good wife and treated him badly. He did nothing to deserve that type of treatment. He was very good to me. I was always convicted for that, and it always weighed heavily on my heart. After much prayer, I called my ex-husband and asked to speak to him in person. This was thirteen years after we were divorced. He was shocked but openly welcomed me. David and I went to his house, and I asked for his forgiveness. He said he had forgiven me a long time ago. I told him I had to ask him for his forgiveness for God to forgive me. That visit was such a big release for me. I was faithful to God, and He, in turn, blessed me. I felt a burden lifted, and I never thought about it again.

My next forgiveness issue to deal with was rape. When I was in fifth grade, I was gang raped by five college basketball players. I had a cousin and was unaware that she was a regular at the basketball house. One night, we went to a local store, and on the way, she took a detour. She said she had to run by a friend's house real quick. When we got there, we walked in, and it was an apartment full of college basketball players. My parents were very strict, and for them to even let me go in a vehicle with someone was a stretch. Here I was, young and sheltered in an apartment with all these guys. I was scared to death. She left me in the living room so she could go into a bedroom with one. After she left, they started surrounding me and touching me. One of the players picked me up and took me into a room with four other guys. I was screaming, but nobody came to help until after they were finished with me. Finally, one of the other basketball players broke into the room and told them to get off of me. I ran out of the apartment and sat in the vehicle crying until she came out. I then demanded to go home. After I got home, I remember showering and feeling so filthy. I felt so violated. I went through many emotions of self-hate and unforgiveness. I thought I was stained goods and nobody would ever want me. I also kept thinking, *What if I get pregnant?* I was so relieved when I realized I was not pregnant. For years I lived with self-hate. I was too young to realize that through all of it, God was there with me and protecting me. I had to let go and forgive those who hurt me and tell my mom so she could know and forgive me as well. I finally told my mom after Shane and I were married. Mom sat and cried because she was hurt that I couldn't trust her. I explained that it wasn't that I couldn't trust her; I just had to forgive the ones who hurt me first so I could heal. Hearing my mom's distress and forgiveness about the situation was healing for me as well.

The final one I had to take care of was my forgiveness of my sisters. There was a lot of conflict between my sisters and me regarding our mother. Many painful things happened that tore us apart. I know it was Satan's way of trying to tear our family completely apart. He did a great job of it temporarily.

Then I decided to dig in and forgive. For two years I listened to a Christian DVD set on forgiveness. I took notes and studied. One day Shaelyn mentioned one of my sisters, and I realized Chance didn't even know who his aunt was. That hit me very hard. I kept praying and studying forgiveness. My sisters and I used to be so close. We used to laugh and have an abundant amount of fun. I considered us a very close-knit family. But that is exactly what Satan hates. He hates family bonds. My sisters and I went from spending every holiday together and taking shopping trips to never talking. Finally one day after prayer, I felt forgiveness for my sisters. This burden I had carried for so many years was gone. I can't explain it, but it was completely wiped away. I gave it all to God, and He took it from me. After so many years of studying forgiveness and praying, God answered my prayers. My mom told me many times that all she wanted was to see her girls together again. Two years after her death, we were finally together again. I just regret that it took so long and Mom didn't get to see it before her passing. We now go on sister trips every year, and we spend every holiday together. Not to mention other little shopping trips too. God is faithful, and once we let go and give it all to Him, He will wipe it all away. I love my sisters with all of my heart. "Then Peter came to Jesus and asked, 'Lord, how many times shall I forgive my brother or sister who sins against me? Up to seven times?' Jesus answered, 'I tell you, not seven times, but seventy-seven times'" (Matthew 18:21–22).

After I forgave and asked for forgiveness, I was launched into a whole new level of Spirit. I was ready to take Mom's mantle. I knew it was not going to be easy, but I believed in my spirit this was what I was supposed to do. The challenges I had ahead of me were part of the growing process in Christ. It was teaching me to have a stronger faith and prayer life.

In these trials, I learned that there is nothing better than God. I am not afraid to show Him my weaknesses. He turns our ashes into beauty. He takes us the way we are. His mercy and grace have a way of finding us. He turns our shame into glory. God is the only One who can. God always takes what Satan plans for harm and turns it into something wonderful.

And provide for those who grieve in Zion—to bestow on them a crown of beauty instead of ashes, the oil of joy instead of mourning, and a garment of praise instead of a spirit of despair. They will be called oaks of righteousness, a planting of the Lord for the display of his splendor.

Isaiah 61:3

Chapter 16: "Surrounded" —Michael W. Smith

Trials kept coming, but God was always faithful. "Consider it pure joy, my brothers and sisters, whenever you face trials of many kinds, because you know that the testing of your faith produces perseverance. Let perseverance finish its work so that you may be mature and complete, not lacking anything" (James 1:2–4).

In second grade, Katelyn received her sixth pacemaker. This one never really made her feel healthy. She never really recovered from the trauma of that pacemaker. I believed for a while that it took a toll on her little body. She still wasn't gaining much weight and always looked sickly. Her coloring was pale, and she always had black circles around her eyes. I look back now at pictures of her, and she looked so weak and unhealthy. She had a twitch in her chest muscle, and it was uncomfortable, which also made her struggle to sleep. She couldn't get quality sleep because of the discomfort of her pacemaker. She always complained of her chest hurting. It didn't seem to be doing its job. We took multiple trips back to her heart doctor, but he never seemed to find anything concerning.

Katelyn was soon to start fourth grade. She was at the age now where she knew exactly what happens when her pacemaker quit working. Once again, she would adapt. She got to the point where she would not tell me if she was feeling bad. Katelyn would just push through and try to hide her symptoms. Fear was starting to set in for Katelyn. It was only natural for this to happen after all she had been through. It was hard for her at such a young age to understand that God was there for her and was going to protect her. And to be honest, with all she had been through, even an adult would have a hard time believing that God was on her side.

Katelyn tried so hard to hide the evidence of problems because she didn't want another surgery. I tried to explain to her how important it was not to cover up her symptoms. It was crucial for us to know for us to get her to a hospital. God used divine intervention to allow me to be able to discern Katelyn's symptoms. I knew I had to listen to God when He helped me discern her ailments. We had been dealing with her heart symptoms at that time for ten years.

Katelyn started fourth grade, and I could tell she wasn't herself. One morning I went into her room to wake her up for school. When I walked in, she was covered in vomit, and I had a very hard time trying to wake her up. After I finally got her awake, she and I just sat in her bed crying. I thought to myself, *All my baby wants is to feel good and live a "normal" life. God, please heal my baby!* I couldn't believe we were once again going through this. It had been only two short years.

After Katelyn and I had our little pity party, I told her it was time to get in touch with the doctor. She looked at me with her beautiful, sad little eyes and finally agreed. I called her cardiologist, and we prepared for yet another trip.

As Katelyn got older, I tried to do something fun with each trip. Lord knows going to the doctor or hospital is not fun. On this trip to her cardiologist, we found a beautiful garden on the roof of the hospital. They had it fixed up with walking paths, beautiful flowers, benches, and a little bridge with a small waterfall. This was a pediatric hospital, and they had it designed for sick children and their families to give them a peaceful break from all the hospital stress. Unless you have had a sick child, you would not know about the pressure. The hardship of losing my mom was unbearable, but the agony of a sick child is unexplainable. As a mom, we naturally want to fix our kids and take away the hurt. With a chronically ill child, it is not in our control. We have to leave it up to God and His timing.

"The Lord sustains them on their sickbed and restores them from their bed of illness" (Psalm 41:3).

The cardiologist did all the necessary tests to check Katelyn once again. This time he found that her pacemaker battery was almost depleted, and it was indeed time for another surgery. He also thought that her pacemaker was misfiring and shocking the muscles around her heart. This was the reason why she was so uncomfortable and couldn't sleep. I believe they knew all along but were waiting until this pacemaker needed replacing to let us know. It wasn't a life-threatening issue, and she had already had so many surgeries and mishaps that I think they wanted to wait until surgery was necessary. Infection is a big problem with surgeries. The doctors took extra precautions to prevent infection with Katelyn since she had already battled with staph.

Our current cardiologist was a very intelligent doctor but had no bedside manner. He had a whole list of credentials but kindness was not one of them. He came off as if he were doing us a favor for being our doctor. That wasn't setting well with me. We bumped heads many times. I didn't like being treated like an idiot because I wasn't an MD. We had the ultimate doctor on our side. God is His name. Jesus said, "If you listen carefully to the Lord your God and do what is right in his eyes if you pay attention to His commands and keep all His decrees,

I will not bring on you any of the diseases I brought on the Egyptians, for I am the Lord, who heals you" (Exodus 15:26).

Katelyn and I stayed at the hospital and waited on Shane. Shane had to make sure our other two kids were cared for. Shaelyn was now in eighth grade, and Chance was in second grade. Both kids were active in sports and school. We tried to get them transitioned without too much disruption. My in-laws were wonderful to come and stay at our house so the kids could sleep in their beds and try to keep normality in their lives. Our family and friends were so great to be on alert. They knew that at any time they could get a call from us for assistance.

As I sat there waiting for Shane, Katelyn began to hit me with questions. In the past, I had asked doctors questions about her health. I quickly found out that doctors did not have all the answers. Katelyn's case was so rare, and not many children with heart block survived past childbirth. Doctors had no clue what to expect. I had to try to answer Katelyn's questions the best I knew how. She looked at me with crocodile tears and said, "Mom, why did God do this to me?" Holding back my tears, I replied, "God did not do anything to you. God chose you to be His special child." She replied, "Well, I don't feel too special. I feel like He doesn't love me." I said, "God loves you with all His heart. He has gotten you this far; He will not let you go!" She then said, "Mom, will you pray with me to have God heal me?" Wow, out of the mouth of babes! What kind of faith is that? It was the type of faith that we all need. She knew at ten years old who her healer was. Do we always have that faith?

"And the prayer offered in faith will make the sick person well; the Lord will raise them up. If they have sinned, they will be forgiven" (James 5:15).

Shane made it to the hospital, and Katelyn was sleeping peacefully. We took the time to go to the garden on the roof to have a little time to talk. I told him about Katelyn's questions. He replied, "We knew that day would come. She is getting old enough now that she will start to have a lot of questions." It was good to be able to sit and have a conversation with Shane. We were both so busy that we didn't get these opportunities often. He always seemed to have a way to put things in perspective that I could understand better. I sometimes thrived for his comfort.

The next morning was Katelyn's surgery. It was time once again to convince her that she was going to be just fine, while in the back of my mind, I was questioning too. I was trying to stay strong for her, but deep down it was ripping my heart out. She was crying and so scared. The older she got, the worse it got. The IV was the worst part. She did not want one. Her little arms and veins were so small that the needles hurt. They decided to just put it in after they got her in the surgical room. After they gave her the happy juice, she could care less about what was happening next.

Katelyn's surgery lasted about four hours. Once they got into her heart, they noticed that her lead was indeed broken, and it was shocking the muscles around her heart. This was causing her discomfort and muscle spasms. The cardiologist changed her pacemaker and her leads for pacemaker number seven. I asked the cardiologist why she had felt so badly for two years and if this was the same broken lead from the last pacemaker. After Katelyn's last surgery, I argued with the cardiologist because he told us that he thought he could make do with her lead even though he could see it was broken. When I asked him if it was the same lead, he would not answer me. He didn't have to say anything because no answer was a "yes" to me. I was not happy that he took that chance with a complete-heart-block patient. Especially knowing her history of near-death experiences. I let him know that I was not impressed with his actions.

After Katelyn was awake in recovery, they let Shane and I go see her. After we got to the recovery room, we heard Katelyn crying for us. She woke up scared to death. The nurse said she woke up yelling for me. As I got to the recovery room door and saw her hooked up to the wires and the look on her face when she turned to me crying, I felt myself almost pass out. Shane had to grab me and sit me in a chair. That was the first time that this had ever happened to me. I think it was possibly the stress and exhaustion. The surgery was easier when she was small and all I had to do was hand her to the nurse instead of being older and more aware of what was about to happen. No surgery is good, but I think it was getting a little harder on her and me.

Katelyn's hospital stay was only three days this time, and we were headed back home. After this pacemaker placement, I could see a big improvement in her. She bounced back quicker than the last surgery. This surgery didn't seem to cause any recurring pains. Katelyn went back to school within two weeks with limitations.

With all three kids in school all day, I had time to concentrate on the Word of God. I spent a lot of time studying and trying to improve my spiritual life to better equip me for when I have to go back into the battle for my family. I constantly felt like our family was under attack. I felt Satan would not be satisfied and leave us alone until he destroyed Katelyn. He was threatened by her. I'm so thankful that when we pray, God releases angels to fight Satan on our behalf. We have to fight with prayer. The moment we start to pray, the Lord releases angels to defend us. Satan can only be in one place at one time, but God is everywhere.

"For it is written: He will command His angels concerning you to guard you carefully; they will lift you up in their hands so that you will not strike your foot against a stone" (Luke 4:10–11).

I look back at all seven heart surgeries with Katelyn. I sometimes felt lost and defeated, but I knew through it all the only way to fight our battles was through Jesus Christ. He surrounds us with His Holy Spirit and His angels. If we stand back and let Him fight our battles for us, life will be so much simpler.

Chapter 17: "God Who Listens" —Chris Tomlin

Pacemaker seven was a reality check for me. I broke down one of my walls and realized that life was short with Katelyn. Every day was special with and for her. In the past, I never wanted to admit how fragile her life was. I was going day by day in survival mode. One day one of my dear friends came to me and asked me about contacting the Make-A-Wish organization for Katelyn. Make-A-Wish is an organization that grants wishes for children who have a life-threatening illness. Most of the time it is for children who, most likely, are not going to survive. It is an awesome organization and does so many wonderful things for children.

My friend only meant to be helpful. But to me, it meant defeat. I felt that if I contacted them, then I would accept that Katelyn's heart defect was more serious than I was ready to admit. I knew if I accepted it, Satan would win. I was not going to claim it! I believe in my friend's mind it was just something for Katelyn to look forward to. Katelyn's life seemed to be surrounded by one disappointment after another. She told me that Katelyn's life to her was a tug-of-war between Satan and God. She wanted to see Katelyn have something special to look forward to in life. My friend loves Katelyn, and her heart was for Katelyn. I was just not ready to accept it.

However, the suggestion took hold. I started thinking and planning. Katelyn always wanted to go to Disney to see the actual "Disney princesses." Katelyn loved princesses, and ever since she was old enough to watch TV, she watched every princess movie made. She had a special recliner after surgeries she would crawl up in and watch movies as she recovered. Katelyn always made her brother watch princess movies with her. He tried to be cool and cheered for the princes, animals, and villains.

A trip that far had never crossed my mind. It seemed as if I was afraid to get too far from Katelyn's heart doctor in case of an emergency. Florida was quite a distance from our home. I checked into flying conditions for Katelyn with her pacemaker. I knew that she couldn't go through security at airports because the magnets would reprogram her pacemaker. I had a lot of preparations to make for a family trip to Disney happen. I was up for the challenge, though, to make my baby's dream come true!

My good friends Kendra and Lynda helped me plan a dream trip for Katelyn to Disney! Did I ever mention that I had the best friends a person could pray for?

In the spring of 2013, Kendra, Lynda, and I had all our plans completed for our trip. We had all the necessary arrangements made. Lynda and I planned to fly with our five kids, and Kendra was driving to meet us. The night before departure, Lynda's father-in-law passed away. Lynda had to stay home, so I went ahead and took the five kids on the flight to meet Kendra at our resort in Kissimmee, Florida. The resort was only five miles from Disney. Every day was planned out and jam-packed with adventures. This was my kids' first trip to Florida and the beach.

One day Kendra took the girls shopping, and I took Chance and Kendra's son, Eli, to Legoland. The boys had so much fun, and Legoland is very interesting. It is intriguing to see all the objects made out of Legos only. We were also able to see our first alligator in the wild. It was swimming around in the lake. It caused all kinds of excitement because it was not supposed to be on the Legoland property. It was rewarding to be able to take the boys to do something special that they thoroughly enjoyed.

The highlight of the trip was Katelyn getting the opportunity to have lunch with the Disney princesses. She was so excited, and it was such a special time for her and me. This was the first time we had the opportunity to leave all the doctors and surgeries behind and just enjoy one another. This was priceless for us. I will forever cherish the opportunity we had together.

Our Florida trip ended at Cocoa Beach. My kids had never been, and it was very exciting for them. They played all day in the sand and sun. All the kids but Katelyn ended up getting lost on the beach. I guess you could say Katelyn was the smart one in the group. She stayed with Kendra and me. After about two hours of looking for the other kids, the security found them quite a distance down the beach. After that excitement, it was time to head back to the resort and prepare for our flight back to Illinois. Our fun and exciting trip to Florida had come to an end.

Katelyn's love for softball started to take shape. Her sister was very active in travel softball and was a very good athlete. Katelyn started playing softball at age eight, and I think this was when she started to see a future in the sport. From age eight, she would watch her sister play at the competitive level and was her biggest fan. She always said she wanted to be a good softball player like Shugs.

Katelyn's heart doctor wasn't completely on board with her playing softball and especially being a pitcher. I knew her heart and desire, so I worked on figuring out a way for her to play. Katelyn wore a chest protector, and we began to coach her on how to move the softball around the bat so the ball did not come back toward her while pitching. With Katelyn being a type A personality, she picked up quickly on how to command her pitches. She placed her pitch wherever she wanted it to go. Just like I said before, this girl was determined, and nothing would stop her.

Shane and I organized a Christian Travel Softball Organization. We started the organization to allow all athletes to play competitive softball. Our area is small, and we knew a lot of athletes that did not get the opportunity to play because of finances or because they were not in the "popular" crowd. They had the ability but were just not given the chance. The Lord laid it on our hearts to start this Christian organization to help all athletes to succeed. We did fundraising to pay for all expenses. When we were playing on Sundays, we would have a devotion, or we would have special Christian speakers come and speak to our athletes. We also worked hard to get our athletes recruited to the collegiate level. If our athletes wanted to play college level, they all got scholarships to play. Needless to say, our summers were jam-packed. Little did we know, but softball would become a huge part of our lives and an open door for Katelyn to be able to spread the Word of God.

"For the revelation awaits an appointed time; it speaks of the end and will not prove false. Though it lingers, wait for it; it will certainly come and will not delay" (Habakkuk 2:3).

I have learned that when I pray, God doesn't answer in my timing. It is always in His timing, and His timing is good.

Twenty thirteen was a big year for the Wilbers. A lot of changes were about to begin. New Hebron Christian School only went from preschool to eighth grade. Shaelyn was now entering her freshman year at a local public high school. This was such a huge adjustment for us. I felt like I was throwing her into a den of lions. I knew at New Hebron she was getting the best Christian education possible. When our kids entered public school, they were a grade or two above everyone education-wise. The public school turned out to be a culture shock for Shaelyn and our family. Shaelyn would come home with stories about kids disrespecting teachers and thought it was horrible. She had never witnessed that type of behavior. Public high school was not a good experience and was a lot of worry and stress. All three of our children struggled at this school. They went through bullying and ridicule. My kids never made good friends and were always considered outcasts. I saw their hurt but tried to always be encouraging. I thank God for New Hebron and the girl's travel teams. That is where they made the best friends that they have to this day. "But I will restore you to health and heal your wounds…because you are called an outcast, Zion for whom no one cares" (Jeremiah 30:17).

This was the year that I was officially diagnosed with lupus. I had been treated with Sjögren's syndrome since 1998. Lupus is a sister disease. I had all the antibodies, but lupus hadn't been confirmed by blood work yet. Sounds crazy, but that is how the medical system works. The disease is not treatable. They can only give medication to help with the symptoms caused by the disease. As I learned about lupus, I discovered lupus flare-ups were typically caused mostly by stress. My doctor told me I needed to control my stress levels, or it would cause my body to destroy itself. I asked him if he was serious. He had forgotten about my life struggles. This was another bump in the road that I had to give to God. I knew I could not handle this on my own. It was so easy for me to pray for Katelyn's healing, but for some reason, it was just hard for me to pray for myself. I had faith, but I was too consumed with Katelyn's well-being to think about myself. I had to learn how to believe in my healing. To this day, God has taken care of this disease, and I have a few problems. My new rheumatologist always tells me that she can't believe how well I am doing. Most patients do not have as few symptoms as I do. I always tell her that I gave it to God, and He is my ultimate healer. I keep planting that seed and praying God will make it grow into my doctor's life.

"Heal me, Lord, and I will be healed; save me and I will be saved, for you are the one I praise" (Jeremiah 17:14).

I will never forget this special memory of when Chance was in kindergarten. My beauty shop window faced the field and woods behind our house. One day, while I was working, I saw him out my window. He was all dressed in his camos with a little camo seat and his bow. He went walking across the yard to a little patch of woods right off the yard. He sat on his little seat with his bow. The bow was plastic with little plastic arrows, but he thought he was a real hunter like his daddy.

Every day we had four deer come into the field to eat. They were accustomed to us because they were there every day, so it did not bother them. I stood there watching Chance, and the next thing I saw was a little arrow arch up and land beside one of the deer. The deer looked at the arrow and kept eating. Here came another arrow, and before long there were four arrows right beside the deer. The arrows never even fazed the deer. I then saw Chance sneak to the arrows because he didn't have any left to shoot. That scared the deer. After they ran off, he grabbed his arrows and dropped his shoulders in defeat. He walked over and got his chair, then came back to the house. Disgusted, he told his dad he needed real arrows to shoot real deer. It was so cute. I will never forget it.

When things seem bad, God always makes things good. Every day is new in Christ. My mom taught me to always look at things in a positive light and not to dwell on the negative.

On a positive note, Chance was now in second grade and started his first year of flag football. He loved it. He was good at it too. Chance was all boy. His goal was to get more flags than anyone else. He also hated it when someone took his flags. He always had the plan to outrun everyone. Chance also planned a special route to avoid getting his flag pulled. He was always a thinker. I loved watching him play sports because he hated to be beaten at anything. When he was in t-ball, my favorite memory was him hitting the ball and running the bases. He slid into every base. It was so funny. No matter what, he would slide.

I enjoyed every season of our kids' lives. Life was never easy, but God always threw in a lot of enjoyment.

"May the God of hope fill you with all joy and peace as you trust in him, so that you may overflow with hope by the power of the Holy Spirit" (Romans 15:13).

As Katelyn got older, she found different struggles in life. I believe all the trials she went through with her health helped her develop into a stronger individual, yet, she was very dependent on me. Katelyn was struggling with fear. In reality, who wouldn't be? She was at the age when her friends wanted to have sleepovers. Katelyn was okay with them coming to her house, but she was scared to stay at anyone else's house. There were many times I made trips at 1:00 a.m. to pick her up from a friend's house. One day I asked her why she was so scared. She replied, "Mom, you are the only one who can protect me! What if I die at my friend's house?" I was learning that she was at the age where her little mind was working. I tried to assure her that she would be just fine and that God is her protector. One day as I was in the kitchen cooking, she came up to me with big tears and said, "Mom, I'm afraid to go to sleep because I may not wake up. What if I never wake up? Will you always check on me at night to make sure I'm still breathing?" She was as serious as she could be. She was gripped with fear. Katelyn has always been the type of child whose mind is constantly working. I hugged her and assured her that God was with us. I told her, "God told me He would never leave us or forsake us. I believe He means that! God has big plans for your life, and He will be here to protect us. We just have to have faith in Him." Katelyn replied, "What if He changes his mind?" I said, "God doesn't change His mind. He loves you and wants the best for you. God is faithful." Katelyn said, "Mom, will you pray with me?" I loved how she knew to ask for prayer because of her faith in God. She believed He answered our prayers and was our protector. Jesus gave us this reminder, "Peace I leave with you; my peace I give you. I do not give to you as the world gives. Do not let your hearts be troubled, and do not be afraid" (John 14:27).

I believe God gives us different seasons in our life. We have good seasons and some that are harder trials. As I walk through each period, I am thankful that God walks beside me. I pray for His strength to help me push through to the other side. The Lord is always faithful. "There is a time for everything, and a season for every activity under the heavens" (Ecclesiastes 3:1).

Chapter 18: "Yesterday, Today and Forever" —Passion

"Mom, are there any other kids like me?" That is a question my soon-to-be eighth grader asked me in the spring of 2016. That was a logical question that I could not answer. In the past fourteen years, we hadn't met any other complete-heart-block kids. The last thing we were told was she was the smallest baby at Riley's to ever receive a pacemaker. We were also told that her condition was one in a million. To be truthful, the thought never even crossed my mind. I was too busy going day by day. I answered her with, "I don't know, but I will find out!" That one little question made me curious. If you haven't found out yet, Katelyn is a little mini-me.

My investigative work began. After many searches and calls, I found a heart-block group on social media. What I found changed our lives forever. We found heart-block kids all over the world, from newborns to age twenty-eight. The closest heart-block kid was in St. Louis, Missouri, where Katelyn's current doctor practiced. After I looked into it, I showed the site to her. Katelyn's face was priceless. So much joy! She said, "Mom, I'm not that weird. There *are* other kids like me! Thank you, *Mom*!" Until this point, she thought she was the only heart-block kid on the face of the earth. Katelyn's confidence and outlook on life changed after I found this group. We spent hours scrolling and looking at the other kids' heart stories. To be honest, I felt a relief reading the other heart mom's conversations. I was finding out that most of them had the same concerns as I did. We were all going through life day by day on autopilot. Cherishing each day we had with our complete-heart-block children.

Katelyn and I got on the site and started conversing with other heart-block families. Katelyn found a friend that was the same age as her. They would talk for hours. Katelyn told me they would ask each other so many different questions. They discussed their fears and their lives with pacemakers. Katelyn also found out that she seemed to be the one with the most surgeries. Nobody on the site had complications as she has endured in the past fourteen years. She asked me again, "Why me, Mom? Why do I still have to be the different one?" I told her she wasn't different; she was God's "special" child. I wouldn't let her focus on that information; I had her look at the positive outlook that there are now kids she can associate with all over the world.

There were a few heart-block kids and families up in Chicago. Chicago is about five hours from us, and they are the second closest group of families. The Chicago families were having a heart-block meet and greet. It was my understanding that they make a point to get together two times a year for the kids and families to socialize. The meet and greet was at Katelyn's friend's house. Her mother invited us to attend and stay with them. At first, I thought Shane would never let us go. He would tell me I was crazy for even considering doing this. I didn't know these people, and here I was, thinking about staying with people I knew nothing about five hours from our home. Not to mention Chicago is known for being the murder capital of Illinois. Not a place people from southern Illinois like to visit. Here's the craziest thought: I felt complete peace about it. After I prayed and God opened these doors for Katelyn, I knew it was God's doing. He placed these wonderful heart-block kids and families in our path for Katelyn's peace.

You guessed it! Shealyn, Chance, Katelyn, and I loaded up and went to Chicago to meet the other heart-block kids and their families. I don't know who was more excited and nervous: Katelyn or her siblings? All I knew was I was following God's lead and showing Katelyn once again that God answers prayers. Big or small, He answers them all.

"And pray in the Spirit on all occasions with all kinds of prayers" (Ephesians 6:18).

When we finally arrived, we were greeted by some of the nicest people we had ever met. There were a lot of hugs and tears. We were introduced to all of these precious miracle babies. I looked around at all these beautiful little kids and thought about how blessed we truly were. We exchanged real-life stories that were good and bad. Most of these families had been in this group since their children were born. I thought about all the years I struggled on my own because I had nobody to ask and the doctors had no answers. I look back now, and I know for sure God was my sole support. If I'd had the group, I might not have depended totally on God and relied on their past experiences instead. I believe it was a test that I passed, and as a reward, God blessed us with this heart-block group.

That evening as we went to our rooms, Chance looked at me and said, "Mom, those people are normal like us!" I asked him, "What do you mean? What did you expect?" He said, "Well, I didn't know if they would look weird or be deformed." Shaelyn joined in, "Yes, Mom! I didn't know what to expect either. I thought the same thing as Chance." I looked at both of them and said, "Is your sister deformed? Is she weird? No, they are just like your sister. Just because they have a heart condition doesn't make them look any different." Shaelyn and

Chance thanked me for bringing them to the meet and greet. Shaelyn said, "Mom, you realize how special this was for Tiny? She needed this so much." I replied, "Yes, Sister, we all did."

I thought about what they said. At first, I thought it was crazy, but then when I thought more, it made sense. All these years, our family thought Katelyn was the only heart-block kid alive. Nobody in our area had ever heard about this condition until Katelyn was born with it. This meeting was exactly what our family needed. We needed to see that God makes us all equal. We might have a health issue, but that doesn't make us weird or strange. God doesn't make mistakes. He makes us all perfect in His sight. I knew God had big plans for all these miracle kids that we had the pleasure to meet and get to know better.

Katelyn and her new heart-block friend spent the evening getting to know one another better. After that meeting, they grew very close. Her mother and I set up meeting points to get the girls together every so often. Their friendship was growing to become a one-of-a-kind friendship. They had something special in common that nobody else could say they had.

While we were at the meet and greet, the kids were hanging out, so we moms got to have our conversations. All of the moms were curious as to why Katelyn had so many surgeries. Out of the group, Katelyn had the most surgeries and complications. I started telling them what had happened. Katelyn's friend's mom told me about their heart specialist. Their pediatric cardiologist specialized in heart block. She said the only downfall was his office was in Chicago, and that was such a drive for us. I couldn't believe what she was telling me! That was exactly what we were looking for! I informed her that miles would not stop me from getting the appropriate attention she needed for her heart condition. Our current heart doctor did not specialize in heart block, and as far as I knew, neither did any of our past specialists. We conversed about our current doctor and how we were not satisfied with him. She said, "Give me a couple of days, and I'll send Dr. Ovadia a text. I don't know if he is accepting new patients, but it's worth a shot!" Within three months, we had our first appointment with Dr. Ovadia.

Here was another one of God's divine interventions. All of this was happening because God set it all into motion.

At our first appointment with Dr. Ovadia, our new heart-block friends met us at his office. As we walked into the patient room, he greeted us with a hug. He said, "Any friends of the heart-block group are friends of mine." Dr. Ovadia was exactly what we had been looking for in a doctor. He was so patient and kind and wanted to know all about Katelyn. He wanted every little detail, whether it be health related or just regular life. We sat there and talked to him for two hours. Two hours! What specialist do you know who would spend that much time with one patient? None that we had met in fourteen years until Dr. Ovadia.

Dr. Ovadia was amazed by Katelyn. He was taken by her at the first meeting. He said he had been a heart doctor for thirty-five years and had never met anyone like her. He told us her story was amazing and nothing as he had ever witnessed. I had all of her medical transcripts sent to him from her various doctors. When we got there, he had already read through all of them and knew her background. He told us he was anxious to meet this very special heart-block girl from southern Illinois. Katelyn and Dr. Ovadia developed a wonderful bond after the first meeting. We left knowing there was no doubt that God was in every part of this divine meeting.

A few months after our first appointment, Katelyn started having some problems with her pacemaker again. It was all the same symptoms again. I called Dr. Ovadia, and he promptly got Katelyn in to check her pacemaker device. His promptness and tenderness were nothing we had encountered in a physician in the past. I can say he cared for all of his patients. They were not considered a burden; they were all special to him, and it was obvious.

Dr. Ovadia always interrogated the pacemaker and then interrogated us. I always felt as if he checked everything thoroughly. He usually spent twenty minutes looking at the pacemaker and then about one and a half hours talking with us. At this appointment, he told us he saw a small glitch in her transmission but wasn't concerned. He adjusted it and thought she would be okay after the modification.

During this appointment, he acted like he had been her doctor for many years. He asked her how she was handling everything mentally. She looked at him as if he were crazy. Katelyn and I have a problem with shoving things away and making ourselves acceptable to the situations that we are dealing with. It was a domino effect because my mom had a problem doing that, then passed it on to me, and I then passed it on to my kids. I'm not saying it is the right way to handle problems, but my kids don't dwell on any one thing. They just adapt and move on. That is what our family had learned to do with Katelyn's heart condition. We dealt with the issues currently and then moved forward. Never carry it with us, almost like we wanted to forget, and it would go away. But it never did.

Dr. Ovadia then told her that he would like for her to write her feelings out on paper. He said she didn't have to show him or anyone else. In his experience, his patients who had done this had dealt with their condition better. He told her that even though she didn't seem upset or depressed, deep down she might have concerns that would help her with getting her feelings out on paper. After he explained that to her, her wheels started turning, and the questions began.

When we reached the car to head home, Katelyn looked at me with big sad eyes and said, "Mom, that makes sense to me. There are a lot of times I have felt alone and wondered why things like these happen to me. I know God has a plan, but I have no clue what it is!" I replied, "If you feel like it will help you, then, by all means, do it! It doesn't mean you are weak or have issues. Maybe it will help you learn how to adapt to your condition mentally." As soon as we arrived home, Katelyn started writing her feelings on paper. Little did we know this was the beginning of her testimony and many doors God was about to open.

Katelyn was a very shy little girl. I believe that goes back to her uncertainty about people when she was little. I also believe it was because she felt so different from everyone else, she was afraid of being judged by her peers. I think it was her insecurities. Katelyn putting her feelings in writing was a big step for her because of being so shy. I figured that the only person who would ever get to see it would be me. God had different plans, though. Katelyn was about to get out of her comfort zone.

The following summer, the heart-block group had a heart-block reunion but this time in St. Louis, which is three hours closer to us! It was over the Fourth of July and consisted of a swim party with dinner at a heart-block member's house and Six Flags amusement park. We had never adventured to Six Flags, so my kids were excited to attend. The group we met in Chicago would be attending, and we would have the opportunity to meet different parents and kids from the heart-block group. We went a day early and made it a long weekend. Shane had to work, so he couldn't make the trip with us. When we arrived, we were greeted by Katelyn's friend from Chicago.

She decided to go to Six Flags with us. We had a great day and a lot of fun. The girls enjoyed each other tremendously, and I enjoyed watching them interact. Katelyn loved hanging around her new friend, who knew exactly what she was going through medically. She could be herself around her and not feel left out or different.

After Six Flags we went back to the hotel and prepared for the next day's swim party. I have to say I was a little nervous. I knew there would be a lot more attending than in Chicago, and I was curious as to how they would accept us. When we arrived the next day, they were all so welcoming to my kids and me. We had the opportunity to meet older heart-block kids and babies too. We also met a couple of families who had two children with heart block. As I observed, I realized we were all there for the same reason. We all needed support and encouragement. Our journeys with our children have been strenuous yet rewarding. God gives these special children to exceptional parents. We are blessed to be part of this extraordinary heart-block group.

Katelyn's eighth-grade year was a maturing and growing year for our family. It seemed like our seasons were ramping up, and multiple changes kept coming. Shaelyn was a senior, and Chance was in sixth grade. I found myself traveling in different directions with all three kids in sports at two different schools. I'm not fooling anyone because I love sports and watching my children play. Katelyn's reassurance in herself after the heart-block reunion exploded. She was more confident, and it showed in her everyday life. She loved cheerleading, and now when she cheered at games, I saw more of a leadership role in her. Instead of standing off, she was up in front yelling and smiling. She was happier because she was content with the life the Lord had given her. I believe she felt that she now had more of a purpose in life and the confidence to take on the challenge!

As long as we keep our sights on God through all the tests and trials, His grace is enough. God's Word is everlasting yesterday, today, and forever. We have to keep the faith and never give up the fight. All of our hope and trust is in Jesus. He is the rock that we stand on and stake our lives on. Katelyn is living proof.

"The Lord is my rock, my fortress, and my deliverer; my God is my rock, in whom I take refuge, my shield and the horn of my salvation, my stronghold" (Psalm 18:2).

Chapter 19: "Million Little Miracles"— Elevation Worship

Twenty seventeen came quickly! Katelyn graduated eighth grade, and Shaelyn graduated high school. Shaelyn moved to college on a softball scholarship, and Katelyn moved on to high school to start her high school softball career. Katelyn was so excited to play high school softball and work on her collegiate recruiting. Her main goal was to play college softball like her sister. The only difference was all the setbacks that she had to endure. I knew that she could do it, though. She had the drive and dedication to make it!

Katelyn was an athlete who was always working out and practicing. She had her routine to pitch or work out every day. Fall is the time for college recruiting, and she was working hard to improve her velocity in pitching. To achieve her goals, we started taking Katelyn to a pitching coach in Cape Girardeau, Missouri. Ryan Medlin was a well-known pitching coach. Years ago, he had coached Shaelyn on a showcase travel softball team, and she would go and play for Ryan at showcases in the fall. When I contacted Ryan about Katelyn, he had no clue that she was Shaelyn's little sister. He thought she was just one of the athletes we coached on our travel team. Ryan and Katelyn hit it off at the first pitching lesson and acquired an unbreakable bond.

For many years to follow, we made countless trips to Cape Girardeau for lessons and to play softball for Ryan. He was a hard case to crack, but Katelyn had a way to do it. She broke down walls that Ryan seemed to always put up around other people. Their bond grew stronger, and I believe Ryan looked to Katelyn for inspiration and spiritual advice. We grew a connection also. I think we had more in common than we both realized. Our hearts were 100 percent for the girls we coached. We loved to see them succeed and would do whatever we could to make that dream happen for our athletes. This relationship between Ryan, Katelyn, and me grew as time went on. Katelyn is thankful to Ryan for her growth and her confidence and pitching. Ryan will always hold a special place in Katelyn's heart.

One day after school, I met Katelyn at the gym. We liked to exercise together at a local gym. We did our workout and then walked to the car together. On our way out the door, Katelyn said she felt strange. As we got to the car, she said, "Mom! Look at my chest! Something is wrong!" She started yelling, "Mom, help me! I'm going to pass out!" She started to go down, and I grabbed her. I put her into my car and started patting her on the face. As she sat there, I looked at her chest, and it appeared her heart was outside of her shirt. It looked as if her pacemaker was coming right out of her chest. She started panicking and crying, "Help me, *Mom*! I'm going to have a heart attack. I have never done this before! Help me, *Mom*!" I hate to admit it, but I started to panic as well. I shut the door of the car and took off to the nearest hospital.

On the way to the hospital, I called Dr. Ovadia's cell phone to tell him what was going on. After filling him in, he called the hospital to communicate with the on-call doctor. Our local hospital is very small, and we do not have a cardiologist. Dr. Ovadia was making sure Katelyn got the proper medical attention until we could get her to Chicago.

After the local doctor interrogated her, Dr. Ovadia came to the conclusion we had. There was a broken lead, and we needed to get to Chicago. It was shocking her chest and making her heart beat so hard it was visible through her shirt. We made plans to head to Chicago.

Katelyn was devastated. Here she was, just starting her freshman year, and it was softball recruiting season. She just cried and cried. I told her everything would be just fine. We had to get her pacemaker fixed first. Surgery was our number one priority right now. Nothing else mattered at this point and time. Katelyn did not look at the situation that way, though. She looked at it as if it were another setback and would lessen her recruiting possibilities.

After Shane and I got her to Chicago, the nurses hurried to get her attached to monitors and prepare her for Dr. Ovadia to interrogate her. As we sat there waiting for Dr. Ovadia, Katelyn looked at me with her big sad eyes and said, "Why can't I just have a normal life like everyone else? Why does this always have to happen to me? This is the worst timing ever! I just want a normal life! Why, *Mom*? Please tell me why." I had to sit there for a minute before I could answer her because I was torn up inside for her. I took her hand and looked her in the eyes and told her, "Sis, this is our 'normal.' We have to live in this season until God completely heals you. I don't know God's plan, but He has a plan for you, and He is here with us to guide us through." Wow, that was a hard one. My teenage daughter just wanted to live life as a regular teenage girl.

I knew I had to keep her faith strong to get her through this hard time. No matter what, I was going to remain positive and reassure her that God had her wrapped in His arms and would never let her go. I reminded her of the words the Lord spoke to me, "Never will I leave thee, and never will I forsake thee." I told her that God would not have told me that encouragement if He wasn't going to take care of her. Katelyn always asked for prayer in hard times. She knew who would answer her prayers. She knew exactly who to put her trust in. Jesus Christ, our Savior and King! It always encouraged me when Katelyn asked me for prayer because she never lost faith that God was there to protect her. We should all learn from this fifteen-year-old "bold" faith.

"If we are thrown into the blazing furnace, the God we serve is able to deliver us from it, and he will deliver us from Your Majesty's hand. But even if He does not, we want you to know, Your Majesty, that we will not serve your gods or worship the image of gold you have set up" (Daniel 3:17–18).

The nurses prepared Katelyn for pacemaker number eight. Katelyn seemed a little calmer this time. I asked her if she was scared, and she replied, "Nope! God's got this! But can we pray?" Shane and I always prayed with Katelyn before they took her to surgery. I replied, "Of course! God does have this!" As we prayed, I could feel God's presence. The Holy Spirit was my confirmation that He was there with us and He was in control.

Prayer is the way we communicate with God and seek His favor. In the past fifteen years, I had a lot of communication with God. God never ceases to amaze me. He lifts me when I am down, and He sets me on the solid rock. When I pray and the Holy Spirit is there with me, I know without a shadow of a doubt the Lord Jesus Christ hears my cries and is there to comfort me.

"Do not be anxious about anything, but in every situation, by prayer and petition, with thanksgiving, present your requests to God. And the peace of God transcends all understanding, will guard your hearts and your minds in Jesus Christ" (Philippians 4:6–7).

As they took Katelyn back for surgery, Shane and I went to the waiting room. In the waiting room were Katelyn's best friend, Madi, and my niece Erica. Madi is Erica's stepdaughter, and we do a lot together. Katelyn and Madi have been best friends and played travel softball together since they were eight years old. Madi got to see Katelyn before they took her back for surgery, and I know that meant a lot to both of them. We all sat in the waiting room and waited.

Four hours went by, and no information from the nurse yet. Typically the nurse will call the waiting room and give us updates on the surgery. I was starting to worry. This was a new hospital and a new cardiologist. All of that added up to make me uneasy. Finally, I went to the receptionist, and she called the operating room. The nurse let us know everything was going well. Two more hours passed before the nurse called to give us an update. Here it was six hours of surgery. Longest surgery we'd had so far. The nurse told us Dr. Ovadia was closing up, so it wouldn't be long. Before we knew it, two more hours passed. It was now midnight. I was starting to stress and pace the floors.

I had many thoughts going through my mind and couldn't understand what was happening. They kept telling us that she was okay, but why was it taking so long? I paced down a dark hallway praying and stumbled across a chapel. Entering the chapel, I started praying and crying on the altar. I kept thinking, *Never will I leave thee, and never will I forsake thee.* That was a promise that our Savior gave me. I knew He was there with me as I was praying. When I returned to the waiting room, Shane said the nurse had called and Dr. Ovadia would be down shortly. As we sat there, everyone was silent. Nobody knew what to say. I knew Erica and Madi had to get going because it was a five-hour drive home, but she wanted to make sure Tiny was okay first.

At 2:00 a.m., Dr. Ovadia came to the waiting room. When Dr. O came and sat with us, he looked extremely exhausted.

I could see the stress on his face as well. He proceeded to give us news that we were not prepared to hear. This is what Dr. O said to us, "I am so sorry to put you guys through all of this. I know this ten-hour surgery was very stressful on all of you. During surgery, I looked at all of Katelyn's scars and thought, *Would my fifteen-year-old daughter be pleased with herself and these scars?* I thought not. So I cleaned up all her scars. I hope she is pleased with them when she wakes up. I also found that the reason why Katelyn keeps running batteries down is that her heart is one big callus. The callus was caused by a staph infection when she was a baby. The staph infection did reach her heart. The callus makes her pacemaker work harder to get the energy through to her heart. The survival rate for someone whose staph infection reaches their heart is less than 20 percent. It is a miracle she survived the infection. As I got ready to put her new leads in place, one of her main veins was 100 percent blocked. I tried for a long time to get the lead through, but it just would not allow me. So I had to route it through her chest and around her sternum. Because she is dependent on this pacemaker, I ended up attaching four leads. If one were to break, we have backups.

"The most amazing thing I found was the 100 percent blocked vein, and out of my amazement, her body adjusted to the blocked vein. Katelyn's thyroid artery rerouted itself to supply the heart with the sufficient blood it needed. What this means is instead of her thyroid artery sending blood throughout her body, the valve flipped and was pumping blood to Katelyn's heart! If her thyroid had not done this, Katelyn would have possibly had a massive heart attack! I have been a heart surgeon for thirty-five years and have never ever seen or heard of anything like this! Do you understand what I am saying? Katelyn's thyroid valve flipped in the opposite direction! This does *not* happen!" I then replied, "Yes, I do! It was a miracle! God performed an amazing miracle on Katelyn! Thank You, *Jesus*!" Dr. O replied, "Yes, it is! I am still trying to process all of it."

"He is the one you praise; he is your God, who performed for you those great and awesome wonders you saw with your own eyes" (Deuteronomy 10:21).

After we discussed the miracle, Dr. Ovadia proceeded to tell us that if Katelyn were his daughter, he would not let her play softball anymore. He said it was too risky. The ten-hour surgery had been extremely strenuous on her. He also said that if she did play softball again, she should wait at least two and a half years. He advised us to discourage her from playing any longer. This news was devastating. I knew she would take this news extremely hard and would possibly give up. Her whole life was centered around softball. In Katelyn's life, she has had one disappointment after another. Softball was Katelyn's "out" in life. She loved it with all of her heart, and her main focus was collegiate softball. When other kids could do other sports or activities and Katelyn could not because of certain restrictions, she had softball. Shane and I talked and cried about this, and we wondered how we were going to break the news to her. We decided little by little because we did not want to overwhelm her with all the information from the doctor.

After two hours in recovery, Katelyn finally got to go back to her room. They gave her good meds to keep her resting through the night. Dr. Ovadia wanted her to sleep because he knew she would be extremely sore.

The next morning Katelyn woke up to Shane and me standing beside her bed. She just started to cry. She said, "Mom, I am so sore. I feel horrible. What happened?" Poor baby could not move. She could barely move her head. Anyone who has had any type of heart surgery will tell you that it is painful. Dr. Ovadia cut out her big scar that ran down her sternum to her belly button. He cleaned it up and restitched it. She had a big scar on her abdomen, and he cut it out and fixed it. The big scar above her left breast is where her heart is. Not to mention running all new leads and putting the new pacemaker in. My baby had been through the wringer. We were happy that Dr. Ovadia took the time and energy to fix all her scars because he thought she didn't like them, and he is that caring of a doctor. He truly cares for his patients, and we are so blessed to have found him. He was a blessing to us, and Katelyn was a blessing to him. He sure will never forget this miracle he witnessed performed on Katelyn through Jesus Christ.

Katelyn had to stay in the hospital for almost a week. She had to get stronger, and Dr. Ovadia didn't want us to travel home and possibly have something dislodged and then have to return. He was making sure everything was firmly attached before we went home. He had her best interest at heart and wouldn't let anyone interrogate Katelyn's pacemaker but him. He was very cautious and protective of Katelyn.

Katelyn is a very private person. Katelyn was devastated because she could not shower, use the bathroom or change her clothes on her own. She would cry and be so embarrassed, but I assured her that I had changed her clothes and wiped her bottom many times. She did not think that was amusing, though. One time when she called for me to help her, she said, "Mom, I feel defeated. Why is this happening to me?" I assured her it was only temporary and that one day she might have to do this for me. I wanted her to know that there was no shame in any of this. She knew that I would move a mountain for her if she needed me to.

A couple of days went by before Katelyn started asking questions. We first told her about her miraculous artery. She was shocked but excited to hear about it. Then she asked the dreaded question, "What about softball? How long do I have to wait before I can start practice? I have to get busy to get recruited! This is a big year for me!" We told her we would talk about it later.

When we got home, some of her softball teammates decorated the house and her room. She lit up like a light bulb. That was the boost she needed. Her softball friends were her best friends. They spent so much time together. Whether it be practice, tournament, or just sleepovers, those girls were always together. They had a wonderful bond on and off the field.

The day finally came when Shane and I had to tell her what Dr. Ovadia told us about softball. Yes, she was devastated. She cried herself to sleep. When she woke up the next morning, she said, "Mom, the Lord said this to me, 'I am within you.' I am not going to let Satan destroy my dreams. God is within me, and I am going to continue to play the sport that I love! I will pitch for my high school softball team. You just watch me!" Katelyn's surgery was in November 2017. Softball season started in May of 2018. Katelyn was back on the softball field pitching in May of 2018. Six short months later, Katelyn was the starting varsity pitcher for her high school softball team and went ahead and won three pitching awards that season. Now, tell me that God is not in the miracle-working business!

"What Jesus did here in Cana of Galilee was the first of the signs through which he revealed his glory, and his disciples believed in him" (John 2:11).

All Katelyn's life she has been carried by grace. She is a true miracle. She has so many blessings and scars to show her faith. I think about it, and I know that it only comes from God. She has miracles upon miracles. We can't even count them all. God has stayed with us, so we didn't give up. I pray that we never forget what He has done for us.

I decided after this horrible surgery that Katelyn's life was very precious. I contacted my friend who had suggested Make-A-Wish. She provided information about the organization and provided a way to contact it. I prayed about it and decided it did not show defeat. It was showing Katelyn that she was special and had earned a reward for all the hardships she had been through. She needed something special to look forward to. My friend told me Katelyn's life was like a tug-of-war between God and Satan. When she told me that, it stuck in my mind because, in a way, it had been.

Within one week, I was contacted by the Make-A-Wish organization for an interview. I told Katelyn they were coming to interview her, and her response was, "Why me? I'm not as sick as a lot of other kids. I'm sure some other sick child needs it worse than me." I told her we would talk to them and go from there.

When the Make-A-Wish counselors arrived, they were very attentive and compassionate. They asked Katelyn about her health and other questions. They asked her what a "dream" trip would be to her. After they were finished getting to know Katelyn, they asked her if she had any questions. They opened the floodgates! Katelyn began to cry, "Why me? I am not as sick as the other kids. This would show I was weak and not appreciative of what God has done for me." Wow, not a dry eye was in the room. Katelyn has always been humble and was never unappreciative. They responded, "This does not show weakness, and you getting a trip would not take a trip away from another sick child. We have plenty of donations for anyone who deserves a trip to get a trip. We believe, after assessing your health records and recommendations from Dr. Ovadia, that you are well-deserving of a special trip." Katelyn said, "Dr. Ovadia? Did he suggest a trip? I don't know what to say." They responded, "You don't have to say anything right now; just plan where you would like to go and let us know!"

Katelyn spent a couple of weeks deciding where her "dream" trip would be. That next summer we all went on a Make-A-Wish trip to the Bahamas! Our trip started with the organization picking us up at the hotel in Indianapolis for the flight in a limousine. This was the first time my kids were ever in a limousine. Then the trip continued wonderfully. We had the opportunity to snorkel in the beautiful clear blue ocean. Swimming with dolphins was one of our favorite excursions. Plus, the guys loved all the delicious food we were blessed to eat. Katelyn was granted to do whatever she wanted. Make-A-Wish is a wonderful organization, and I believe God had His hand on all of this. There is no doubt this opportunity was a reward from God to His faithful servant. This trip gave Katelyn a much-needed escape from reality for a short time. "His master replied, 'Well done, good and faithful servant! You have been faithful with a few things; I will put you in charge of many things. Come and share your master's happiness!'" (Matthew 25:23).

Never Will I Leave Thee...

Chapter 20: "Even If"—MercyMe

Katelyn's ten-hour surgery and Dr. Ovadia's suggestion to journal her feelings and thoughts opened doors for testimonies of God's wondrous miracles in Katelyn's life. From this point forward, God got all the praise from Katelyn Grace. Katelyn began to get bold in her faith.

Two months after Katelyn's surgery, her travel team, Future Prospects, entered a tournament in her honor. I had jerseys made that said, "Heart Block Warriors Team Katelyn." The girls were proud to sport the jerseys and play in Katelyn's honor. Most of the girls on the team had played softball with Katelyn for at least three years. They were a close-knit team and always supported one another. Three of the athletes came and decorated our house and her bedroom for her arrival after the surgery. The news of the critical surgery spread fast, and it affected all who knew and loved her.

After one of our games, I had a coach ask me the meaning of the jerseys. I directed him to Katelyn, and this was the first opportunity for her to share her testimony publicly with a stranger. I was so proud of her for stepping up and putting her shyness aside to witness God's miracles in her life. As the coach turned around from talking to her, he had big tears rolling down his face. He shook my hand and said, "That player is one amazing young lady." He walked over and told his team Katelyn's testimony. They all came over to get a picture with Katelyn. After this opportunity, Katelyn told me, "Mom, people do care about my story." I told her, "Yes, Sister, your story gives many people hope, and they can see the wondrous work of our God. Never stop telling your story."

When Katelyn went back to school after her surgery, she had to take a CPR class at a local junior college. I dropped her off and then went back to pick her up. When she got in the car, I could tell she had been crying. I asked her what was wrong. She said, "Mom, you won't believe this. I asked the CPR lady if anyone could do CPR on me because of my pacemaker. She then wanted to know all about my heart disease. I had my first witnessing opportunity! We were both crying. How does this even happen?" I replied, "It happens because God is opening doors for you to witness. God wants you to be bold in your faith."

"So do not be ashamed of the testimony about our Lord or of me his prisoner. Rather, join with me in suffering for the gospel, by the power of God" (2 Timothy 1:8).

Never Will I Leave Thee...

Katelyn had to go to Dr. Ovadia for her six-month check-up. Before this checkup, Katelyn asked me if it was normal for breasts to be different sizes. I told her that most women have different-sized breasts. She said, "Half the size?" Her left breast, where her pacemaker was implanted, was half the size of the right breast. I thought to myself that it was not normal. I told Katelyn we would ask Dr. O about it. She was appalled because there was no way she was going to talk to him about her breasts! She is a very private young lady. That was too intimate to discuss. I thought to myself, *We have a five-hour drive to talk this over.*

As we arrived closer to Dr. O's office, I brought the breast discussion up again. I told her that he would want to know because it had something to do with her heart. To much of her dismay, she agreed to discuss it with him. He handled it very well. He is a private individual as well, and he knows how she is. He said that because of the blocked vein he found in her last surgery, her left breast was not getting the blood flow it needed to produce growth like the other breast. Now that she was a teenager, her physical body meant more to her than before. I never worried about it because I was more concerned with her overall health. This appearance aspect was important to a teenage girl. Dr. O told her that if it were a big concern of hers, he knew a lot of really good plastic surgeons he could contact for her. He also told her that he thought since he fixed the nonflow problem with her heart, her breast might catch up with the other one. Katelyn decided to wait and see what the future held. She didn't want another surgery.

This was when Katelyn shared her journal with Dr. Ovadia. Katelyn also shared with Dr. O that she was playing softball again. After our two-hour appointment, Dr. Ovadia looked at me and said, "Have you ever thought about writing a book about this amazing young lady?" I laughed and said, "Well, actually, I believe the Lord is leading me to write one." He said, "You need to because she is one of a kind."

That summer, Katelyn decided to go with a local church to a big church camp down in Kentucky. This was definitely out of her comfort zone. Katelyn had one friend on the trip. About an hour after Katelyn was on the church bus, she texted me. "Why am I going to this? Nobody will talk to me, and I feel really out of place." I assured her she would be fine and to have fun! During the weekend I got quite a few texts like that one. However, her last text said, "Mom, something amazing happened! You will be so proud of me! I can't wait to tell you!" After I picked her up off the bus, she proceeded to tell me the good news. Katelyn said, "We split up into groups with around a hundred kids. There was a kid in my group that all weekend constantly argued with the group leaders about anything and everything we discussed. Until this kid said, 'How do you know there is a real God? I don't believe in Him!' I felt like God was shoving me out of my seat. Next thing you know I am giving the whole group my testimony. I looked right at the boy and said, 'This is how I know God is real!' It was like God took over. I don't even remember all that I said, but there was not a dry eye in the group. God seriously was talking through me. After the session was over, I had three leaders come to me and thank me for sharing such a touching testimony. I even had some kids from the group say thanks to me. I believe now that I was there for a reason. I was completely out of my comfort zone, but God used it to glorify Him!" I can't even express how proud of Katelyn I was. This was huge for her. You see, these kids who were on the trip always treated Katelyn like an outcast. They always looked down on her because they thought she was different from them. She is different. She is a warrior for Christ. Katelyn proved it to those kids that day.

These stories were just the beginning of how God started using Katelyn. Katelyn took her journal thoughts and turned them into a testimony. Katelyn took that testimony and started a journey of telling her miraculous story. Word quickly got out about Katelyn's testimony of her miracles. We live in a small 300-person town, and word travels fast here. This shy little girl was turning into a bold spiritual speaker!

This is her first testimony at her first speaking engagement at a local church.

"Hello, everyone, my name is Katelyn Wilber. I am seventeen years old, and I live in Flat Rock, Illinois. I want to thank you all for inviting me to share my testimony about everything that I have been through with my health. I would not be standing up here if it weren't for God, and He deserves all of the credit. I am here as living proof that God does exist and still performs miracles every single day, not only in my life but also in everyone else's, even if you don't realize it. Before we start, let's all bow our heads and pray.

"I wrote a devotional testimony after my doctor told me that I needed to write my feelings out. These feelings I wrote about have been used as my testimony. Why not spread God's Word and all the goodness He does to bring people closer to God? *Just like in the Bible:*

> Now the tax collectors and sinners were all gathering around to hear Jesus. But the Pharisees and the teachers of the law uttered, "This man welcomes sinners and eats with them." Then Jesus told them this parable: "Suppose one of you has a hundred sheep and loses one of them. Doesn't he leave the ninety-nine in the

open country and go after the lost sheep until he finds it? And when he finds it, he joyfully puts it on his shoulders and goes home. Then he calls his friends and neighbors together and says, 'Rejoice with me; I have found my lost sheep.' I tell you that in the same way, there will be more rejoicing in heaven over one sinner who repents than over ninety-nine righteous persons who do not need to repent."

Luke 15:1–7

"Man, God is just that good. He's just so kind. He's a Father that never gives up, even when you think you are that lost sheep. He's a Father that loves you no matter what, no matter if you feel that you cannot be loved by anyone else. He gives us His love so completely, and we don't deserve it, yet He forgives us for doing wrong again and again. There is a God out there that created the heavens and the earth, and He knows my name. Think about that. I speak my testimony because if I can touch just one person and bring just one person or that one lost sheep to Christ, then everything that I have been through is worth it. I want to start by asking this one question. When someone asks you, 'What is your worst fear?' most people would say spiders, snakes, or the darkness. But if you really think about it, everyone's worst fear should be nothing but dying. Dying is a scary thing; no one understands how you know or how you feel unless you have felt that pain where you don't know whether or not you were going to go to sleep and never wake up again. You wouldn't think that a seventeen-year-old would think about dying. But if I'm gonna be honest, I think about it quite frequently, and I might even say almost every day. Even though I stand up here to talk to you about my story and all God has brought me through and you might think I have it all

Never Will I Leave Thee...

together, I am still human (even if I am part bionic), believe it or not. I still sin, and I still have my insecurities and doubts every single day. I still get scared, wondering why this had to happen to me. I've spent my whole life asking myself these questions. I've had so many close calls to dying that now that I'm older, I ask myself, 'Why am I still here? Why has God still kept me on this earth? What is my purpose? What have I been called to do?' I've had eight pacemaker replacements and nine heart surgeries to fix my, I guess you could say, 'disease' I was born with. I am only seventeen and have already been so close to death and not only seen but been through so much more than most people go through in their entire lifetime. But these past couple of years, these questions have come into focus more than at any other time in my life. Not only have these questions popped up, but I have had to change my outlook on how I view my life. I have learned that not only I but everyone has a purpose for being on this earth. We may not know what it is right now or even in ten years. But we all have a purpose, and it's all in God's timing.

"Anyone here that knows anything about chronic illnesses knows what I mean when I say that it never goes away. You have your good days and your bad days. You spend time in denial. But it's still there waiting on you. So my story begins with being diagnosed with a congenital heart defect called complete heart block. What that means is that I was born with something wrong with my heart, and it is incurable. I will have to deal with it for the rest of my life. You know how you hear about people with stage four cancer, and the stages tell you how bad it is? Well, I have third-degree complete heart block (also the worst degree), and this is a condition in which the electrical signals in my heart are completely dead. So when blood goes into the top of my heart, the ventricles, which are the bottom part, do not know to pump the blood back out. This means that I have a pacemaker that works twenty-four seven to keep my heart pumping. For those of you that don't know what this is, it is a small metal device in my chest that connects to my heart in my arteries by little wires called leads. Without a pacemaker, my heart only pulsates at twenty beats per minute. I was diagnosed when my mom was twenty-four weeks pregnant. The cause of this is that my mom has a severe disease called lupus and Sjögren's. Lupus causes my mom's antibodies to attack her vital organs, so in return when I was in her womb, lupus went straight for the main organ of the baby, my heart. After I was born, I went straight into surgery and had my first pacemaker implanted at only six hours old. The smallest and youngest person to ever get a pacemaker at Riley's Children's Hospital in Indianapolis, Indiana. I kind of wonder if I still hold that record…anyway, a couple of weeks later, I came home, and my mom noticed my incision wasn't healing properly and didn't look right, so we went back to the doctor, and I was diagnosed with a staph infection. I went in for another surgery and another full system replacement, pacemaker, leads, and all. The staph infection was crawling up my lead and was centimeters from my heart, so we thought that if it had reached my heart, I would have died instantly. This will come in later in my story. Fast forward many years, and I don't remember a whole lot until the fourth grade. By the time I was in fourth grade, I had gone through eight heart surgeries and seven pacemaker replacements. This is because I am very active, and my body produces excessive scar tissue, so every surgery has been an emergency. None have been scheduled because my leads are breaking all the time. I remember my surgery in fourth grade and from then on because that is when I was old enough to realize how serious my condition was. It was more of a realization of 'Hey, this thing is real, and your life revolves around it,' except it never has. My life has never revolved around my condition. I have always lived my life like a normal kid, and no one would ever know any differently. You see, you can't live your life in a bubble and wonder what will happen if you make a wrong move and make your condition worse. You will miss out on all the good things that will happen or do happen in your life. The pacemaker I received in fourth grade was the longest I had ever had until my freshman year of high school. Another life-changing experience happened to me once again. I was at the gym working out when my lead broke and was shocking me through my skin. We went to the emergency room, then to my doctor in Chicago, and I went into surgery the next day.

"Remember the staph infection I mentioned from when I was an infant? Well, the staph had reached my heart. The staph had made a callus (which is a tough or rough surface) around my heart that makes the pacemaker work harder than it needs to get the good part of my heart because the outside is basically like dead tissue. That is why the battery drains so much. For those of you who are not familiar with the anatomy of the heart, veins in your heart are what supply your heart with blood, and arteries are what take the blood from the heart and spread or transport it to your body. Dr. Ovadia had realized that one of the main veins to my heart was blocked, and he was amazed to find that my thyroid artery, instead of pumping blood through my body, had flipped and was supplying my heart with the blood that it needed. Do you realize how miraculous that is? Dr. Ovadia said, 'Because that also means that the valve in the artery had to completely flip to pump the blood to my heart!' Telling my parents this after a ten-hour surgery after a scheduled three-hour surgery, and they wondered why I hadn't had a heart attack yet. He said, 'In thirty-five years of being a cardiologist, I have never in my life seen this. I discovered her thyroid artery had rerouted the blood and now compensates for the loss of blood to her heart.' My parents said, 'We know exactly what caused that; the Lord saved her!' If that isn't God's work, then I have no idea what is. Once again God was working in mysterious ways to help me overcome that fear and to keep me pushing through. My God never fails me and always takes care of me no matter how hard it gets. I have a pretty high pain tolerance, and I don't like to show up when I am in pain. I've just been raised to tough it out and throw some dirt on it! But when I can't even lift my arms to feed myself and my mom has to give me showers for about a month, it makes me feel defeated. They cut so much more than just the scar that gets reopened every time. I now have five scars on my chest and abdomen. This surgery was absolutely mentally and physically exhausting, for I had never been in so much pain in my life. But after all this happened, I felt the best I have ever felt in my entire life. Praise God!

"In my surgery in 2017, any surgery I have had in fact, I thought about the possibility of having the thing I love the most in my life taken away from me. Most of you know me, know that I play softball. I have lived and breathed softball ever since I can remember, and in this situation where softball was going to be taken away from me, I was feeling like everything was going to cave in, and I was never going to do it. Anyone who knows me knows that I am not the type to give up easily. I'm pretty hard headed and determined just like my mom. Well, after this surgery my doctor told me that I wasn't supposed to play softball for two and a half years or possibly never again. Little did he know, he didn't know whom he was talking to. I reacted just like anyone else would in that situation. I was so mad at God, thinking, *Why, God, would You take the thing I love the most away from me?*

"I was so upset day in and day out. I was upset thinking about what my teammates would think if I never played softball again. I was so frustrated, and I didn't know what to do, but it's hard to get that negativity and doubt out of our lives after something like that gets taken away from us. It's easy to praise God when things are going right in your life, but what will you say when things aren't going your way and you feel like the whole world is crashing down and going against you? It only takes just a little bit of faith to do big amazing things. I had a little bit of faith in this situation. But when God chooses to give you a situation that you have no power to do anything about or to change what has happened, He will give you the strength to say, 'It is well with my soul.' After I had my pity party for a little bit, I decided, 'You know what? This isn't who I am! After all of my surgeries, I have bounced back so quickly, and I am going to do the same for this one.' So that's what I did! I started to heal, and the next thing I knew, I was back on the softball field. I was the starting varsity pitcher at my high school, and I went on to win three awards that year.

"Going to the doctor and having him control the way my heart beats, how fast or how slow by a machine, is the hardest thing that has ever been done to me continuously. I get so sick and worked up that I have to distract myself by moving my legs up and down. One time recently at a doctor's appointment I didn't get upset. Dr. O looked at me after the visit and said, 'Tell me what you're thinking. You're more calm than usual.' I just said to him, 'Well, after so many years, I have come to the conclusion that this is just something that I have to do and go through.' What I was thinking in my head that I didn't say out loud was that *I'm not scared.* God had brought me through this so many times; what makes me think that He will bail on me now? I realized that I need to be calm with myself and trust that God is in control and there's nothing I can do to control what happens.

"The devil targets the weakest part of me, my mind. I will admit I really struggle with self-confidence and what other people think of me. I also struggle with saying these two little deadly words to myself: *What if?* What if my story is not worthy enough to share? What if I am not strong enough or as good as everybody else? You know what? Who cares what other people say about you? Because you know what? God says *I am good enough*, and God says that *you are good enough*!

"Something that has been in my heart lately is listening to a song called 'Even If' by MercyMe. You see, right before my surgery in 2017 is when this song came out. I had tickets and was supposed to go see MercyMe in concert a week after my surgery. Sadly I didn't get to attend the concert. So one day my mom and I were talking about this song, and if you don't know the movie and song 'I Can Only Imagine,' Bart Millard is the writer of that song, and the movie is about him and his childhood. His dad abused him. He talked about how music got him through these tough times in his life and about how his dad came to God after years of trying to change him. In his dad's final days, he saw God change his father from a man that he hated into the man that he wanted to become. One night my mom and I were watching this movie, and I said, 'You know, I think this is my favorite song that they sing.' I said, 'Is it yours?' My mom turned to look at me and said, 'Their song "Even If" is my favorite song written by them.' She said, 'It reminds me so much of you.' So it got me thinking; the next day I looked it up on YouTube with the testimony, and almost every day on my drive to school, I listen to my praise and worship music, and that's just my alone time with God in my car. So I listened to this specific song with the testimony on the way to school, and I just started bawling my eyes out. Anyone that knows me knows that I am already an emotional person because I believe I am so filled with the Holy Spirit. Little things in life make me emotional because I know it was a blessing from God. I just get emotional about spiritual things when I know the Holy Spirit is present. I was just praying in my car as I do frequently, and I just started to lift my hands and say to God, 'Thank You. Thank You for showing me this.'

"In his testimony, Bart's son has diabetes, and he says later in it that a family friend asked about what he has been through and stopped him and said, "Let me pray for complete healing for Sam." Bart said he was having a bad day, and it ticked him off a little bit. He thought in his head, *Really? Healing for my son, like that never crossed my mind before? What a novel concept!* This same thing has happened to me before. Deep down it's hard to hear that because we know God has the power to heal me. But for whatever reason, He's not. But you know what? It's okay. I know that He is able, and I know that He can, and maybe that is not what He wants me to do right now, and that's okay. You may look at me weirdly and think, *She's crazy* after I say this next thing. But I am actually happy I have complete heart block. I am happy that I have been through nine heart surgeries, and I am happy that God has put me through hell and back because you know what? This has made me who I am today. I wouldn't be the person I am today without the power of prayer and God saving my soul through it all. I am happy that even if I am not healed yet or even get healed, it is still well with my soul. I can change the world as a person with complete heart block, and guess what? It's okay. Maybe the ending to my story and the finisher to my testimony and my mom's book that she is currently writing is that one day I will be healed. I just have to trust in Him and wait for that to happen. God knows my sorrow and hurt, but my hope continues to be in Him. Sometimes it's hard to think about this because I just don't think that things in life are always fair. But If I'm being honest, sometimes it doesn't feel okay. Sometimes I wish I had the courage like Shadrach, Meshach, and Abednego to stand in front of the fiery furnace and say, 'I know God can deliver us, but even if He doesn't, I'm still not going to surrender to the doubt and fear because *He is worth it!*'

"When there are times when I forget to rely on God and forget who I am, luckily He still remembers me. And there are times when I don't think that I'm going to be okay and I don't have the courage to stand up, but the bottom line is the only way I can get up every day and go through this is what Christ has already done for me. No circumstance will change who I am in Christ. It'll try, and sometimes it feels like it's going to win, but it won't. So I don't know what anyone here is going through. I know that we all go through something, and if you haven't been through anything yet—God bless you—it's coming. When we go through these hardships, the first question we normally ask ourselves is, 'Why me? Why do I have to go through this?' It always seems to be that as soon as we start to feel sorry for ourselves, He places someone in front of us that has it worse. I am so blessed to be in the condition I am right now rather than a worse one.

"Let me tell you a little story about someone I encountered who showed me to be less selfish about my heart condition even if it is really bad. I knew during my freshman year that I would be having another pacemaker surgery soon. I just didn't know when. The anticipation is what gets to me. When I was down and upset, it was when they couldn't find out what was wrong with me. I was at an appointment in Chicago with my doctor. As we were in the waiting room, there was this little girl, only three years old. I remember it like it was yesterday. She was wearing pink; she was so tiny, just like how I was when I was sick and little. She was eating some applesauce that her mom was feeding her. She finished the whole thing, and her mom was so happy! After she got done eating her applesauce, she looked at me with a sparkle in her eye and a great big smile on her face, clapping and cheering! Then she asked my name, and she was talking to me while our moms shared heart stories. The little girl had a disease where twice a month she had to go to Boston Children's Hospital in Massachusetts. Her disease consisted of an open heart surgery where she had to get her arteries pulled back open twice every month because they kept closing. This little girl was three years old and was not supposed to be living. Her mom had told my mom that she doesn't know how much longer she has to live. When I got to the patient's room, waiting on Dr. Ovadia, I immediately started crying. Mostly because of that little girl and the other reason because I couldn't stop thinking about how blessed I am to be in the condition I am right now rather than a worse one. I believe we are supposed to be thankful for every little thing that we have in life. I learned that from that point on. I was going to be more relying on God and let Him take control over all of the problems I ever had. He's the only One that can cure us of diseases. He's the only One who can calm our minds and thoughts in times of trouble. He's the only rock we have to support us. Just know you're not alone because there is a God out there that loves you and is with you every step of the way. Sometimes bad things happen to us as life lessons to show us and the people around us how to come close to Him. But instead of saying and praying to God, 'Can You change these things? Can You stop all the hurt and sorrow?' we should be praying, 'God, can You change *me* so that I can handle the things that You're walking me through?'

"He will not give you any more than you can handle. Psh-hh. Yeah right. That is a lie. God will give you *more* than you can handle, but He wants to see what we will do with it. How we will handle *that* is how He puts us to the test. I like to say a lot—it's kind of like my life motto—He gives His toughest battles to His strongest warriors. I know I am one of His strongest warriors, and I am proud of that! I would not change everything I have been through for the world. It has led me here to preach to you guys about the Word of God through my testament. I think that's pretty cool. I beat the odds when the doctors said I was not going to live. I am one out of a million babies who have complete heart block. To the fact that only 75 percent of babies born with a critical congenital heart defect are supposed to only survive to the age of eighteen, I can stand up here to say that I have won the battle as a child of God. I am accomplishing my dreams because of God on my side, and He deserves all of the credit! I believe I will and have touched so many lives. Possibly I have touched a lot even without knowing it. I know that even if I have a severe congenital heart defect and I may never get healed, I know with God on my side I can change the world and everyone around me.

"'Have I not commanded you? Be strong and courageous. Do not be afraid; do not be discouraged, for the Lord your God will be with you wherever you go'" (Joshua 1:9).

"I pray today that I planted that seed to change your lives as well. So let me ask you this, 'Do you believe that God still performs miracles?'

"What do you think? Is God still in the miracle-working business? I believe He is!"

Never Will I Leave Thee...

Chapter 21: "Gratitude"—Brandon Lake

"For our struggle is not against flesh and blood, but against the rulers, against the authorities, against powers of this dark world and against the spiritual forces of evil in the heavenly realms" (Ephesians 6:12).

God was blessing Katelyn with different speaking engagements, and of course, Satan did not like it. God was launching Katelyn, but much resistance came with it. I have believed for years that Katelyn was covered by so much prayer and God had such big plans for her that she was protected. Satan began attacking those closest to her. It seemed as if, for a couple of years, it was one thing after the other. We had a blessing, and then "*bam*," here came Satan. This went on for years. It was a spiritual "tug-of-war" from day to day.

Satan always knows what our weakest point is. Mine is my family, and he was attacking them with both barrels. Our marriage was very rocky. Katelyn's health problems were a big stressor in our marriage. Shane and I never had time together. Shane's way of dealing with Katelyn's problems was to hide in his cabinet shop. We did need the extra money, but there were times I needed him more. I am one of those who keep my feelings bottled up, and that caused a separation between Shane and me. I knew it was Satan trying to destroy our family bond. I spent a lot of time praying and studying to keep our family together.

Satan also went after Shaelyn and Chance. He was attacking anything that created a little crack to get in. It was a constant battle. I knew exactly what Satan was up to. He wanted nothing more than to destroy our family to prevent Katelyn from carrying out God's plan. He knew that was the only way to get to Katelyn.

When things got stressful was when I would miss my mom the most. As I had said before, she was my spiritual advisor and best friend. One day, I needed to just get away and pray. I decided to go to the cemetery. It was a cold and cloudy day, but I felt the need to go there to pray.

Pulling into the cemetery, I began to sob. I felt such deep sadness and failure. The way Satan was attacking Shaelyn and Chance made me feel like I failed them as a mom. I then felt unsuccessful as a wife. There were such heavy burdens on me. It was a feeling that I had never had before. I got out of the car and walked sobbing to Mom's tombstone. When I reached the tombstone, I dropped to my knees. It was almost like time stood still. I have no idea how long I was there crying and praying. Then out of nowhere, I felt a warm ray of sunshine on my face. I stood up and looked at the sky, and it was like the Lord had opened it up just for me. The sky parted, and the sun's rays were only on me. As I stood there, I was consumed with God's grace and love for me. At that moment I realized it was God confirming that I was a good mom and wife. I stood there just giving "thanks to my Lord!" I was in awe of God's confirmation of me. The beautiful, warm sun rays stayed on me until I finally walked back to the car. When I looked over my shoulder, the sky closed back up. It was the most amazing confirmation I have ever witnessed. After that, I knew God was pleased with me and He was giving me the strength to fight Satan for my family's sake. God said, "I have given you authority to trample on snakes and scorpions and to overcome all the power of the enemy; nothing will harm you" (Luke 10:19).

After this confirmation, I changed how I prayed for my family. I knew with the Lord excelling at Katelyn and working through her, I had to make sure we were all covered by the blood of Jesus Christ. We needed to have our whole armor on and not partially. My prayer life changed, and so did the effects of Satan's attacks.

"Put on the full armor of God, so that you can take your stand against devil's schemes" (Ephesians 6:11).

Katelyn was now a junior in high school and actively looking at colleges. She and I had already traveled to colleges in Kentucky and Tennessee. We were now going to travel to a couple in Missouri that she was interested in. It was a process because she had to find a college with her degree and also catch the softball coach's eye for recruiting. One day we went for pitching lessons in Missouri, and her coach suggested on our way home to detour and look at Missouri Baptist University. Katelyn had not checked into Missouri Baptist, but she thought she'd take her coach's advice and go look at it.

Katelyn and I were always up for adventures! She and I love to go to different places. Many times I would load up softball girls, and we'd take off to play softball and add impromptu adventures. I always have a good time with those athletes.

Katelyn and I mapped out a couple of colleges to go see on our way home. Missouri Baptist was our last stop before we headed back to Illinois. As soon as we pulled up, Katelyn said, "This is it! This is the college!" I always told her that she would know the perfect college for her when she stepped foot on campus. We had visited seven previous colleges, and each one of them was not "the one," she would say. As we traveled back home, she and I started talking and making arrangements for an official college visit and to meet with the softball coach.

Katelyn had offers from other colleges' softball programs, but she had her heart set on Missouri Baptist. We started praying and working on recruiting. Everything just fell into place. Before we knew it, she was accepted at Missouri Baptist University and was given a softball scholarship for six years! We had discussed that if this were the college God wanted for her, then God would open doors and she would walk through with ease. That is exactly what happened! God opened multiple doors, and she marched right on through. Katelyn was to start at Missouri Baptist University in the fall of 2021 with a softball scholarship. Her dream had come true!

Shortly after Katelyn got recruited, she had a heart doctor appointment. She couldn't wait to see Dr. O and tell him of her softball scholarship. During the summer Katelyn had not felt her best. We were at a softball tournament in the early spring, and Katelyn was warming up by hitting off the tee when she felt something "pop." After that, she had episodes of her pacemaker acting up. She wanted to wait to see Dr. O until after the summer season because she knew it was her critical time to get recruited. She was once again pushing through. I was clueless that her heart was out of rhythm during the summer. When her heart is out of rhythm, she is very weak and feels sick. She had learned to cover it up very well.

On our way to Chicago to see Dr. Ovadia, Katelyn said, "Mom, I need to talk to you about something." This is a five-hour drive provided traffic is not bad. So we had a lot of mother-daughter talks on our Chicago trips. I said, "What do you want to talk about?" Katelyn proceeded, "I had a dream, and I've never dreamt like this before. I thought maybe you would know why I had it or what it means. I heard God say, 'I am within you.' He said it all night at random times. I knew it was Him because I wasn't scared. You always say that if it is peace, then it is God, and fear is Satan. I was not scared." I told her, "Seems to me that God is reassuring you that His Spirit is within you. God loves you, and He has big plans for you. He just wants you to rely on Him and not be fearful. If His Spirit is in you, nothing can harm you. Does that make sense?" Katelyn replied, "Yes, thank you. I am not scared. I know He is within me." The conversations Katelyn and I would have reminded me so much of the conversations my mom and I would have. It was a reminder of how special my mom was to me. God said, "The Spirit of truth. The world cannot accept him, because it neither sees him nor knows him. But you know Him, for He lives with you and will be in you" (John 14:17).

"On that day you will realize that I am in my Father, and you are in me, and I am in you" (John 14:20). Tell me that is not powerful. The Holy Spirit lives in us and speaks to us to guide us on our journey here on earth.

When we reached Dr. Ovadia's office, he was so excited to see Katelyn and hear all about her fantastic news! Dr. Ovadia always wants every little detail from Katelyn. Katelyn has a way with people. Once someone meets her, they love her. One of my customers told me one time that Katelyn has a "glow" surrounding her and draws people near. After she said that, I noticed it to be true. Once you meet her, you won't forget her.

Dr. Ovadia started to interrogate Katelyn's pacemaker. During the interrogation, he saw an irregular incident. He asked her if something happened on May 13, 2020. Katelyn said, "Yes, that was a softball tournament, and I was warming up to hit, and I felt a 'pop' in my chest. Ever since then, I have not felt very good." Dr. O found that she had indeed broken a lead that day. He said, "Since you broke that lead, the other lead I implanted did its job and rerouted. But your pacemaker went into shock mode because it knew something had happened. Now your pacemaker has been on 100 percent voltage since then, and your battery is depleted. We are going to have to replace the pacemaker, but hopefully, the leads are all intact except for the one you broke. This will be the simplest replacement you have had so far. Let's get you on the schedule so you have time to recover for college softball!" Even though Dr. O advised us not to let her play softball, she pleaded her case to him, and he knows her heart. He knows that it means the world to her and he is not going to be the one to stop her. In his way, that was an encouragement to her.

Katelyn's ninth pacemaker replacement surgery was set for November 2020. We dreaded another surgery, but we were happy to have a scheduled surgery and not an emergency like the last eight pacemakers. We also looked at it as if she would have a new pacemaker before she started college and prayed it would last until she graduated college. In the past, we learned that anytime there is something dark in your life, God always makes a bright side.

The excitement of signing up to play softball for Missouri Baptist and all her speaking engagements kept her from thinking about her upcoming surgery. November crept up on us fast. Before we knew it, it was time for pacemaker surgery.

The week before we traveled to Chicago for surgery, the Lord awakened me at 2 a.m. with these words, "This surgery will be another chapter in your book." I thought to myself, *Wow! I have got to start working on this book!* This was just one of the many hints and signs that God continued to give me. He set people in my path with suggestions, and God would randomly give me words for my book. But I still did not believe that I could write the book that He had laid on my heart after Katelyn's surgery in 2017. I do have to say, though, that after this last word, I was starting to try and figure out how I could make this happen.

The time had come for us to once again head to Chicago for yet another surgery. Dr. O came in to talk to us and Katelyn. Dr. O asked Katelyn if she had any questions or concerns. Katelyn said, "I'm not even scared this time! I know it is going to be a breeze. I have to get ready to play college softball!" Dr. O replied, "Okay then, let's get this over with! See you after the procedure." After he left the room, Shane and I did our normal prayer routine. I looked at Katelyn after we prayed, and she was so calm. She had no doubts whatsoever about this surgery. I thought to myself, *If only everyone could have her faith.*

This surgery took about five hours. This was a little longer than we anticipated. Dr. Ovadia came out to talk to Shane and me. He said, "Katelyn did very well. This girl never ceases to amaze me, though. I never know what I will encounter with her. I tested some old leads in her pacemaker pocket in her abdomen and found a lead that was still good. I decided to replace the one that was broken in the spring with the old lead in the abdomen. As I ran the lead through her chest, I ran it through the area, not thinking about where her old staph infection was. I doused the lead with medications to kill any infection that might be lying dormant in the tissue. We will have to keep watch on this area to ensure no infections arise. I ran into another snag, though. As patients reach adulthood, we like to use an artery in one of the legs to run the lead through to save on incisions in the chest area. When I went to put the lead in Katelyn's right leg, I couldn't get the lead to go through. I tried for quite a while to get it to go through, and it would not. We ended up doing a few scans, and we found out that the main artery in her right leg is 100 percent blocked. We looked further into it, and she has a mass amount of big veins that run all over her leg and up her back to her chest. These veins are supplying her leg and chest with the amounts of blood that her leg artery is not producing. This is the most amazing thing! Once again, this is nothing I have ever seen before." Shane and I just sat there speechless. I told Dr. Ovadia, "Here we are with another miracle!" As the doctor turned to walk away, he looked at me smiling and said once again, "When are you writing this book?"

After he left, Shane and I sat there in the waiting room and discussed what he had just told us. I know God is in the miracle-working business, but He still amazes me. The miracles He has performed on Katelyn are nothing but amazing. We decided not to tell Katelyn about the blocked artery in her right leg for now. We didn't think she needed that extra stress at this time with everything going on in her senior year and preparing for college softball. I knew this was the reason the Lord told me that this surgery would be another chapter in my book. Another miracle to tell the world about!

I always feel like I fall short in how to express my gratitude to the Lord for all He has done for us. God is always there when we need Him. All I can do is praise God again and again. All I can do is sing hallelujah to God. I raise my hands high to praise God again and again. I don't have much for God, but all I have is my heart that sings hallelujah to praise Him for all He has done for our baby girl.

"Praise the Lord, for the Lord is good; sing praise to his name, for that is pleasant" (Psalm 135:3).

I think Katelyn bounced back so quickly after this surgery because she was so focused on preparing for high school graduation and college. Katelyn's story was getting around quickly. She had people contacting her all the time for speaking engagements. It was amazing to me how quickly word was traveling about her testimony. Softball opened so many witnessing doors and was special to her in more ways than she thought. God was starting to use it to open some really big doors for witnessing.

CHAPTER 22: "THEN CHRIST CAME"—MERCYME

"Now to him who is able to do immeasurably more than all we ask or imagine, according to His power that is at work within us, to Him be glory in the church and in Christ Jesus throughout all generations, forever and ever! Amen" (Ephesians 3:20–21).

God never ceases to amaze us. God was launching this little, shy, untrusting, big-hearted child of God to a whole new level. As word spread, she was getting multiple speaking engagements. The more she spoke, the more confident she became. I started to see such maturity and change in Katelyn. This fragile little girl of mine had turned into a warrior for God.

Katelyn told Ryan about her speaking at local churches and church camps. He asked if she would speak to his fourteen-and-under travel team in Cape Girardeau, Missouri. Katelyn was so honored to have this opportunity because of the respect and love she had for Ryan. He had done so much for her that she felt this was the least she could do for him. Katelyn was nervous about this opportunity. She had spoken at church camps in front of kids, but this was her first softball team. Her other speaking engagements were at churches. But with her love for softball and the age of the kids, it hit a little closer to home for her. Katelyn had played for Ryan's older team that weekend, and he arranged it to that she would speak after she played her last game of the weekend. After she finished, she walked over to the younger team's diamond to prepare to speak. When she began to convey her testimony, I noticed Ryan walking away and standing at a distance. Ryan had a hard time dealing with Katelyn's condition. He thought the world of her, and he couldn't bear to hear her testimony. To this day, I don't believe he has ever heard it. Each person deals with heartache differently. I have noticed through the years that men closest to her distance themselves and have a hard time accepting the condition. I know Ryan admires her strength and how she overcomes any obstacle that she is confronted with through Christ. He commends the courage and determination that she conveys to athletes.

This is the testimony she composed for Ryan's travel softball team.

"I wrote a devotional testimony a couple of years ago after my doctor told me after everything I have been through I needed to write my feelings out. But these feelings I made into a preaching life lesson rather than writing down my feelings and feeling sorry for myself. A little bit about me so you'll know how I got here to talk to you all today. I met Ryan a little over a year ago through my sister, who used to play for him. My mom took me to my first pitching lesson at Lindenwood University. Later in the lesson, I said something to my mom that I used the words 'mom.' Ryan looked at me confused and said, 'Mom?' I said, 'Yeah…Heather is my mom!' He had no idea that I was Shaelyn's little sister or Heather's daughter. I think a few lessons later, as I was framing, he said, 'I couldn't help but notice the scars on your chest. What are they from?' I said, 'Oh, I just have a pacemaker.' He looked at me shocked, and then I pretty much spilled the whole story to him about my health complications. Tears came rolling down Ryan's face, and with everything you know about Ryan, he shows little to no emotions. This was a shock to me as well. Ever since that day, Ryan and I have had a friendship on another level. I would like to consider it a spiritual level. Now you know a little back story of how I met Ryan. I'll tell you the back story of my life."

Katelyn continued with her previous testimony but ended it differently to keep her younger audience engaged. She learned to adjust each testimony. Katelyn concluded the softball team with this:

"Sometimes we wonder, 'Why me? Why do I have to go through this?' It always seems to be that as soon as we start to feel sorry for ourselves, He places someone in front of us who has had worse. And I am so…blessed to be in the condition I am right now rather than a worse one. Just know you're not alone because there is a God out there that loves you and is with you every step of the way. Sometimes bad things happen to us as life lessons to show us and the people around us how to come closer to God. He will not give you any more than you can handle. I like to say a lot—it's kind of like my motto—He gives His toughest battles to His strongest warriors. I know I am one of His strongest warriors, and I am here to preach to you guys about the Word of God through my testimony, and I think that is pretty *cool!* I believe I have touched so many lives and a lot without me even knowing it. I know that even if I have a severe congenital heart defect and I may never get healed, I can change the world by keeping a positive attitude and not letting the devil get me. You can all do the same, and I hope today I have planted that seed to change your lives as well. Thank you."

One week after Katelyn spoke to the team, the mother of one of the athletes contacted me. She thanked me for Katelyn's boldness in giving her testimony. Her daughter was touched by it and told all her friends and their church. She asked if Katelyn would be willing to travel to their church to speak. She accepted the invitation but didn't have the opportunity that summer to travel there. She hoped to eventually honor the invitation. Katelyn's "bold" testimony gave this young athlete a "bold" testimony as well.

After speaking to the softball team, Katelyn was contacted by our local Fellowship of Christian Athletes organization to speak at their next meeting. FCA is a Christian organization for high school athletes to meet and learn about God through sports. She, at first, was nervous at the thought of speaking to local teenagers that were acquaintances. As I said before, Katelyn didn't want to be treated differently because of her illness and never used it as an excuse or a way for sympathy. She was concerned that sharing her testimony with her peers would show weakness. I told Katelyn teenagers have daily struggles. It may be the one life she saves. That is how God works. Sometimes we have to get out of our comfort zone to see God's big plan.

We pulled up to the school to park. Katelyn said, "Mom, please pray for me. This is one of the hardest things I've had to do. What if they make fun of me? You know these kids have never accepted me, so why would they want to come and listen to my testimony?" I turned and looked at her, and she had big tears in her eyes. I could see the fear on her face. I understood how she felt, and my heart broke for her. We prayed and asked God for comfort and confidence. I told her to not have fear because God was with her.

> Praise be to the God and Father of our Lord Jesus Christ, the Father of compassion and the God of all comfort, who comforts us in all our troubles so that we can comfort those in any trouble with the comfort we ourselves receive from God. For just as we share abun-

dantly in the sufferings of Christ, so also our comfort
abounds through Christ.

2 Corinthians 1:3–5

The FCA leader introduced Katelyn, and she walked up
to the podium to speak with confidence. Katelyn gave her
testimony, and there was not a dry eye in the building. To her
amazement, the one girl she was most concerned about was
the first to approach her with big tears in her eyes. She told
Katelyn her testimony was exactly what she needed to hear at
this time in her life. God knew Katelyn needed to speak there
to help save this young girl's life. We have to be humble and
trust God because His ways are better than ours. Jesus said,
"Come to me, all you who are weary and burdened, and I will
give you rest. Take my yoke upon you and learn from me, for I
am gentle and humble in heart, and you will find rest for your
souls. For my yoke is easy and my burden is light" (Matthew
11:28–30).

Katelyn was then contacted by her cousin, Mykala, who
was currently studying at Indiana State University in Terre
Haute, Indiana. Indiana State sponsors a Riley's Children's
Hospital dance marathon fundraiser every year. Mykala asked
Katelyn if she would speak and be a special guest since she
was a Riley's kid. She was honored by the invitation. When
we arrived, we were greeted with open arms and treated like
special guests. There were mainly students attending except
for the speakers for the evening. Later in the evening, Katelyn
gave a small portion of her experience at Riley's. She was very
young when she was treated there, and she did not remember
many details. I helped her before we arrived with some of the
details. We respect Riley's Children's Hospital because they
helped save Katelyn's life when she was born. We never know

what doors God will open for us. We need to be ready to serve when we are called.

Katelyn's speaking invitations continued to a local church. Katelyn spoke at Outer West Market in Palestine, Illinois. We had family and friends who attended this church. One Sunday morning she boldly told her testimony. As I scanned the audience, there was not a dry eye in the auditorium. Katelyn stood up there with such confidence as she professed the love of God. The congregation's response to Katelyn's testimony was overwhelming. She received letters and cards with notes from people that we didn't know personally. They were messages of how she changed their lives and how they could feel the Holy Spirit that day.

One week after she spoke, a lady at Casey's convenience store stopped me. She told me that she attended Outer West Market occasionally and felt the desire to attend the day Katelyn gave her testimony. She said Katelyn's testimony had changed her life. She informed me that she was a negative and bitter person because of her circumstances lately. As she heard Katelyn speak of all the miracles and what the Lord had brought her through, it was clear to her that her situations were not big compared to Katelyn's. She said she thought to herself, *How can this little girl stand up here and praise God after all she has been through, and all I can do is complain? I have nothing to complain about!* She began to pray and ask God to take those feelings away from her and make her a strong warrior like Katelyn. She thanked me for raising such a Spirit-filled individual and to be sure and tell her how her testimony changed her life. She now looks at life from a different perspective. When she feels down and discouraged, she thinks of Katelyn and her faith then, which raises her to face her challenges.

"Consequently, faith comes from hearing the message, and the message is heard through the word about Christ" (Romans 10:17).

Katelyn has no idea how many people she touches with her testimony. It is a domino effect. You plant that seed in one person, and then they go and plant it in many more.

You see, God uses us in so many ways. Katelyn, with each speaking engagement, gets stronger in her faith, and it shows. You never know whom you can touch with your story. God gives us many opportunities to give our story. How "bold" are we?

"He proclaimed the kingdom of God and taught about the Lord Jesus Christ—with all boldness and without hindrance!" (Acts 28:31).

Chapter 23: "I Speak Jesus"—Charity Gayle

In 2021, Katelyn graduated as the salutatorian of her high school class. She was not only athletic but also intelligent. Katelyn received eight scholarships on top of her softball scholarship and multiple awards at graduation. She also had the honor of giving a speech at graduation. The administration was not prepared for her speech to turn into an actual sermon. Can you imagine a sermon and prayer at a liberal public school? Well, it happened, and we were very proud of her. She was finding her boldness in Christ.

Katelyn took extra classes at the local junior college and entered Missouri Baptist University with thirty-six college credits. She decided to major in biology with a concentration in biomedical sciences and a minor in medical technology. After she receives her degree from Missouri Baptist, her goal is to transfer to a physician assistant program for pediatric cardiology. She wants to treat babies and kids with heart defects like her. This girl has some big goals, but if anyone can do it, I know it will be her.

The summer of 2021 had many endings and beginnings for our family. We had a lot of adjusting to do because our world as we once knew it was going to be very different. I am one of those moms who love to have my kids at home. I never wanted summer break or Christmas break to be over. I love the atmosphere when we are all home laughing and enjoying each other's company. It was a complete blessing with my three kids getting along so well. Our softball girls always said that our home just felt so "homey" and "peaceful." I believe it feels peaceful because our home is God's home. We always welcomed anyone with open arms.

Shane and I decided this would be our last summer to have our travel organization, Future Prospects. We have had this organization for twelve years. We coached a lot of athletes and made a lot of friends. It was our life for many years. Shane and I spent many hours working with our athletes. We practiced and played all year long. We turned our garage into an indoor practice facility. We were dedicated. At the end of the summer, it was going to end. I believed the thing I would miss the most about our teams was the girls coming here just for my cooking and to relax at our house. Our home had an open-door policy, and all of them were always welcome. Many times I had athletes who came to practice and stayed to sit for hours and talk and eat. I had many phone calls from mothers looking for their daughters because they took so long at practice. Those teenagers told me some things I probably did not need to know! I always said I'd rather hang out with my softball girls than adults. Adults tend to worry too much about what people think, and these girls just want to eat and have fun. We as adults need to act more like kids sometimes and just loosen up and have good clean fun.

We had coached most of these girls since they played twelve-and-under softball. They were like our family, and soon they would all be going in different directions. We had athletes playing college softball in New York, Missouri, Kentucky, Illinois, and Indiana. Our athletes worked hard, and they would soon be reaping the benefits. We made some wonderful memories. Shane and I have talked about having a Future Prospects reunion. I'd love to see what all of our athletes have done with their lives. We coached a lot of athletes in twelve years. Some years we had as many as four teams to coach. The hardest thing for me was knowing that this special time in my life was about to end. I do know that God gives us seasons and seasons change. The next phase of our lives seemed to come too quickly.

This was Katelyn's last summer of travel softball. She had played travel since she was eight years old. Travel softball was Katelyn's life. It was all she knew for many years. Katelyn is not big on change, so I knew this would affect her. Katelyn told me one day, "Why do things have to change? I like them just the way they are!" Her whole world was about to be altered here in a few months. One of her best friends on the team was going to New York to play softball, and that was a hard adjustment. Life was changing rapidly.

This would be Shaelyn's last summer as a Wilber. She was going to marry in October 2021. She found her future husband,

Kody, while she was in college. Shaelyn went to Kaskaskia College in southern Illinois for their radiology program. She also went to college on a softball scholarship. After she graduated from Kaskaskia, God opened doors for her at a great job in Springfield, Illinois, in a level I trauma hospital. She was hired in the neurology department, and there she worked for two years in neurosurgery. She and Kody survived a long-distance relationship and would soon be married in the fall. After the wedding, they moved to St. Louis, Missouri, where Shaelyn works in neurosurgery and the heart cath lab at two different hospitals. To say the least, I am very proud of the young woman she has become.

We had our last family vacation in the summer of 2021 with just us five family members. It was a wonderful time in Florida. We didn't do a lot of sightseeing, but our family just enjoyed quality time together. We had been too busy lately for family time. Shaelyn worked three hours away and didn't get to come home as often as we would have liked. I knew once Katelyn left for college, family time would be sparse with her also. My mom always said that once they made it to high school, don't blink your eyes because they would be gone. She was once again correct.

With every ending, God blessed us with new beginnings. God gifted us with so many new beginnings this summer. Experiences that changed all of our lives.

"Forget the former things; do not dwell on the past. See, I am doing a new thing! Now it springs up; do you not perceive it? I am making a way in the wilderness and streams in the wasteland" (Isaiah 43:18–19).

Katelyn had a special invite to speak at the Softball Nationals in Louisville, Kentucky. The tournament director asked her to speak at the opening ceremony. This observance starts the tournament off, and all the teams and fans will be attending. This was the largest crowd to which she had ever given her testimony. Not to mention some of these girls were her age, and she had played with many of them. She was a nervous wreck but yet honored to have the opportunity.

Chance started playing travel baseball. He played for a team five hours away. We played a lot of baseball in northern Indiana and Illinois. We spent a lot of time on the road. I enjoyed it because it gave him and me some quality time together. I felt like he finally got to do something special like his sisters. When the kids were growing up, Chance sadly got put on the back burner. Don't get me wrong—he had fun playing with our athlete's brothers, but he always had to come wherever we went with softball. I dealt with guilt for a lot of years and still do because I feel he was left out a lot. Shane and I were so busy with softball, work, and Katelyn's health that Chance was left to find ways to entertain himself. With that came a lot of social media complications. This is when we opened our eyes to problems and decided to get him into something he would enjoy. I knew it would be a little bit of a strain to swing everything, but I was up for the challenge for Chance to be able to participate and make him feel like he was also worthy of our attention. I was just on autopilot trying to make everything work and didn't realize how he was also struggling with his sister's health. They were very close, and he couldn't understand for a long time why I always had to leave with Tiny and be gone for days. After realizing the struggles he was having, I spent more time assuring him that he was loved. I also learned that boys express their emotions differently than girls. My girls would cry and tell me everything. Chance would distance himself or try to find things to do away from home. He worked hard at avoiding us. This broke my heart because I was feeling a wall being built between Chance and the family. I knew this was not of God. Satan was trying to pull him away, and I was not going to let that happen. This was the summer that turned the tables for Chance. I never want my kids to ever feel unloved or unworthy. I thank God that we conquered Satan's schemes that summer. Chance and I had a blast traveling, and it led to an essential connection that we both longed for.

If Chance had a tournament the same weekend as the girls, I would take him to his tournaments and then meet up with our softball girls later. Nationals weekend, he had a tournament, so I was late to the girl's games. By the time I arrived, Katelyn had already finished speaking at the opening ceremony. I was greeted by some of the parents of our athletes that had never heard Katelyn's testimony. They were in tears, telling me how they enjoyed her speaking and how it touched them. Most parents knew that Katelyn had a heart condition but had no idea to what extent. They were humbled by her loyalty to her teammates now knowing her real health struggles.

I went into our dugout to help Shane coach, and I noticed a man walking in and out of the dugouts. He came to our dugout. I asked him if I could help him. He said, "I'm looking for the young lady who spoke at the opening ceremony. The tournament director said she plays for your team." I said, "Yes, she does. She's out there on the pitching mound. Can I help you?" He said, "No, I need to talk to her." After Katelyn came into the dugout, the man came up to her and shook her hand. He handed her a new softball and said, "I just want you to have this new softball as a souvenir from me. I am an umpire here at the tournament. I wanted you to know that your testimony completely changed my life. I am the one sheep that God left nine-nine to find. Thank you for changing my life." This was such a miraculous event. In her testimony, she talked about God leaving the ninety-nine sheep to find the one lost sheep. He is talking about leaving ninety-nine saved souls to find the one lost soul. Katelyn stated in her testimony that if she touched one person and brought them to Christ, it was all worth it. This day at the Nationals, her testimony moved one lost soul and brought him to Christ. God is just that good! To God, we give all the glory! Jesus said:

> What do you think? If a man owns a hundred sheep, and one of them wanders away, will he not leave the ninety-nine on the hills and go to look for the one that wandered off? And if he finds it, truly I tell you, he is happier about that one sheep than about the ninety-nine that did not wander off. In the same way, your Father in heaven is not willing that any of these little ones should perish.
>
> Matthew 18:12–14

After Nationals the tournament director contacted me about how great Katelyn did and that people were approaching him about her testimony. He was very impressed and informed of how she had touched so many people. He then asked if she would speak at the opening ceremony of the Softball World Series in Johnson City, Tennessee! Katelyn was honored by the invitation. She couldn't believe what this meant. The opportunity to speak to thousands of people about Jesus Christ. How many lives could she save by just being herself and talking about God's wonderful miracles? How could she pass on this opportunity? I was going to do everything in my power to make this work into our schedule. There is no mile too far to spread the word.

She had a couple of scheduling conflicts, speaking at a church camp and a church the same week of the World Series. Johnson City, Tennessee, was a nine-hour drive one way from our house. I told her we would pray about it, and if God wanted us to go, He would pave the way for us.

The new beginning that Katelyn had worked so many years to accomplish was rapidly approaching. She was busy preparing to move to college. She was excited about her softball scholarship. God had highly blessed her with this opportunity. She had always wanted to go to a Christian university but had no idea that she would have the honor to play softball there also. It was a dream come true. I told her that when you follow God and do His will, He will reward you. She was doing what God laid on her heart by giving her testimony, and He was greatly repaying her. I knew in my spirit that God opened the doors for Katelyn to attend Missouri Baptist University, and He had "*big*" plans for her there.

Katelyn was almost overwhelmed with all her opportunities and how quickly summer was coming to an end. I kept praying about Katelyn speaking at the Softball World Series. I knew this opportunity was a very special one. With her prior speaking engagements already made that same week, I wasn't sure how we could make it all happen. I knew that if God wanted her to speak at all of them, He would make a way. One night, the Lord put on my heart that Katelyn was to go to speak at the World Series. I believed she would touch many lives there.

The next morning I woke up with peace, knowing that God had already paved a way for her to speak at all of her prearranged speaking engagements and the World Series! I contacted the tournament director and confirmed that we would be attending. The church camp administrator worked with us, and so did the church. I had everything worked out for us to make the trip to the Softball World Series! It was going to be a big week. I knew God would bless many people of all ages with

Katelyn's testimonies. I have learned that when God says go, we must go. This would be an awesome way to end our summer!

"You need to persevere so that when you have done the will of God, you will receive what he has promised" (Hebrews 10:36).

The last new beginning I was working on that summer was Shaelyn's wedding plans. I could not believe my firstborn was to be married in October 2021. It was her dream to have a beautiful destination wedding. We went the previous fall and found the perfect wedding venue in the mountains of Gatlinburg. Not only did we find the venue, but that was also the weekend she was proposed to. It was a great trip, and we made amazing memories. Gatlinburg has always been our family's favorite place to vacation. Now, we would be busy planning and preparing for the "big day" at our favorite location. Shane and I were excited for Shaelyn but yet a little sad too. It was hard to believe our baby was old enough to get married. She was our firstborn and will always hold a special place in our hearts. We were learning that every ending had a new beginning, and our lives were full of them on this particular summer.

Katelyn was speaking the name of Jesus over all the people who were hearing her testimony. She was giving people hope and freedom in Jesus Christ. She was living proof that miracles still happen. She was speaking about life, miracles, and blessings to anyone that heard her testimony. I knew that her next three speaking engagements would be life-changing for her and for all the people she would speak to. God was using her in miraculous ways!

Never Will I Leave Thee...

Chapter 24: "My Testimony" —Elevation Worship

"As I sat here anxiously waiting to walk out onto this AAA Baseball stadium to speak to thousands of softball players and parents, I asked myself, 'How did I get here? Why did they pick me to speak at the Softball World Series in Johnson City, Tennessee? What if I mess up? What if they laugh me out of the stadium? These athletes are my age, and I've played against some of them. Will they take me seriously? Why do I get this honor? I'm just a little country girl from Flat Rock, Illinois.' My nerves started to take hold. Then I looked over at my mom. She smiled at me and reassured me that God has me here for a reason and reminded me of the lives I was going to touch with my testimony. Then I heard the tournament director say, 'Katelyn Wilber, our special speaker for the Softball World Series Opening Ceremony.' As I got up and started to walk onto the field, every emotion and all my fear just left me. Yes, God completely took away the fear! I walked out there with such confidence, and I knew I was there for a reason! I was chosen to give my testimony of God's love and to touch as many athletes and parents as I could.

"I stood out on the field and could feel God's presence in what I was doing to honor Him. You see, me being out there speaking to thousands of athletes and parents is a huge miracle in itself. I have always been such a shy and quiet person until about two years ago. Then I realized that I have to tell people about what God has done for me, and if my testimony can save one person and bring them closer to God, it will all be worth it. As I looked around at all the people who were there to hear me, I began to tell them what God had done for me and what He could do for them.

"'My name is Katelyn Wilber. I am eighteen years old, and I live in Flat Rock, Illinois. I play for the Future Prospects travel organization out of Flat Rock, Illinois. I have been playing travel softball since I was eight years old. My plans for the future are to go to Missouri Baptist University to play softball on a scholarship and study biology with a concentration in biomedical sciences and a minor in biotech. When I graduate with my bachelor's degree, I plan to get into the physician's assistant program at Washington University. It's one of the top medical schools for physician assistants. I hope to help treat kids with heart defects and give them genuine comfort and assurance because I have been through this.

"'Now that you know a little about my background, I want to talk about overcoming challenges in our lives. I also want to talk about being thankful and giving glory to God for all of our successes. Throughout my whole life, a series of miracles have been performed in me and in my life time and time again. Even when we can't see it, God performs miracles in every one of our lives every single day. I want to share with you the challenges I have overcome in my life that have led up to this point and have made me who I am today. I would not be standing here if it weren't for God. He deserves all of the credit. I am living proof that God does exist, and this is why I want to share my testimony. If I can just touch one person and bring that one person to God, then everything that I have been through has been worth it.

"'Physically you can't tell that anything is wrong with me. I just look like a normal teenage girl. But, underneath all of this,

I have five big scars on my abdomen and chest that I once was ashamed of. Ladies today, at our age, a lot of us tend to worry about our outside appearance compared to other body types. I used to be the same way. I was so ashamed of my scars and scared to wear bathing suits, especially bikinis, because my body didn't look like the other girls. But let me tell you something, the game of softball is one of the most unique sports because no two girls look alike. We are all different shapes and sizes, all playing for the same goal. Don't worry about what other people think about you or how you look for a guy because you know what? God only cares about what is on the inside, not the outside. The good thing about Him is we don't have to come to Him as someone else; we can come to Him just as we are. So wear those scars proudly. Every time I look in the mirror, they are a reminder of how strong I am. Even on those days when I don't think I am. My scars are from multiple heart surgeries and pacemaker replacements throughout my life. How many people in the world can say that they have had ten heart surgeries and nine pacemaker replacements by the time they were eighteen years old? I'd like to think not many!

"'My story begins with being diagnosed with a congenital heart defect called complete heart block. What that means is that I was born with something wrong with my heart, and it is incurable. I have to deal with it for the rest of my life. You know how you hear about people with, for example, stage four cancer, and the stages tell you how bad it is? Well, I have a third-degree complete heart block (also the worst degree). This is a condition in which the electrical signals in my heart are completely dead. When blood goes into the top of my heart, the ventricles, which are the bottom part, do not know to pump the blood back out. This means that I have a pacemaker that works twenty-four seven to keep my heart pumping. Without a pacemaker, my heart only pulsates at twenty beats per minute. Only one in a million babies in the world are born with complete heart block. Less than 20 percent of these babies will survive the birth. Because of this, the doctors wanted to abort me. The doctors did not give my mom any hope. Little did they know, but my mom is stubborn and believes in Jesus Christ! Abortion was not an option.

"'I was diagnosed when my mom was twenty-four weeks pregnant. My mom has lupus. Lupus causes my mom's antibodies to attack the main organs in her body. When I was in her womb, lupus went straight for the main organ of the baby, my heart. After I was born, I went straight into surgery and had my first pacemaker implanted at only six hours old. The smallest and youngest person to ever get a pacemaker at Riley's Children's Hospital in Indianapolis, Indiana. I kinda wonder if I still hold that record… Anyway, a couple of weeks later, I came home and had a staph infection. I went in for another surgery and had another full system replacement, pacemaker, leads, and all. The staph infection was crawling up my lead and was centimeters from my heart, or so we thought. If it had reached my heart, I would have died instantly. It didn't because God was saving me for a greater purpose. This will come in later in my story.

"'Fast forward many years, and I don't remember much until my fourth grade. By the time I was in eighth grade, I had already gone through eight surgeries and seven pacemaker replacements. This is because I am very active, and my body produces excessive scar tissue. Every surgery has been an emergency because my leads break all the time, except for the last surgery, which I just had in November.

"'My surgery in fourth grade is when I realized how serious my condition was. It was more of a realization of, "Hey, this thing is real, and your life revolves around it!" Except it never has. My life has never revolved around my condition. I have always lived my life like a normal kid, and no one would ever know any different.

"'The pacemaker I got in fourth grade was the longest I had ever had a pacemaker last, until my freshman year of high school. Another life-changing experience happened to me once again. I was at the gym working out when my lead broke and was shocking me through my skin. We went to the local emergency room. The next day we went to Chicago to see my doctor for yet another surgery.

"'Remember that staph infection I mentioned from when I was really young? Well, the staph infection had actually reached my heart. The staph infection made a callus (which is a tough or rough surface) around my heart. This makes the pacemaker work harder than it needs to to get to the good part of my heart. The outside is basically like dead tissue. That is why the battery drains so much. For those of you who are not familiar with the anatomy of the heart, veins in your heart are what supply your heart with blood, and arteries are what take the blood from the heart and spread or transport it to your body. Dr. Ovadia had realized that one of the main veins to my heart was blocked. He was amazed to find that instead of pumping blood away from my heart, it had flipped and was supplying my heart with the blood that it needed. Dr. Ovadia said, "Do you realize how miraculous this is?" This also means that the valve in the thyroid artery had to completely flip to pump the blood to my heart. Telling my parents this after a ten-hour surgery that was only supposed to be three hours, Dr. Ovadia was wondering why I had not had a massive heart attack yet. He said, "In my thirty-five years of being a cardiologist, I have never in my life seen this! If that isn't God's work, then I have no idea what is!" Once again, God was working in miraculous ways to help me overcome that fear and to keep me pushing through.

"'My God never fails me and always takes care of me no matter how hard it gets. I have a pretty high pain tolerance, and I don't like to show when I am in pain. I've just been raised to tough it out and throw some dirt on it. But when I can't even lift my arms to feed myself and my mom has to give me showers for about a month, it makes me feel defeated. This surgery I had my freshman year was absolutely mentally and physically exhausting. I had never been in so much pain in my life. But after all this happened, I have felt the best I've ever felt in my entire life. Praise God!

"'During my surgery in 2017, any surgery I thought about things that might be taken away from me. Most of you know me because I play softball. I have lived and breathed softball ever since I can remember. In this situation where softball was going to be taken away from me, I was feeling like everything was going to cave in on me. I was never going to be able to do anything if I didn't have that one thing I love in my life. I didn't know what to do. Anyone who knows me knows that I am not the type to give up easily. I'm pretty hard-headed and determined just like my mom. After this surgery in 2017, my doctor told me that I wasn't supposed to play softball for two and a half years or possibly never again. Little did he know he didn't know whom he was talking to. I reacted just like anyone else would in that situation. I was so mad at God, thinking, *Why would God take the thing I love the most away from me?* I had that doubt, and the devil was telling me, "You can't even lift your arms to feed yourself. Do you think that you'll be able to pitch a ball again the same? Do you think you'll be able to play college softball and not make your health worse?"

"'I was so upset day in and day out. I was upset wondering what my teammates would think of me or wondering how I would handle possibly never playing softball again. I was so frustrated, and I didn't know what to do. It's hard to get that negativity and doubt out of our lives after something like that gets taken away from us. It's easy to praise God when nothing is going wrong in your life to bring you down, but what will you say when things aren't going your way? It only takes just a little bit of faith to do big amazing things. I had a little bit of faith in this situation. But when God chooses to give you a situation that you have no power to do anything about or change what has happened, He will give you the strength to say, "It is well with my soul." After I had my pity party for a little bit, I decided, "You know what? This isn't who I am! After all of my surgeries, I have bounced back so quickly, and I am going to do the same for this one." So that's what I did! I started to heal, and the next thing you know, I was back on the field as the starting varsity pitcher at my high school. I went on to win three awards that year.

"'I am now about to live out my lifelong dream of playing college softball at a Christian university on a softball scholarship. Isn't that just amazing? I have always dreamed of being a college softball player ever since I was a little girl. I have always been a great player, but I didn't always have the confidence in myself from past coaches and my health. It always seemed to be that anytime I thought I was right where I needed to be, bam, another surgery or another thing going wrong with my heart would happen. I have always had to work extra hard to get where I wanted myself. I have always compared myself to others, and sometimes I still do. I compared myself to others knowing that they didn't have any health issues. I was jealous that all the time I was out for surgery or not feeling well, the other girls were still practicing, playing, and getting better. But you know what? That's okay because all of those extra hours at the field were worth it.

"'As my travel softball career is coming to an end and a new chapter of my life opens, it is a very bittersweet moment. Some of you may know what I am going through. I will be eternally grateful for the friendships I have made, the new places I have seen, and the memories I have made. Don't take this time for granted! Much too soon, softball will be over, and we will have to grow up and move on with our lives. Girls, I want to leave you with this. All those times that you showed up to the ball field after work, school, or after a family situation and you didn't want to be there, someday you're going to look back and miss those days. You will miss the chances you had to be on the field. Not everyone gets the chance to play softball and live out their dreams of playing the sport that they love. Some kids have medical issues and aren't dealt the same cards that we were given. Those kids wish they had the chance to do what we do. We need to be thankful that we get to play the game of softball. When you leave here, take a minute to stop and thank your parents for everything that they have done for you. They are the only reason that you all are here right now. They love softball because you love softball. They pay for your hotel rooms, food, traveling expenses, and fees because they love you. Never take that for granted because one day softball will be gone, and your parents and anyone who supported you through this season of your life will still be there to support you. Most importantly, thank God for all of your many blessings because without Him none of this would be possible! Thank you!'"

"As I turned to walk off the field, I received a standing ovation. I looked at the thousands of people who had heard my testimony. I have to say I will never forget this wonderful opportunity."

These were Katelyn's own words of her testimony of the World Series experience. As Katelyn walked off the field and I saw the standing ovation, it was one of the proudest moments ever. I knew that she touched multiple lives that day. God was working through her, and as she stood out there with confidence and spoke, I could feel the presence of God there with us. The Holy Spirit was consuming. Yes, we were having church on the AAA baseball field!

We gathered our things to leave, and Katelyn was stopped by a line of people to speak with her. There were people with their testimonies. Some just wanted to shake her hand and thank her for the encouragement and hope she gave them. A lady came to her in tears because she was a new Christian, and Katelyn's testimony was a confirmation to her. Another testimony was of a woman whose husband was standing there with her. She told us that he was questioning if God was real, but after hearing Katelyn he looked at her and said, "There is no doubt God is real. Look at that girl. She is a miracle." She told us this as she wept and thanked Katelyn for her boldness. There was a lot of healing that day. God was moving, and that was maybe the only church some people had experienced. The seeds Katelyn planted that day God will bless and make grow in countless people's lives. I believe we need to always tell our stories because you never know whom you may impact. No matter if your story is small or big, God can use all of them to glorify Him. "May the God of hope fill you with all joy and peace as you trust in him, so that you may overflow with hope by the power of the Holy Spirit" (Romans 15:13).

Katelyn and I made our way to the car. We even had people stop at our vehicle to talk to us. I was humbled by the way people responded to her courage. I have always known she was special, but to have all these people confirm it was more than I could have ever hoped. I looked over at her, and she was glowing. God was shining through her, and it was obvious. People drew to her, and through teary eyes they confessed how great our God is. The Spirit I felt that day was unmeasurable. We are the church. It doesn't matter where we are to proclaim God's greatness. He is there with us.

We started our journey home. We called Shane because he was anxiously waiting to hear how it went. Katelyn was excited to tell her dad how awesome it was! I could hear how proud he was of her. His shy baby girl cleansed the AAA ball stadium with the Holy Spirit!

Katelyn had her last two speaking engagements in the next two days to finish out our summer and get ready to move to college. God richly blessed us with a wonderful summer. One we will never forget.

CHAPTER 25: "OCEANS (WHERE FEET MAY FAIL)"— HILLSONG UNITED

Summer was ending, and Katelyn had one last witnessing opportunity before she moved to college. She was asked to be a counselor at our local church camp that she attended in her younger years. Now too old to be a camper but old enough to be a counselor. This was another milestone in her life.

The camp counselors had a meeting to discuss the upcoming youth who were attending. This generation had been affected by a pandemic and Satanic attacks. Satan promoted fear and targeted our youth in multiple ways. Drugs, sex, and physical abuse were plaguing them. Suicide was destroying our community. Children were crying out for help. It was our obligation to teach the kids only Jesus Christ can save them from their ungodly situations. To the best of our ability, we had to surround them with God's unfailing love. Katelyn's testimony and loving nature were exactly what the campers needed at this time.

> Love is patient, love is kind. It does not envy, it does not boast, it is not proud. It does not dishonor others, it is not self-seeking, it is not easily angered, it keeps no record of wrongs. Love does not delight in evil but rejoices with the truth. It always protects, always trusts, always hopes, always perseveres.
>
> 1 Corinthians 13:4–7

The camp dean asked Katelyn to speak at one of the chapel services. She was not prepared to speak but took on the task. She said, "God will lead me!" Her sermon targeted the hurt in the youth. Katelyn's struggles but victory through Jesus Christ was the confirmation they needed to believe that God was the only way to defeat their worldly strife.

"Open my eyes that I may see wonderful things in your law" (Psalm 119:18).

At the end of her sermon, she had a bag of small wooden crosses. Katelyn prayed over them and handed one to each camper. She told them that the Lord would always be with them. If they ever needed anything, they should hold their cross and pray. God would hear their prayers. I watched the campers as they approached Katelyn and the love in their eyes. God was there, and they witnessed freedom in the Holy Spirit that night.

"Now the Lord is the Spirit, and where the Spirit of the Lord is, there is freedom" (2 Corinthians 3:17).

As summer came to an end, we loaded up our packed vehicles and took Katelyn to move in for her first year of college. I would be lying to say that I wasn't super emotional. The baby who I spent nineteen years watching and taking care of was moving away to college on her own. I was so proud of the young woman she had become. My flesh wanted her to stay home with Mom, but I knew it was time for her to spread her wings and fly. Katelyn had worked so hard to get to this point, and she was ready for her reward.

> He gives strength to the weary and increases the power of the weak. Even youths grow tired and weary and young men stumble and fall; but those who hope in the Lord will renew their strength. They will soar on

wings like eagles; they will run and not grow weary, they will walk and not be faint.

Isaiah 40:29–31

Katelyn seemed to be transitioning into freshman year with ease. She loved her coaches and her teammates. Her professors were very helpful, and she really liked the small classes. She wanted to keep a personal class situation like she was accustomed to in high school; her graduating class only had seventeen students. Katelyn didn't think a big university would be a positive choice for her.

Katelyn called one day, and with great excitement, she exclaimed, "Mom, I am finally a college softball player! Can you believe it? All my hard work finally paid off!" She was living her dream as a college athlete. Katelyn's social life was always put on hold because of pitching lessons, practice, or games. She always chose softball over any other invites from friends or classmates. Her ambition to become the best she could be was her main objective in life. It didn't matter if it was academics or softball—the sky was the limit.

God was also setting Katelyn up to give her testimony to her coaches and her teammates. I told her I believed the Lord told me in my spirit that she would soon be giving her testimony to her teammates. She replied, "Mom, it's too soon. I just want to get to know everyone first. I don't want them to look at me like I am weird. I'm just a freshman, and I don't want to hurt my chance of making friends because I'm different." I was a little shocked because she had never responded like that before. I think she forgot that the Lord has the final say because little did she know He was about to move in miraculous ways.

It seemed like I turned around, and it was October. We had such a busy summer and the beginning of fall. I couldn't believe it was time to take our trip to Gatlinburg for Shaelyn's wedding. I remembered the day I brought her home from the hospital. It seemed like yesterday. Now, here I was, about to watch her walk down the aisle. Shaelyn and Kody were about to become one in a covenant with God, and it was such a special time in both of their lives.

"For this reason a man will leave his father and mother and be united to his wife, and the two will become one flesh" (Ephesians 5:31).

In my mind, I first thought a destination wedding would be a lot of work. The natural beauty was most of the decoration for the ceremony. The reception area was already decorated beautifully for fall. We just had to do some of our personal touches to make it complete. My family jumped in and helped to make everything run smoothly. I delegated, and they didn't hesitate. We will be forever grateful for their hard work and dedication to help make this day special for Kody and Shaelyn.

During the ceremony, Chance walked me down the aisle to my seat in the front row. I sat there just admiring God's natural beauty in the surroundings. The fall leaves and the mountain scenery were perfect for this special wedding day. I would have given anything for my mom to be able to attend Shaelyn's wedding. My mom would have loved the beautiful leaves and the scenery. Shaelyn, or "Toodle," held a very special place in Mom's heart. As I sat there, I played back in my mind the day we picked out Shaelyn's wedding dress and the beautiful bridal shower. My mom missed the joy on Toodle's face, and now she was missing the most special part of her life. Before she passed, she told me she wanted to live long enough to see her babies walk down the aisle. She didn't get the opportunity, but someday, we'll be able to tell her all about it.

My mom loved jewelry, and before her passing, she made sure the girls had a ring in remembrance of her. I saved the rings to give to the girls on their wedding day. One week before the wedding, I gave Shaelyn her special ring to wear in memory of Meemaw. We stood and wept because of the special meaning behind the ring. I catch sight of her wearing her ring to this day.

Katelyn was the maid of honor. As she stood at the front waiting on the bride, a ray of sunshine shone through the mountains and radiated right on Katelyn. The sun was not on anyone else. I sat there looking at her as she glistened. As Shaelyn walked down with Shane, I noticed the gleam of sunlight on her as she reached the front with Katelyn. During the whole ceremony, the sun was beaming on my girls. The radiance was not shining on anyone else at the wedding party. I knew it was just like when I went to the cemetery to pray that humbling day. It was God shining on both of my girls! He was blessing them. I sat there thanking God for His constant watch over my family. I knew this was a confirmation that He was there with us and blessing this ceremony. It was truly a marriage blessed by God. As the ceremony ended and the girls walked back down the aisle, the ray of sunshine left. Just like it did for me at the cemetery.

After the wedding, my sister pulled me to the side. She had taken pictures, and she wanted to show me the glow on the girls. The pictures clearly showed the sun's rays shining directly on my girls. They were radiant as they stood there before God. She said, "Look! Mom was smiling down on the girls at the wedding!" I have those pictures. It is a reminder to me that God is always with my family.

"The Lord bless you and keep you; the Lord make his face shine on you and be gracious to you; the Lord turn his face toward you and give you peace" (Numbers 6:24–26).

The wedding was a ceremony out of a bridal book. Typically weddings have at least one issue. Not this one. I can proudly say it was perfect. God blessed all of us, and I believe it was a union made in heaven. Will it be perfect? I'm sure not, but I know without a shadow of a doubt that God was there that day to bless Shaelyn and Kody's covenant with Him.

After the wedding, we all traveled home. Katelyn opened up to me about school. She was getting homesick, her classes were hard, and softball was a struggle. She said it was wearing her out. They were doing two practices a day, which were workouts at 6 a.m. and then practices at 3:00 p.m. Pitchers would go at 2:00 p.m. for extra practice. Katelyn is the type of athlete who, if there was softball practice of any kind, would always be there. Katelyn only wanted to work hard and prove herself to her new coaches even if it meant wearing herself out.

Never Will I Leave Thee...

I asked Katelyn if the coaches had told anyone on the team about her heart condition. She said she thought they were starting to talk about it. Katelyn was afraid to tell anyone because, being a freshman, she was still trying to make a place for herself on the team. Katelyn didn't want her heart to keep her from making the varsity team or cause her to be excluded. She did not like to be singled out as a weaker athlete because of her circumstances. I think that made her push harder.

Katelyn was able to do everything in softball except run distance. Her heart would not allow her to run long distances or long periods. Even with her pacemaker, her heart would not beat fast enough for those exertions. Other than that, she could do everything else.

Shane and I had never told Katelyn, but we worried that a college would never sign her up to play softball. We were afraid she would be considered a liability because of her heart. With the possibility of a ball hitting her in the chest or a heart attack on the field. We believed it was another miracle and blessing that Missouri Baptist would give her a chance. Coach A saw her hard work, determination, and character. Like I said before, when anyone meets Katelyn, they are drawn to her. She and Coach A had an instant friendship.

Coach A had seen Katelyn's World Series testimony live on Facebook. He knew Katelyn's battles with her heart. Coach A and Katelyn had many personal conversations. This opened the door for Katelyn to share her testimony with the Missouri Baptist Fellowship of Christian Athletes group. Katelyn once again called me, "Well, Mom, you were right. Guess what? I'm speaking at FCA! Coach A wants me to tell my testimony to all the athletic teams on campus. What do you think about that?" I laughed and said, "Well, I hate to say I told you so, but I told you so!" This was bigger than I first anticipated. She had only been at school for a few months, and they were already asking her to speak to the athletes. Katelyn was honored with a special night to share her testimony for FCA. Her softball team, which included the coaches and their spouses, attended. There were also athletes from other Missouri Baptist athletic teams that attended. This was God's way of opening doors for Katelyn once again.

Her testimony matured each time she shared it. I could see her spiritual growth with each speaking arrangement. This time she had a PowerPoint with pictures of her surgeries to explain her health better. It was very impressive. She was becoming quite the little speaker. Her testimony is so big and covers so many situations in life that she can adjust to fit any audience she speaks to. I was so proud of her, and I knew God was smiling down on her. She was doing all this to honor Him.

Katelyn's testimony started the same as her last testimonies. She started with an introduction and explanation of her illness. She concluded and changed it for her college peers. I have included below her conclusion.

"Now I am here at MBU on a softball scholarship, getting to play the best game in the world, softball! But the best part of it all is I get to stand up here to share my testimony with you all. This is something I have always prayed for. Isn't that just amazing? I have always dreamed of being a college softball player ever since I was a little girl. I have always been a great player, but I didn't always have the confidence in myself from past coaches and my health. I have always had to work extra hard to get where I wanted myself. I have always compared myself to others, and sometimes I still do.

"During my search for the right college for me and the perfect place to play softball, I found Missouri Baptist. I always planned on playing at a Christian university for as long as I can remember. But as I got older and learned more about the recruiting process, I kind of strayed away from that idea. It was always in the back of my mind. I thought, *You know? If going to a Christian university doesn't work out, it'll be okay as long as I'm happy getting an education and playing softball somewhere.* I believe I was starting to settle for less. I didn't realize it at the time. But God knew exactly where He wanted to put me. I know since I have been at Mobap, He has blessed me in many ways. I believe that I have a mission here to lead people to the Lord whatever it may be.

"The devil likes to target the weakest part of me: my mind. I will admit I struggle with self-confidence and what other people think of me. I also struggle with saying these two little deadly words to myself: 'what if?' What if my story is not worthy enough to share? What if I'm not strong enough or as good as everybody else? You know what? Who cares what other people say about you? God says *I am good enough*, and God says that *you are good enough!*

"There are times when I forget to rely on God and I forget who I am. Luckily He still remembers me. There are times when I don't think that I'm going to be okay and I don't have the courage to stand up, but the bottom line is the only way I can get up every day and go through this is what Christ has already done for me. No circumstance will change who I am in Christ—it'll try, and sometimes it feels like it's going to win, but it won't. So I don't know what anyone here is going through. I know that we all go through hard times. If you haven't had any yet—God bless you—it's coming! When we go through these hardships, the first question we normally ask ourselves is, 'Why me? Why do I have to go through this?' It always seems to be that as soon as we start to feel sorry for ourselves, He places someone in front of us that has it worse.

I am so blessed to be in the condition I am right now rather than a worse one. I get to attend Missouri Baptist University, study what I love, play what I love, and be with the people that I love. All because Jesus died on the cross for my sins and saved a broken soul like mine.

"I believe we are supposed to be thankful for every little thing that we have in life. I have learned over time that I was going to be more reliant on God and let Him take control of all of the problems I ever had. He's the only One that can cure us of diseases. He's the only One who can calm our minds and thoughts in times of trouble. He's the only rock we have to support us. Just know you're not alone because there is a God out there that loves you and is with you every step of the way. Sometimes bad things happen to us as life lessons to show us and the people around us how to come closer to Him. But instead of saying and praying, 'God, can You change these things? Can You stop all the hurt and sorrow?' we should be praying, 'God, can You change me so that I can handle the things that You are walking me through?'

"'Have I not commanded you? Be strong and courageous. Do not be afraid; do not be discouraged, for the LORD your God will be with you wherever you go' (Joshua 1:9).

"I pray today I have planted that seed to change your lives as well. So let me ask you this, 'Do you believe that God still performs miracles?'"

God opened bountiful doors for Katelyn after her testimony at Missouri Baptist. Her assistant softball coach asked her to speak at his church. The head FCA leader asked her to become an FCA leader. Most important of all, Katelyn's teammates and coaches gained a new respect for her that was unmeasurable. Katelyn opened spiritual doors that evening. Spiritual doors that only God could have blessed.

To the angel of the church in Philadelphia write: These are the words of him who is holy and true, who holds the key of David. What he opens no one can shut, and what he shuts no one can open. I know your deeds. See, I have placed before you an open door that no one can shut. I know that you have little strength, yet you have kept my word and have not denied my name.

Revelation 3:7–8

CHAPTER 26: "IMAGO DEI"—SEAN FEUCHT

For you created my inmost being; you knit me together in my mother's womb. I praise you because I am fearfully and wonderfully made; your works are wonderful, I know that full well. My frame was not hidden from you when I was made in the secret place, when I was woven together in the depths of the earth. Your eyes saw my unformed body; all the days ordained for me were written in your book before one of them came to be.

Psalm 139:13–16

God is mourning how easily the unborn are destroyed today. Millions of abortions are performed every year. Social and political acceptance of this ongoing issue makes believers accept or ignore what is happening. Every life is precious to God, but the unborn need special care because they are the most vulnerable. They do not have a voice and cannot defend themselves. We have to pray for protection for the unborn.

This subject holds dear to my heart because of the pressure to abort Katelyn and Chance. If I had listened to Satan's schemes and not held fast to our faith, Katelyn and Chance would not be here today to use their testimonies to speak in honor of God's miracles. God has placed them here for a time such as this. They are advocates for the unborn.

My heart breaks for all of the soon-to-be mothers who were persuaded to abort the unborn child they were carrying inside of them. The song used for this chapter was written specifically in support of the life of the unborn.

Satan does not take defeat lightly. Chance has had multiple Satanic attacks in his life. From a very young age, Chance would see demons trying to destroy him and me. He was too young to understand, but I knew exactly what was happening. Satan was trying to destroy him because of God's calling on his life. Chance survived near-death experiences and social media destruction. I believe God is not finished with Chance yet. God is opening doors for Chance every day, and sometimes he acknowledges it, and sometimes he does not. He is a harder case to crack to convince that he, too, is worthy. His story will be told in book form just like his sister's. As a family, through Christ, we overcame these attacks. "Have I not commanded you? Be strong and courageous, Do not be afraid; do not be discouraged, for the Lord your God will be with you wherever you go" (Joshua 1:9).

The Lord laid it on my heart that Chance was going to be a preacher. I told him I believed God wanted him to be a minister. Chance's response was, "*No*, Mom, they don't make any money!" I don't think he realizes God has the final say in his future.

Satan's attempts of destruction on Katelyn and Chance have only made them stronger in Christ. I believe they have a glorious calling in their lives. God has placed them here for a time such as this.

Chance's struggles in the past have brought forth rewards! When Chance was sixteen, he was asked to give his testimony at church camp and church. After he gave witness at church camp, one of the preachers said, "I didn't know Chance was going to be a preacher." That was a proud mom moment. I then looked at Chance and said, "Told you so." I got the traditional teenage "eye roll."

After Chance spoke at church, I told him God had big plans for him and his testimony. He replied, "My testimony is nothing like Tiny's. Nobody wants to hear mine." This response broke my heart. His disbelief and lack of confidence come from all of his struggles in his past. I told him, "You have a tremendous testimony. It's not like Tiny's, but it is just as glorious, and the Lord is going to use you to touch people just like Tiny. You wait!" After he delivered his testimony at church, I could see a change in him. God healed him and softened his heart that day. I believe God will open doors for him to share his testimony. I also believe I will write a book about the miracles in his life.

Chance wrote a testimony of how he saw his life growing up with a sister who had a chronic illness. I am proud of the understanding Katelyn's siblings had of her illness.

Chance wrote:

"Growing up with a sister who has complete heart block like Katelyn doesn't change your everyday activities as some people may think. When people hear of someone having a complete heart block, they think, *How could that person live a normal life if only half of their heart is beating?* Doctors may try to explain how Katelyn has lived a fairly normal life based on science, but little do they know they are trying to take the glory away from God, who is the real One who has gotten Katelyn through all of her struggles. We have spent our lives at hospitals visiting different doctors, and it was not until Dr. Ovadia that we finally had a doctor tell us that God was the One performing all these miracles in Katelyn's life.

"Katelyn was in the hospital a lot when she was little in between appointments and surgeries, which means Shaelyn and I had to stay at relatives' houses. We spent a lot of time at my grandparents' house or my aunt's home while my parents were with Katelyn. Dad worked at Marathon, which meant that he worked a lot of night shifts. Shaelyn and I were too young to stay home alone, so that is why we had to go to our grandparents' or our aunt's. This was kind of confusing for me because I was too young to understand what was going on, and sometimes I would get mad because I thought that they were leaving just because they could. A lot of things like that were confusing to me because I was too young to understand what was going on, but the older I got, the easier it was to understand that they were taking my sister to the hospital to get the help that she needed.

"Katelyn's testimony is one of the most impacting things that has happened to my family because it allows us to share God's miracles with the world. It is our duty as Christians to share God's Word and to touch as many people's lives as we can by showing them the miracles God has performed. Katelyn's testimony has opened up the opportunity for me to be able to include her in my papers anytime I'm writing about something that has changed my family's life. Katelyn has had the opportunity to share her testimony with thousands of people speaking at churches, events, and even the Travel Softball World Series in Tennessee. Although Katelyn has had lots of problems in life, she never fails to praise God and thank Him for getting her through every step of life, and that is why she tries to spread God's Word as much as she can."

Katelyn has no clue how she has impacted her siblings. I know with all the disappointments Katelyn has encountered in her life, it's hard for her to see the people she has deeply touched. Witnessing her struggles yet always trusting God and never losing faith, I believe, has shown her siblings the power of God.

"My message and my preaching were not with wise and persuasive words, but with a demonstration of the Spirit's power, so that your faith might not rest on human wisdom, but God's power" (1 Corinthians 2:4–5).

I am humbled by all the struggles we have overcome and will continue to overcome as a family to glorify our Savior, Jesus Christ. I guess you can say all of Satan's attacks have backfired. I will never let my guard down. I will do everything with God's strength to continually defeat Satan's schemes for my family.

We are thankful for God's works in our children. I pray God continues to increase their spiritual maturity. I trust they know all too well where their strength comes from and will never forget. "But those who hope in the Lord will renew their strength. They will soar on wings like eagles; they will run and not grow weary, they will walk and not be faint" (Isaiah 40:31).

Chapter 27: "Run to the Father"
—Cody Carnes

Katelyn's freshman year in college was full of trials, but once again God blessed her with rewards. Katelyn had a special bond with her head coach, A. He was the main reason she picked Missouri Baptist over all the other colleges. She had other college softball offers but felt led to accept Coach A's offer. Katelyn would randomly go to his office just to talk. He valued her opinion, and she valued his.

Katelyn was having issues with one of her assistant coaches. It was making Katelyn struggle and question her position with the team. Katelyn texted me one morning after workouts. She was very upset. The two-a-day workouts and practices were wearing her out physically and mentally. She also had a full load of classes. Katelyn had her generals finished before she went to college, so she went straight into her biology program, which is one of the hardest programs on campus. Satan found a little crack and started creeping in. She began to doubt her abilities and self-worth. When I heard that, I knew it was time to pray it up! The kids always know that when they have problems, I dig in the Word, and God comes to the rescue.

Katelyn was never treated in the past differently because of her health condition. But I knew this was very hard for her having a heart issue on top of all the normal college studies stress. The average college athlete with good health has struggles. I was concerned that, eventually, stress would affect her health, so I prayed this would not be the issue. She was not one to give up easily or lessen her work ethic, so I knew she was pushing the limits to impress the coach. Knowing her determination, I prayed her health would allow her to accomplish her goals in softball. I kept the faith that God would pull her through, knowing her heart and loyalty to Him.

I called Katelyn to pray with her. I then told her she needed to take a step back. Turn on her favorite praise and worship song and just be silent. Let God lead her and give her peace. Sometimes God just wants us to be silent and listen for His guidance.

"Yes, my soul, finds rest in God; my hope comes from him" (Psalm 62:5).

That afternoon, Katelyn called me. She said, "Well, Mom, God showed up! We were in the chapel, and the service was so good. After the service, they played the song 'Run to the Father' by Cody Carnes. That was the song I was listening to this morning when you told me to step back and wait on God. Coach A came up to me and said, 'Hey, Poky, what are you doing?' I told him I was taking my time because I loved the song and was wanting to hear it. The coach said, 'Well, I'll just listen to it with you!' Coach sat down beside me, and we sat there listening to the song, and I just cried. Mom, God was there! I could feel the Holy Spirit!" Isn't it wonderful how God sends little confirmations when we need them?

The fall and winter did not get much easier for Katelyn and softball. Coach A announced that he would be retiring. He had a health condition that was forcing him to retire. This was a big letdown for Katelyn because she felt so highly of him. She was very upset to see her coach rapidly declining in health. Katelyn was his go-to person at softball games and practices. He always sat by her, and she was the one to help him when he needed it. She was dealing with the coach's declining health and the mistreatment from the assistant coach. I am sad to say college softball was not turning out as she had envisioned.

Katelyn's hard work and determination were not paying off for her in softball. Her talent was there, but for some reason, the play time was not. All she hoped for was to get a fair opportunity to show her talent on the field. For some unknown reason, this was not the case. Sometimes, Satan puts distractions in our way to keep us off God's path. God has a path already paved for us, and sometimes it's not what we think our path should be.

Katelyn loved the university as a whole. She was making friends on and off the softball field. She liked her professors and felt she was getting a quality Christian education. She also enjoyed interacting with the activities on campus. Her academic grades were very good, and she was adjusting to city life. She still felt in her spirit that she made the right decision for her college.

I always tried to be uplifting and encouraging when Katelyn would call upset over softball. I reminded her that God always makes good out of bad situations. I believe that we all need small words of encouragement. We don't realize how this can change someone's outlook on what they think is a bad circumstance.

"When Jesus spoke again to the people, he said, 'I am the light of the world. Whoever follows me will never walk in darkness, but will have the light of life'" (John 8:12).

I was blessed with having the opportunity to travel to Florida to watch Katelyn on her softball spring break trip. I am a people watcher. I noticed the softball team loved Katelyn. Coach MB and her main assistant coach admired her and loved her too. They all looked up to her. She was a bright spot on the team. If they had issues, they would come to Katelyn for guidance. I quickly saw Katelyn's purpose on the team. I knew why God had her there and what He was setting her up to be. Katelyn just wanted to play softball, but I believe God wanted her to be the spiritual advisor for the team.

Instead of riding back with the softball team from Florida, we took a couple of extra days to ourselves before I drove her back to college. She is a lot like her mother. We both love the beach. We took an extra day at the beach and then, of course, the pool at the resort. She and I are very easy to please. Our idea of a perfect day is lying in the sun. We don't have to sightsee or be very active. Not only that, but she needed mom time before she went back to school. The fourteen-hour drive home was a night road trip. Katelyn said, "Mom, I miss our road trips. This is so much fun! I'm so glad we had this time alone together." Those words melted her mom's heart.

As soon as Katelyn made it back to college, it was time to start softball's spring season. Spring season in college softball is the most important part of the year. Katelyn once again had a disappointment. She worked hard but did not make the varsity team. She was heartbroken. She felt like a failure and that she was not "good enough." Once again I received a phone call from a broken-hearted little girl on the other end. My heart broke for her because I knew how badly she wanted this. She was devastated. She told me, "Mom, I can't keep working this hard with no reward. I'm afraid my health can't handle it. The workouts are too much for me if I'm not going to make the team." As I sat there, I just listened. She just needed to hear my voice and know that I was there listening. How many times do we come to Jesus like that? Many times I go to Jesus in prayer because I know He is listening to my broken heart. Sometimes we just need His comfort.

Never Will I Leave Thee...

"The Lord is a refuge for the oppressed, a stronghold in times of trouble. Those who know your name trust in you, for you, Lord, have never forsaken those who seek you" (Psalm 9:9–10).

Katelyn was appointed to play on the junior varsity team. During this meeting with Coach, he asked her to be the team's SAAC for the following season. Each varsity team at the college has a representative. This is the SAAC. She would be the one who takes care of all the team's meetings with the athletic director and the coaches. If anyone on the team had issues, they would take it to Katelyn, and she would present it to the coaches or the athletic director. She was the only one on the team who could contact the athletic director directly. This was a big honor. It showed that the coaches highly respected Katelyn and trusted her with this opportunity. She was honored to be appointed to this position but was very disappointed to not make the varsity team.

I encouraged her by telling her it was a way that she could grow in the collegiate program. Katelyn was talented enough to pitch for varsity, but for some reason, the coaches were not giving her the opportunity. I told her this, too, should pass. We would adjust and adapt once again. To some people, this disappointment over softball would be stupid. But to Katelyn, softball was her life. This situation was devastating to her. She battled extra hard to get this opportunity only to be let down again. When anyone told her she couldn't do something, that moved her to work harder. That is exactly what this did. She was determined to overcome it. She spent any extra time she had at the field or in the batting cages practicing. Her main goal was to play on the varsity team, and she was determined to make it happen.

During this time, Katelyn was getting other wonderful opportunities. As I said, God will bless you with rewards if you are loyal to Him. Katelyn is one of His loyal warriors. It seemed like her softball doors were being shut for this season, but God was opening different doors.

Katelyn was approached by three of her professors to be their teacher's assistant for the following fall. This would be for her sophomore year. This was a big honor as well! The three classes were Intro to Biology lecture, Intro to Biology Lab, and Anatomy and Physiology II Lab. Three of the hardest classes at school. She accepted all three of the offers. She was shocked but excited about this opportunity. She knew it would look good on her physician's assistant application.

I know she did not make the varsity team and that was her heart, but He was making her excel. In her sophomore year, she was already a teacher's assistant for three courses, plus softball SAAC and an FCA leader. She continued to touch lives. God was moving!

"And we know that in all things God works for the good of those who love him, who have been called according to his purpose" (Romans 8:28).

There was no doubt in my mind that God put Katelyn at this college for a purpose. I saw her mature so much in her first year. My baby was no longer a child who depended on her mom. She was learning to navigate on her own. She was also comforted knowing that Shaelyn lived only twenty minutes from her. On weekends or evenings, they would get together and have some sister time. It made me feel more comfortable that they were both in St. Louis together. Katelyn looked up to her sister, and I was thankful they could have adult talks when she needed them. It was healing for both of my girls.

Softball conference time came, and all the athletes were allowed to travel to the conference tournament. Katelyn was very excited because she wanted to support her team! Everyone on the team got to dress for the games too. Before the first game began, the team lined up on the first baseline for the national anthem and team awards. Katelyn said she knew she wouldn't get an award because she wasn't on varsity, but it was exciting to be included in the whole process. As they stood there during the announcements, Katelyn's name was called. She said she just stood there looking around, and her teammates were yelling for her to walk out on the field. She couldn't believe they had called her name! Katelyn walked out to Coach, and he was standing there and greeting her with a great big smile! She won the Academic All-American and Championship of Character Awards for her spring softball season. Katelyn said she stood there hugging the coach and crying. God once again showed up for His warrior.

The conference marked Katelyn's end of her freshman year at Missouri Baptist. She was moving home for the summer. Time was flying by. I was excited to have her home. I missed her this past year. As I said before, she and I have a close connection. I couldn't wait to have her home for the next two months.

As I looked back at her freshman year of college, I knew softball was rough, but I saw such maturity in her. I, at one time, told Shane that if Katelyn could move away to college and not cry to come home, anyone could! I can't express how proud I am of her. She set her goals and accomplished them.

During the summer, I spent a lot of time catching Katelyn as she practiced pitching. She worked hard to improve for her fall softball season. Katelyn was very determined to make her sophomore year a new start in her collegiate softball career. She was not giving up on the sport that she loved easily.

In the past eighteen years, I spent many hours catching my kids as they practiced pitching. Shaelyn, Katelyn, and Chance all were pitchers. I have always enjoyed catching. I loved watching them improve and grow in their pitching power and technique. It was very rewarding for them and me to watch them grow in the sport they loved. Catching Chance was very challenging for me. Catching a small baseball is very different from catching a large yellow softball. Anytime the kids asked me to catch them, I never hesitated. I knew that this special time was short and my kids would not be playing the sport they loved forever.

Katelyn was also busy giving her testimony throughout the summer. She once again shared at church camps and churches. Katelyn didn't realize, but she shared her testimony as she gave softball lessons to her little athletes too. I loved watching those little girls as they looked up to Katelyn when she was instructing them. They all loved her. Katelyn's gentleness and positive attitude were a testimony to them. Katelyn is compassionate, and young athletes pick up on that attribute. Athletes of all ages need a godly influence to show them they can play the sport they love through Christ.

"I can do all things through Christ who gives me strength" (Philippians 4:13).

One big part of Katelyn's life that I have failed to mention in the past was a young man named Wyatt Kennedy. Katelyn met Wyatt when Shaelyn was dating his best friend in high school. She thought Wyatt was the cutest thing she had ever seen. Katelyn was probably in sixth grade when she first met Wyatt. Fast forward to her freshman year in high school. Wyatt no longer looked at Katelyn like a little girl. He asked Katelyn to homecoming and has been in her life ever since. Katelyn was worried about a long-distance relationship when she left for college. I told her that if it were meant to be, God would make it work. So far, it looks like Wyatt is here to stay. He made that clear when he gave Katelyn a "promise ring" on their fifth anniversary.

It was time for Katelyn to move back to Missouri Baptist to start her sophomore year of college. She worked hard all summer to prepare for her fall season. She knew she had to earn her position on the team. I prayed all summer for a new start for Katelyn and her collegiate softball career. Over the summer Missouri Baptist hosted a softball camp, which allowed Katelyn to meet her new softball coach. She was staying positive but was not 100 percent sure about the coach. When you've played softball for years and have different coaches, you learn to have discernment.

While Katelyn was home, we had different opportunities to have heart-to-heart talks. She was excited and humbled by the new opportunities she was blessed with for the upcoming sophomore year. She was still concerned about her upcoming softball season. She told me that she could not physically and mentally deal with what she had dealt with the previous year. The idea of her feeling not worthy and not enough in softball just broke my heart. The Lord tells us we are enough! No man has the power to define us. God made us perfect in His sight.

"For you created my inner being; you knit me together in my mother's womb. I praise you because I am fearfully and wonderfully made; your works are wonderful, I know that full well" (Psalm 139:13–14).

The health challenges that she endured her whole life and overcame made it hard for me to not give in and get upset. I believed my job as her mom was to pray and believe God knows her heart and will bless her. I have learned through the years that sometimes what we think we need, God knows better. He blesses us in ways we sometimes don't understand.

"I the Lord search the heart and examine the mind, to reward each person according to their conduct, according to what their deeds deserve" (Jeremiah 17:10).

As we dropped our baby off for yet another year of college, I looked at her beautiful smiling face and began to feel myself well up with tears. I was so proud of her and the young woman she was becoming. They were tears of happiness and gratefulness for what God has done for us. Katelyn was turning twenty in two weeks, and our journey here became refreshed in my mind. The whole drive home, God was reminding me of our journey to this point in life. The baby Satan tried so hard to kill in my womb was changing people's lives. It's so clear to me why Satan wanted to end her life. He feels threatened by her. Satan knows the big picture of what God has planned for her and the lives she is going to change with her testimony. The whole journey was God's divine plan for all of our lives. Her miracles have made us stronger in Christ and have shown us that only through Christ could we have survived these trials and hardships. I've learned you cannot advance the purpose of God without suffering.

> Be alert and of sober mind. Your enemy the devil prowls around like a roaring lion looking for someone to devour. Resist him, standing firm in the faith, because you know that the family of believers throughout the world is undergoing the same kind of sufferings. And the God of all grace, who called you to his eternal glory in Christ, after you have suffered a little while, will himself restore you and make you strong, firm, and steadfast. To him be the power forever and ever. Amen.
>
> 1 Peter 5:8–11

CHAPTER 28: "RAISE A HALLELUJAH" —BETHEL MUSIC

"Whether you turn to the right or to the left, your ears will hear a voice behind you saying, 'This is the way; walk in it'" (Isaiah 30:21).

After Katelyn left for college and Chance started his senior year of high school, I had time to myself. Every morning, I took my devotionals and Bible out to our front porch. I had a little sitting area set up just for me to pray and seek God's guidance. This was my favorite time of the day. I also had opportunities to travel and listen to some wonderful preachers. I felt my spiritual life growing.

One day in my beauty shop, Laura June, my client who was the final push for me to start my book, came in for a haircut. She had a stroke in the previous months. I was told by her husband that she was a miracle. The doctors told them the type of stroke she had no one typically recovered from it. By God's grace, she was gaining strength and recovering. I was so happy and blessed to see her walk through my beauty shop door. We had a nice visit as I was cutting her hair. When I finished, her husband looked at me and said, "How is the book coming along?" I turned and looked at her, and she smiled her beautiful smile at me, and I instantly felt the Spirit of the Lord all over me! I said, "It's not. I have been busy all summer." Instantly I felt conviction. I let Satan distract me from God's plan. Once again God had to shake me and get my focus back on glorifying Him in His book.

"I will instruct you and teach you in the way you should go; I will counsel you with my loving eye on you" (Psalm 32:8).

On this journey, God has guided my book the whole way. There is no way I could have done this without Him. Just like putting that wonderful woman in my life, God put so many Spirit-filled people in my life to inspire me. God used people who were clueless about how God was using them. I had clients who would come in and say inspirational things to me, and I'd say, "Hold on. I have to write that down. It's going in my book!"

We are God's church. My clients all know that you will hear about Jesus when you sit in my beauty shop chair. Many times I'd say, "Whew! We just had church!" I loved this! I believe my beauty shop is my way of sharing God's love with everyone who enters. I am a witness that our family's testimony touches many lives, not only in my beauty shop but in the people my clients share the testimony with.

"For we are co-workers in God's service; you are God's field, God's building" (1 Corinthians 3:9).

God continued to give me insight for my book during the night hours, and I continued to type it out. I started carrying my notebook around because God abundantly gave me words for my book. I had many customers ask, "How many chapters will be in your book? What's the ending of your book?" I would always respond with, "I have no clue. God is writing this book. I'm just the vessel He is using to type it out." That is exactly how I see it. I will type and not realize what I have typed. I will reread it and think, *Wow! I just typed that! Thank You, Jesus!* It was so exciting to see it all come together.

"The Lord makes firm the steps of the one who delights in him; though he may stumble, he will not fall, for the Lord upholds him with his hand" (Psalm 37:23–24).

It took me to the final chapters of my book to understand how important my little beauty shop was on this journey. God placed the right people at the right time for me. When I needed a little encouragement, God placed the client to encourage me. When I needed a little shove to get me back on track with the book, God placed the right customer to give me a little shove to get me started again. God even blessed me with people who, without hesitation, agreed to read my book and edit it for me. Everywhere I looked, God was opening doors to get this important testimonial book published.

I caught myself telling people that I couldn't believe how God was using me to write a book. I always said, "I am not a writer! I don't even read books!" As time went on, I was convicted. Because the truth is I am a writer through Christ. God gave me this awesome story to write and tell of what He did for us and what He can do for others.

My client Laura June, who just had a stroke, had a setback and was in the hospital. As soon as I heard this, I knew in my spirit I had to go see her and pray for her. That was the least I could do for her after her spiritual influence on me and my book. I felt such a spiritual bond with her. I was told they probably wouldn't let me in the hospital room because of the contagious nature of the illness. I just happened to have a doctor's appointment in the same hospital that week. Coincidence? I think not. After I finished my appointment, I prayed, "God, if I am to go and pray with her, they will let me in the room." As I drove over to the entrance, I felt the urgency to pray for her. I entered the hospital and went toward her room. I knew God placed me there for a purpose. The nurse stopped me and asked if I was family. I said, "No, I'm her hairdresser!" The nurse looked at me unamused. I proceeded to tell her that I was there to pray for her. The Lord told me to come and anoint her. I talk a lot when it comes to witnessing. I proceeded to tell her how Laura June helped me with my book and the whole story. During this time, another nurse came around the corner and heard the conversation. She said, "You realize her illness is very contagious?" I told her, "Yes, but I am supposed to pray for her." The nurse smiled and said, "Come on, let's get you equipped to go in." I had to put on a gown, mask, and gloves to enter the room. As I entered the room, Laura June saw me. Even though she felt terrible, she still had a big smile for me. I instantly felt the Holy Spirit and began to tear up. I went over to her, and she said, "What are you doing here? They let you in?" Through my tears, I replied, "Yes, God told me to come and anoint you. You have done so much for me; it's the least I can do for you." The nurse looked at her, and her right arm was purple, swollen, and freezing. The nurse replied, "I have to go call the doctor; something is not right with her arm." The nurse left the room. Laura June looked at me and said, "I feel so bad. I am ready for the Lord to take me." I said, "Let's anoint and pray. We will let God lead us." As I began to pray, the Lord kept giving me the word "peace." I began to pray "peace" over Laura June and "healing." As I stood there holding her right hand and praying, I felt warmth enter her hand. I looked, and the purple was leaving, and it was starting to turn a reddish-pink color. After we finished praying, Laura June thanked me over and over again. I said, "No, thank you for being the spiritual advisor that I needed." I told her I was committed to getting the book finished so she could read it since she was a big part of getting it written. Two days later, she was transferred to a hospital closer to home, and her health was improving. Laura witnessed multiple health setbacks. Her family members would tell me that no matter how she felt, she never missed an opportunity to witness at the hospitals or nursing

Never Will I Leave Thee...

homes. This did not surprise me because of her strong faith. I later found out that Laura loved to read books. I felt this was fitting for the Lord to use her as the final witness to convince me to write His book. Three months after I prayed with her in the hospital, she went to be with our Lord and Savior. Laura passed away during Holy Week, which was so fitting for her with her amazing faith in Jesus Christ. I am blessed to have had the opportunity to pray with her. It was healing for me, and I pray it was healing for her as well.

When we listen and obey God as He leads us, we will see miraculous things. I am learning to "go" when God says, "Go!" Praying for Laura June was a reward to be able to help someone so special to me. "The Lord makes firm the steps of the one who delights in him; though he may stumble, he will not fall, for the Lord upholds him with his hand" (Psalm 37:23–24).

One day I called Katelyn about a church that wanted her to set up a date and time to speak. Katelyn responded, "Mom, why aren't you giving your testimony? You have as big of a testimony as I do! Where is your boldness?" Wow, I never thought of that! God's power is when we speak. When Katelyn speaks her testimony, she shows God's power. I need to declare God's will to open doors with my mouth and not just my hands. After that comment, it was on my mind. I'm thinking God used her to plant a seed of what may be coming next in my future.

"The man who saw it has given testimony, and his testimony is true. He knows that he tells the truth, and he testifies so that you also may believe" (John 19:35).

I believe everything has a purpose and nothing is a coincidence. God always has perfect timing. I have been working on my book for exactly one year now. This year, God has placed multiple revelations in front of me. I caught myself many times saying or thinking, *Why is this book taking so long?* I thought I would have it written in a couple of months. This is "God's" book, and it is being written in His timing, not mine. As I am writing it, He is making it clear why His timing is perfect. The experiences He has placed before me this past year are making me into the author that He has planned for me.

"In their hearts, humans plan their course, but the Lord establishes their steps" (Proverbs 16:9).

I am excited to see how God uses this book for power and energy to praise Him. As I said before, I believe everything happens for a reason. Numbers have meanings in the Bible; it's called biblical numerology. As I wrote chapter 28, I felt in my spirit to look up what twenty-eight means in the Bible. The Hebrew meaning of twenty-eight is "power" and "energy" in spoken words. Hallelujah appears twenty-eight times, and the phrase "The Lamb," which means Jesus Christ, occurs twenty-eight times.

I believe that sums up this chapter. I'm saying hallelujah to Jesus Christ for the power and energy in the spoken words in my book. I'm praising God for the trials and tribulations to get to this point in our lives. I'm saying hallelujah for the unknown spoken words of my clients who have helped me to get here. It has all happened in God's timing.

"Consider it pure joy, my brothers and sisters, whenever you face trials of many kinds, because you know that the testing of your faith produces perseverance. Let perseverance finish its work so that you may be mature and complete, not lacking anything" (James 1:2–4).

Chapter 29: "God Really Loves Us"
—Crowder

Shortly after Katelyn started her sophomore year at college, she had to return to Chicago for a pacemaker check-up. Once a year she has to get a release from Dr. Ovadia to be able to play softball. I tried to make this long trip into a fun trip. Our day usually consisted of different places to eat and Katelyn's favorite, shopping. Katelyn loves to shop!

Katelyn was still wondering about her career path. She was anxious to see her doctor and ask him questions about different medical careers. Katelyn wanted to major in some type of medical career but didn't want to go to school for ten or twelve years. He means a lot to Katelyn, and she values his opinion.

Shane, at one time, told me in private that he believed Katelyn would be a well-known Christian speaker. He believes that when my book launches, she will be busy traveling and speaking. I've always said that she would be a world-known female evangelist. We can voice our opinions, but only God knows how He is going to use this special young lady to continue to touch people's lives. The Lord gives us this confidence. This is what He said:

> You are the light of the world. A town built on a hill cannot be hidden. Neither do people light a lamp and put it under a bowl. Instead, they put it on its stand, and it gives light to everyone in the house. In the same

way, let your light shine before others, so that they may see your good deeds and glorify your father in heaven.

Matthew 5:14–16

This five-hour trip gave Katelyn and me an opportunity to talk about college. I could sense she had a lot on her mind. She proceeded to tell me how overwhelmed she felt with everything. Katelyn was carrying a full load of classes, softball workouts and practices, softball SAAC, three teacher assistant jobs, and being an FCA leader. Somewhere in her day, she had to find time to eat, study, and sleep.

Katelyn has always been one of those very organized kids. All through high school, she was the leader of her class. The teachers knew that if they wanted something done and finished the correct way, they had to put Katelyn in charge. She doesn't like attention brought to her, but she likes things done the correct way. With this being said, every obligation she has in college, she puts pride in it and makes sure it is done promptly and correctly. To succeed in this manner, Katelyn puts a lot of pressure on herself.

Katelyn told me there was not enough of her to go around. Some of her obligations were being put on the back of her list, and it was upsetting her. The one obligation she did not have enough time for was her FCA leadership role. She was upset about it because she knew God put her in that leadership role for a reason. Once again, I let her talk and cry while I sat back and listened. I was waiting for God to guide me with the comforting words she needed. But for now, I was just there to listen.

As we entered Dr. Ovadia's office, he was standing there waiting for us with his usual big smile. He is always so excited to see Katelyn. My girl holds a special place in his heart. He has seen more miracles in her life than any of his other heart patients in thirty-five years. No matter who you are, those miracles will always be in your heart and mind. Jesus tells us, "'Unless you people see signs and wonders,' Jesus told him, 'you will never believe'" (John 4:48).

Dr. Ovadia interrogated her pacemaker. Katelyn told him she felt the best she had ever felt. Physically, Katelyn looked so healthy. He was pleased with Katelyn's overall health. Her pacemaker did not have any extra battery usage since our last visit, which meant no lead breaks. This does not happen very often. He told her everything looked great, and she was released to play softball for her sophomore season!

As Katelyn conversed with her doctor, I sat there watching her and remembering how these visits used to be. I believe this was one of the easiest appointments in twenty years. I have been the one who has taken her to all her doctor's appointments, from emergency visits to routine visits, plus the near-death experiences and the trauma of it all. I can't even begin to add up the miles we have traveled together. I was enjoying sitting here watching her converse with her doctor. This moment made me the happiest and most blessed mother. To be honest, I knew God was taking care of her. Katelyn looks the healthiest physically she has in her entire life. I believe God is healing her body. I cherish every moment that God allows me to have with this precious child of mine.

"Children are a heritage from the Lord, offspring a reward from him" (Psalm 127:3).

Dr. Ovadia talked to Katelyn about her academic goals. He asked her, "Do you realize how many little kids' lives you could change being a pediatric cardiology physician? Not only are you intelligent, but you also have your own experience as a heart patient. Not many doctors have the advantages you do. Most doctors just have the intelligence, but you have been through it all. You know firsthand what it is like to be a cardiology patient." Katelyn said, "Yes, but I don't know if I want to go to school for ten or twelve years." Dr. Ovadia responded, "Don't limit yourself. You are living proof that you can do anything you set your mind to." Katelyn said, "I know. I am considering it." He said, "Just think of the little children's lives you will impact."

Katelyn needed to hear his opinion on what he thought her capabilities were.

He then asked Katelyn, "Are you still dating Wyatt?" With a big smile, Katelyn responded, "Yes!" Dr. Ovadia said, "Does Wyatt realize what he has? He probably thinks he has a gem, but he has something golden!" Katelyn and I laughed. I was not expecting that response. As I said, he never ceased to amaze us with each visit.

Katelyn assured Dr. O that she would consider pediatric cardiology. We said our goodbyes and started our trip back to college. Once again our doctor's appointment turned into two hours, and only about twenty minutes was a pacemaker exam. I do have to admit we have the most considerate and best cardiologist anyone could be blessed with. I thank God for putting Dr. Ovadia in our lives.

We stopped for dinner, and Katelyn began to talk about the visit. She said, "Mom, I'm never scared at the appointments anymore. I am confident in who I am, and I know that God will take care of me. I used to be so scared. I remember as a little girl I thought I was going to die when the doctors would shut my pacemaker off. It was the worst feeling ever. But today, it didn't bother me. I'm going to be just fine." I remember the visits all too well too. Very frightening to watch the doctors control her life with a computer. They could give her life, or they could take it away. We both know where our strength comes from.

"God is our refuge and strength, an ever-present help in trouble" (Psalm 46:1).

Katelyn told me that Dr. O was her confirmation that she was to be a pediatric cardiology physician's assistant. She can get this degree in six and a half years and possibly five years. She said she wanted to take care of babies just like her. Katelyn believed she could give moms support so that their babies have a chance. I encouraged her and told her that this would be a wonderful witnessing job. Her testimony and godly witness needed to be heard by struggling mothers who had no hope. I remember when I was in their shoes. The only difference was I had hope in Christ. Seeing Christ in Katelyn will be the evidence they need to have faith in God for their sick babies. I believe God laid it on Katelyn's heart, and He will direct her path. After Katelyn finished talking about her career direction, we started talking about softball. "Trust in the Lord with all your heart and lean not on your own understanding; in all your ways submit to him, and he will make your paths straight" (Proverbs 3:5–6). Little did I know, but softball once again was not starting as well as she had hoped. She told me that it was a repeat of last year. The only difference was she did not have Coach A to rely on. She said, "I'm pouring my heart and soul out for softball, and the coach does not even give me the time of day. He could care less about my work ethic and determination to play." To hear this broke my heart. I know Katelyn, and she is by far the hardest worker I have ever coached. She never complains and is the first to volunteer for extra practice. I also know the hard work she put forth this summer. I was the one catching her as she pitched. I was feeling the hurt she was feeling.

As Katelyn was explaining the softball situation to me, things were not adding up. For instance, Katelyn had the highest batting average on our travel team. She was our third batter and led our team in home runs. Katelyn said at their first fall practice the coach let her hit. Her first at-bat and her first pitch she hit the ball to the fence. He never let her hit after that. Then she was only allowed to pitch to four batters. Then he'd take her out. It didn't matter if it was at practice or a game. I had never heard of anything this crazy before. I told her to keep working hard and that she might just have to have a meeting with him. She was so upset, and I understood her frustration.

Katelyn then said, "Mom, softball is distracting me from my other responsibilities. I am so upset about softball and trying to practice extra to prove myself to the coach that I don't have time to spend on FCA. I'm ashamed, and I don't feel as if I am a good leader. I don't study as I should, and I am not attending meetings. I don't have enough time for everything. I'm so stressed. I'm grouchy all the time. I cry at the drop of a hat, and I am miserable. What should I do?" That was a loaded question. I thought, *Please, God help me with wise words*. I said, "Well, what's the number one thing we know to do in times of struggle?" Katelyn replied, "Pray." I said, "You are absolutely correct. God wants us to come to Him with all our concerns. Big or small, they all matter to God." We sat in the restaurant and prayed. I then told her, "God has this! God placed you at Missouri Baptist for a reason. He wants you there, and He will handle all your concerns. He will lead you in the right direction for softball, and He will make the paths straight for your other obligations. Do not give up or lose hope. God has big plans for you." After we had our talk and prayer, I could see the relief on her face. When we come to God, He gives us peace and comfort.

"Now may the Lord of peace himself give you peace at all times and in every way. The Lord be with all of you" (2 Thessalonians 3:16).

We decided our next best thing to do before we started back to college was to go to the mall. We figured a little shopping therapy was in order. Shopping always makes Katelyn feel better. We went to one of her favorite shopping malls and had time to take our minds off college and softball for a short time. She and I always enjoy our time together. No matter what she and I have by way of struggles, we can always find a way to comfort one another. It is a very special bond we cherish.

After I dropped Katelyn off at college, I spent the rest of my drive home listening to praise and worship songs and praying. I could not wrap my mind around the softball situation. I couldn't understand why the coach would not even allow her to prove herself to him. In a couple of days, Katelyn was having a softball tournament, and I assured her I would be there to support her. I love watching my kids play their sports. Katelyn told me, "Mom, don't waste your time and money. He's not going to play me." I said, "You never know! Be positive, and don't speak negatively." Katelyn responded, "I'm not speaking negatively, Mom. I'm just speaking the truth."

I traveled to Missouri to watch Katelyn play in her softball tournament. Out of six games, she pitched four innings and was not in the batting lineup. During this day, I saw multiple home runs hit off of one pitcher. This pitcher was never pulled. Multiple strikeouts from multiple players, and Katelyn never saw the batting lineup. Those were just a few situations that, as a coach myself, I saw were not logical. You don't pay scholarships to twenty-eight athletes and only play eleven. I knew deep down there was more to Katelyn not playing. Situations were not adding up. Then to see the hurt on my baby's face, knowing how much she has poured her heart and soul into this game that she loves. I once again encouraged her even though my flesh wanted to take care of the situation myself. Mama

Bear wanted to come out! I knew I had to hand this over to God. It was His battle, not ours.

After the tournament, I said my goodbyes to my sad and once again defeated baby and headed home. All the way home I prayed and worshiped God. I asked for His guidance in this situation. I knew He had a bigger plan. But for the life of me, I could not figure it out. All I knew was the pain in Katelyn's heart was tearing me up. She worked too hard to be treated with this disrespect. "'For my thoughts are not your thoughts, neither are your ways my ways,' declares the Lord. 'As the heavens are higher than the earth, so are my ways higher than your ways and my thoughts than your thoughts'" (Isaiah 55:8–9).

Once again after I got home, I received a phone call from a very heartbroken little girl. She had time to get to the dorms and think for a little bit before she called me. Katelyn is a very bright individual. She always processes things thoroughly. We used to joke when she was little that she would be an attorney. I never knew a child who could ask the same question in fifty different ways. She would wear you down asking the same question. My friend told me, "Katelyn is going to be an attorney, and they would just plead guilty to get her to shut up and leave them alone!" She never jumped to conclusions; she would process it over and over before she would bring up the situation. As she cried on the other end of the phone, I was quietly praying on my end. I was expecting the call. My prayer time on the drive home helped me to prepare for her broken-hearted phone call.

I know to most people this situation compared to what we had already been through with her health was no big deal. But to Katelyn, it was a very big deal. I believe that softball was her way of helping her cope with her health. Softball was the one thing that she knew would always be there in the natural to help her push through her health situations. When Satan told her she couldn't go back to softball, God would step in and yet perform another miracle. Softball helped her in multiple ways. It gave her confidence, which encouraged her to speak to thousands of people about her miracles from God. It helped her with determination to succeed in whatever she did. It showed her that no matter what doctors would tell us about her health, God would step in on her behalf. Most importantly, it strengthened her faith in Jesus Christ. God used softball to open doors that would not have been opened without this awesome sport. Katelyn used her softball platform to touch thousands of lives with her testimony. So yes, softball is very important to Katelyn.

> As for me, I will always have hope; I will praise you more and more. My mouth will tell of your righteous deeds, of your saving acts all day long—though I know not how to relate them all. I will come and proclaim your mighty acts, Sovereign Lord; I will proclaim your righteous deeds, yours alone. Since my youth, God, you have taught me, and to this day I declare your marvelous deeds.
>
> Psalm 71:14–17

"Mom, I just can't do this anymore. I can't keep putting myself through this stress. I've prayed, but God hasn't given me any answers. I don't know what to do. I feel like it is pulling me away from God. All I know is I'm miserable. I've decided I am going to go to Coach and let him get to know me personally. He needs to know where my heart is and what all I have worked through to get to this point in my life. He needs to know!" Katelyn told me through her tears. I confirmed with her I thought that was a great idea. I believed he did not know her and her heart. I thought if he got to know her and what she had overcome in her life, he would maybe have a change of heart and at least give her a chance. She wasn't asking for the coach to give her special attention; she just wanted a fair chance to prove herself.

"But in your hearts revere Christ as Lord. Always be prepared to give an answer to everyone who asks you to give the reason for the hope that you have. But do this with gentleness and respect" (1 Peter 3:15).

I was very proud of Katelyn for taking the initiative to talk to her coach. I did not know anyone who could hear her story and not want to give her a chance. As a coach, if I had an athlete come to me and pour her heart out, I would allow her to prove herself. All I could do was wait for her call after her meeting and trust that God was in control.

"In the same way, let your light shine before others, that they may see your good deeds and glorify your Father in heaven" (Matthew 5:16).

Never Will I Leave Thee...

Chapter 30: "Too Good Not to Believe" —Brandon Lake

I woke up out of a deep sleep crying with my chest hurting and my heart pounding. I looked over at the alarm clock, and it read 3:10 a.m. I continued to weep with my heart hurting. I felt like my heart was broken. I knew it was God communicating once again to me in my spirit. As I lay in bed weeping, God was speaking so many things to me. Finally, I got up and grabbed my red notebook to write all these words down. God was saying multiple words; it was a rapid-fire moment with provision.

"For God does speak—now one way, now another—though no one perceives it. In a dream, in a vision of the nights, when deep sleep falls on people as they slumber in their beds" (Job 33:14–15).

I sat in the kitchen writing these words and thinking to myself, *God, You are so good and faithful! Thank You for blessing me with this opportunity to glorify You!* These words were almost too good to believe. I was writing and weeping at the same time. I had never felt this before. God spoke to me at night for my book, but this was a different visitation from the Lord. I sat there writing, weeping, and giving God my gratitude.

The morning before this incident, Katelyn called after she met with her coach. Shane and I put Katelyn on the intercom so we could both hear her. Through her tears, she proceeded to tell us about her meeting. "Mom, Dad, the meeting did not go so well. First of all, I introduced myself because he seemed to not even know who I was. I told the coach a little about my history with my heart and all the obstacles I had overcome to play softball. I felt he needed to hear this from me. He sat there just looking right through me. No expression or compassion was expressed at all. He told me that I would probably never pitch for him. He said that I could be his bullpen pitching coach or a manager. I told him that I wasn't a pitching coach. I was an athlete! I said I did not go through all I have to be a bullpen pitching coach. I am getting a good scholarship to play here. I don't understand why I am not playing. I pitch just as well as the other pitchers that we have on the team, but you have not allowed me to prove myself to you. You never take the time to watch me!" Shane and I sat there with big tears in our eyes hearing the hurt in Katelyn's voice.

Katelyn said, "I told him I was a utility player and could play another position if I wasn't going to pitch. He told me he had plenty of other players for the other positions. I told him about my batting average and home runs. I asked him why I couldn't hit. He just said I wouldn't hit without any explanation. I told him I would work extra hard for an opportunity to prove myself, and he told me it wouldn't matter. The coach was cold and expressionless. He had no compassion toward me. He said someone told him that I wear a chest protector on the field. I told him I did because of my pacemaker. Mom and Dad, I don't see why wearing a chest protector matters." After Katelyn told us this information, Shane and I knew the reason for her not playing. It was exactly what we anticipated and prayed wouldn't happen. We couldn't understand how a coach at a Christian university could be so heartless toward one of his athletes. Shane and I knew beyond his cold heart God had a bigger plan.

"The Lord is close to the brokenhearted and saves those who are crushed in spirit" (Psalm 34:18).

She said, "He told me that my pitching speed was not fast enough, and he was afraid I'd get hurt on the field. I told him that I learned to move the ball when I was eight years old around the bat to protect myself. I may not be the fastest pitcher, but I can move the ball. The coaches who recruited me knew this. Why else would they have given me such a big scholarship to play for them?" Ever since Katelyn was eight years old, she learned to move the ball around the bat and keep the batters guessing so no balls would come back at her on the mound. It was a way that she learned to adjust to playing at a competitive level. She didn't throw super fast, but she could control her pitches. With pitch control, she could command, for the most part, where the ball would be hit on the field. When there is a will, there is a way, and Katelyn had the will to succeed.

As Katelyn cried to Shane and me, she said her coach told her that if she wanted to be a manager, he would gladly "red shirt" her so she could continue to get her softball scholarship. Needless to say, she was completely devastated. She felt rejected and unworthy to be called a collegiate softball player. Her dreams were shattered in a few hours. To say the least, Shane and I were devastated as well. When she told me this, I reminded her that no man defines her. Through Christ, she was made perfect in His sight, and she is fearfully and wonderfully made. I told her it was obvious that the coach needed Jesus to soften his heart. I knew we needed to pray for him, but my natural feelings wanted to contact the college for discrimination. I know that we do not battle against flesh and blood but against the principalities of Satan. I knew this was spiritual warfare. Satan was trying to destroy Katelyn's confidence because he knew that was her weakness. God was using her in miraculous ways to reach multitudes of lost souls through softball, and Satan's focus was to try and destroy her through the sport she loved. I told her this battle was not over with her coach because God always has the final say! He would hear her complete story, and it would humble him!

Jesus said, "See that you do not despise one of these little ones. For I tell you that their angels in heaven always see the face of my Father in heaven" (Matthew 18:10).

Katelyn said, "So many times in my life, I have been threatened to have the one thing in my life that I love to be taken away from me. I worked and overcame that threat. Now, I am what I worked hard to accomplish, and it is being taken away from me. There is nothing I can do to change it. This time, it is out of my hands. What will I do without softball? I feel like my life is crashing down around me." At this point and time, Katelyn's situation was devastating to her, but God had a plan.

> Not only so, but we also glory in our sufferings, because we know that suffering produces perseverance; perseverance, character; and character, hope. And hope does not put us to shame, because God's love has been poured out into our hearts through the Holy Spirit, who has been given to us.
>
> Romans 5:3–5

After we got off the phone with Katelyn, Shane and I talked about the conversation. The coach did not say it, but our feelings were that he was not playing Katelyn because she was considered a liability with her heart condition. Nobody said those words, but it was easy to read between the lines. Shane and I feared this day would come but never believed it would. Then it happened!

I wanted to make sure that Katelyn did not feel defeated. In times like these, it's hard to see the bright side. Like in our past, God always makes good out of bad. I know my God can do more, and He does. I texted Katelyn to check on her and reassure her that Shane and I were always here and supported her in any way she needed.

"Now to him who can do immeasurably more than all we ask or imagine, according to his power that is at work within us, to him be glory in the church and in Christ Jesus throughout all generations, forever and ever! Amen" (Ephesians 3:20–21).

That week seemed so long. I couldn't wait for Friday to get here because Katelyn was coming home. It was only Monday when all this happened. That week, God was working with Katelyn at college and me here at home. God was opening doors for Katelyn and giving me a lot of revelations for my book. I was walking around with my red notebook in and out of the beauty shop. God was rapidly firing information for my book! I told one of my very special clients what was going on. She and Shane were the only two that knew what God was doing. As I was telling her, she was consumed with the Spirit and began to cry. She said, "I feel God all over that word!" It was very spiritual. I believed the word God gave me on Monday at 3:10 a.m. was a confirmation from God of Katelyn's future. He was moving amazingly in Katelyn and my life. This week was a turning point for both of us. I love how God shows up and shows off!

Katelyn called and told me that she had so much to tell me when she got home. I had not told her about the visitation from the Lord on Monday night. It was for sure something that I needed to tell her in person. I prayed the blood of Jesus Christ over my family continually that week. I know when God is moving, Satan is too! I was not about to let Satan try to destroy how God was blessing us. God's blood would fill any crack that might be open for Satan to try and sneak in.

"They triumphed over him by the blood of the Lamb and by the word of their testimony; they did not love their lives so much as to shrink from death" (Revelation 12:11).

When Katelyn got home, she and I sat in the kitchen and had a very emotional talk. We were having church! The presence of the Lord was all over us! She proceeded to tell me about her week. Katelyn told me she talked with one of the other FCA leaders, whom she respects as a spiritual advisor. He helped make some of her paths straight with softball through Christ. She had the opportunity to meet the chapel pastor at Missouri Baptist while she was talking with the FCA leader. The leader introduced Katelyn to the pastor and gave him a little background about Katelyn. The pastor was very interested in Katelyn and asked to meet with her to get to know her story better. Katelyn was so excited about meeting the pastor. She was a sophomore and had never met the pastor. She told me, "Mom, don't you think that meeting was a little strange? The pastor has never said a word to me the whole time that I've been here. Now he wants to meet with me?" I did not think it was strange at all. I knew the answer to this. God was working!

Katelyn's pitching coach, Ryan, traveled two hours to take her out for supper and to comfort her. Katelyn and Ryan have a wonderful bond, and when she hurts, he hurts too. He gave her insight from a college coach's view on the news she received from her coach. This helped open her eyes from a coach's perspective. God was using spiritual advice and also friendship insights to comfort Katelyn through this hard time in her life. As she was telling me all this, I could see God working in amazing ways.

During this week, Katelyn also met with her advisor. She told her advisor what was going on with softball. Her advisor told her if she didn't have to work around softball, she could take a couple of extra classes and graduate one year early. Katelyn could get a major in biomedical sciences and a minor in medical technology in three short years! She could then apply for physician assistant school one year early. How amazing is this? God was taking care of His warrior.

I let Katelyn tell me about her week and pour her heart out to me. She and I both needed this for our healing. As she was talking, I could see how God was restoring her through this trauma. Katelyn's strength surpasses anyone that I know. It brought to mind once again when the Lord said, "Never will I leave thee, and never will I forsake thee!" God has never left us. He has always been by our side through everything Satan has thrown our way.

I remember when there were times we had struggles. I'd be praying when difficulties surfaced. I would start praying against Satan. I knew these trials were Satan trying to once again destroy our family and faith. Many times I'd say, "Are you finished yet? You know you can't touch us! We are God's servants. All you are doing is making us stronger in Christ!" That is exactly what happened. The harder Satan pushed, the harder I dug into God's Word, the Holy Bible. I'd think He'd given up by now. It's been twenty years!

"Be strong and courageous, Do not be afraid or terrified because of them, for the Lord your God goes with you; he will never leave you nor forsake you" (Deuteronomy 31:6).

After Katelyn finished and the Spirit was still moving, I told her it was my turn to tell her about what the Lord had given me Monday at 3:10 a.m. To my amazement, her week matched up perfectly with my divine word from the Lord.

Through tears, this is what I told Katelyn the Lord told me, "At 3:10 a.m. on Monday, I woke up with my heart hurting.

I knew it was breaking for you. The sadness and hurt I had were for the hurt you were feeling. As I lay in bed weeping, the Lord spoke these words to me in my spirit, 'This "*is*" the ending of your book. I want *all* of her! I don't want parts of her; I want *all* of her! I placed her at this college to honor Me. Katelyn's time with softball is over. Give time to honor Me. You will excel in FCA, and you will speak at the chapel during the time you are there. I want *all* of her!' Softball was a stepping stone. It was a big part of her life but didn't hold a candle to what God's big plan is. These words were so powerful! As I told Katelyn, she sat and wept. She knew in her spirit these words were true and from God.

The Lord continued to give me words throughout the week. I thank God that He uses me as His vessel. This has been the most amazing journey I could have ever prayed for. I'm humbled that God chose me.

The Lord continued in my spirit, "God has much more in store for Katelyn. Katelyn's story is not over, but this season of her life has been fulfilled. It's the end of this season but just the beginning of so much more to come."

The Lord continued with the rapid-fire discernment for this time in Katelyn's life, "Restore in boldness. She'll continue to be a blessing to so many people. Insight on collegiate sports. Too much emphasis on collegiate sports and need to focus more on salvation." These words God was giving me were extremely powerful and perfect for this time.

Then the Lord said, "She wanted to prove to herself that she could do it. She did it! I want to be number one, and the one thing she can't live without is not softball. Everything has a season, and all seasons must end for new ones to begin."

For the Lord said, "For it will not be you speaking, but the Spirit of your Father speaking through you" (Matthew 10:20).

Never Will I Leave Thee...

As you can see, the Lord lined up Katelyn's experiences at school during the week with the word God was giving me. This was not coincidental. Everything happens in God's timing, and this was His timing. That is exactly how our God works!

When God told me, "This is the ending to your book." I thought, *What? The ending? This is not what I thought the ending would be.* But God's ways are better than mine. I believed the ending would be the complete healing of Katelyn's heart here on earth, which would add to her testimony. Then I realized this book has been healing for Katelyn and will add to her testimony. This is the "ending" to this book but the "beginning" of another. God's not finished with us yet. That season is over, but a new one has only begun!

"Be strong and courageous, do not be afraid or terrified because of them, for the Lord your God goes with you; he will never leave you nor forsake you" (Deuteronomy 31:6).

CHAPTER 31: TESTIMONIES

We have known Katelyn Wilber since she was a baby, and she has always held a special place in our hearts. If Katelyn and her siblings were together with our daughters and they wanted something, which they anticipated the answer to be *no*, the solution would be to have Katelyn ask. Everybody knew it was hard for us to say no to Katelyn. She overcame many obstacles, even while in the womb. There is no doubt that Katelyn has been through numerous challenges that have become her testimony. The little girl who was born with half of her heart not functioning has one of the best hearts we've ever encountered. She is tender-hearted, kind, loving, compassionate, and full of the love of Christ.

—Lynda and David Vaughn
Longtime friends

The first time I met Katelyn, she was super tiny and was hiding behind her mother. I was teaching first grade at New Hebron Christian School, and Katelyn had come with her mother to pick up her sister from kindergarten. My good friend Lynda introduced me to Katelyn's mom, Heather, and immediately told me that God had big plans for Katelyn. That was eighteen years ago, and when I look back on that now, I can see that Lynda was right. God did and still does have big plans for Katelyn.

Over the past eighteen years, I have watched Katelyn struggle over and over with her many surgeries and have been amazed at how Heather and Katelyn have been able to trust God and still find joy in life. I have a son who has special needs and health issues as a child. I know firsthand how easy it is to be overprotective and shelter a child with health issues. Heather really did a great job of letting Katelyn live a normal life and participate in all the activities that healthy children do.

When in grade school, Katelyn was cautious and always seemed happiest when close to her mother. That wasn't always a bad thing. Heather and I once decided to take all of our kids, plus our friend Lynda's girls, with us to Florida. The trip was a lot of fun, but we did have a bit of an incident when, at Cocoa Beach, we managed to lose all of the children except for Katelyn. All of our kids and Lynda's girls wanted to go for a walk down the beach. We didn't dream that they would get lost. But after an hour of not seeing them, we were a bit panicked. The kids eventually made it back to us safely, and I remember Hannah, the leader of the group, saying that Katelyn was the smart one.

Over and over I have seen God do amazing things with and through Katelyn. I would love to be able to say that God has completely healed Katelyn and that she will never need another surgery, but I can't. What I can say is that Katelyn is an amazing servant of our awesome God, and she has been a blessing to everyone who knows her. I'm confident God will continue to do amazing things through Katelyn!

—Kendra Jones
Longtime friend

We knew Katelyn was "special" before she was even born. God held her in the palm of His hand, and we held her in our hearts. We had to wait to hold her in our arms for quite some time. She has been an inspiration to so many people. Always a fighter and so brave. She gave me courage when I faced brain surgery. God has always had a plan for her. She listens to Him and follows His direction. I can't wait to see where He leads her next.

Jeremiah 20:11.

XOXOXO,
Grammy

Katelyn is very special. She was born tough and only got tougher as she grew older. I've never heard her complain or ask God, "Why me?" She accepts her problem and thanks God it isn't any worse. God is a very important part of her life, and it shows through her testimonies. God has gotten her through many trials, and He will not let her down now.

Love,
Papaw

I met Heather about fifteen years ago as a customer. I have gotten to know her wonderful family through the years and remember Katelyn as this little girl coming into her mother's shop to have her hair fixed for school. I know of all they have been through with Katelyn's heart blockage and Heather's lupus. Being a mother myself, I cannot imagine how hard it's been for Heather and Shane to see their little girl go through all the surgeries and issues with the pacemaker that Katelyn has experienced.

A mother's instinct is to cushion and protect, but Heather has complete faith in God to take care of her children. Heather and Shane have coached their children's teams and taught them the value of hard work and sportsmanship, teaching them values that are lost in today's world.

I am amazed at Katelyn! She loves softball and has played for several years on traveling teams. She has taught other children pitching in a building at her house. Katelyn used her talent as a pitcher to get a scholarship at the school she chose, with the goal in mind of getting an education geared toward helping other children who have heart problems not letting fear keep them from living their lives.

She has given testimonies at several places, including the church I attend. Katelyn knows that it is all because of God that she is who she is today and gives all the glory to Him. What an inspiration she is!

It is through faith in God and His guidance that this family lives. It is evident the minute you walk into Heather's shop and hear the Christian music and share each other's life stories that God is the center of their life.

—Sue Lockhart
Client and friend

We often think of miracles as things the Bible tells about that only happened thousands of years ago. Truly miracles are happening every day around us. The world has become so skeptical that we fail to open our eyes and hearts to recognize God is indeed at work in our lives constantly, ever so miraculously as He was thousands of years ago. Katelyn's story is undeniable proof of one miracle after another throughout her entire life and the lives of her whole family.

I have gotten to know Heather over the past seven years and have been a witness to many of these miracles unfolding. As we sat in her beauty shop and Heather told me about the things that were happening, I always literally got goosebumps and teary eyes. There were acts of God! Now seeing this entire story put together is an even stronger testimony and witness to the countless miracles God has performed in Katelyn's life. I have personally found that knowing Heather and Katelyn's story has strengthened my faith. God is here. He is faithful and merciful. He will never forsake us!

Katelyn's story is a story that needs to be told. The world needs to know not only of all the miracles but also of faith and the power of prayer.

Katelyn's witness to God's love and constant care has been very inspirational to me. She never gives up, no matter what obstacles confront her. She knows she is in God's care, and she is excited to share her testimony and encouragement with the world.

There is no doubt that God has great plans for Katelyn and no doubt that she will spend the rest of her life following and doing His will.

This story is powerful, inspiring, encouraging, and a true blessing.

—Martha Edgington
Client and friend

About the Author

Heather Wilber is a hairdresser from Flat Rock, Illinois. In 1996, Heather married her husband, Shane. They have three beautiful children, Shaelyn, Katelyn, and Chance. Heather was the fourth of five daughters of Charley and Barbara Neeley. She was raised in a Christian home with a preacher for a father. If blessed with children, Heather vowed to raise them in a Christian home like herself. Because of her trials in life, she knew God had a special purpose for her life. In 2017, the Lord made the aspiration clear. She was to be the author of Katelyn's inspirational book. Through Christ, she is now an author.